"Edmund Metatawabin's voice is clear, brave and full of the grace of his Cree homeland. *Up Ghost River* is a powerful and unsettling read, full of heartbreaking truth-telling, resistance and Metatawabin's uncompromising love of land, his people, his language and his culture. These stories are full of the real lived violence of colonialism and of the beautiful tiny moments that our Elders and storytellers wrap around our children to teach them, protect them and nurture them. Metatawabin is a gift to all who are lucky enough to read him, and the key to reading Metatawabin is a willingness to simply allow these stories to transform you."

Leanne Betasamosake Simpson, author of
Dancing on Our Turtle's Back and *Islands of Decolonial Love*,
and recipient of the RBC Taylor Emerging Writer Award

"*Up Ghost River* arrives at an important time in the ongoing national debate over Canada's reconciliations with its native communities, adding personal perspective and emotional texture to a debate far too many of us get to see only through an ideological lens. . . . A book that has the potential to be a valuable cultural document. . . . *Up Ghost River* succeeds in turning one man's personal account into a telling testament of an entire people's trials."   *Toronto Star*

"The horror of Metatawabin's account seem almost unbelievable, but it is all too factual, backed up with official documents. Nor can Canadians dismiss this as a tragedy from a now bygone era; Metatawabin argues that recent legislation from the Stephen Harper government is a continuation of oppression. This work is a harrowing but enthralling account of an aspect of Canadian history that the country would prefer to forget but which continues to haunt."   *Publishers Weekly* (starred review)

"A searing memoir about a young boy and the legacy of trauma inflicted on Canada's First Peoples by the residential school system. A gripping read."
Karyn L. Freedman, author of *One Hour in Paris: A True Story of Rape and Recovery*, quoted in the *Globe and Mail*

"This aptly titled, well-crafted book is an especially poignant reminder of the harm [residential schools] caused. . . . *Up Ghost River* is a memoir containing a polemic wrapped in native history. . . . By weaving together memoirs and indigenous cultural practices, the case that he makes for a louder voice in the country's political, economic and environmental decisions is cleverly strengthened." *Winnipeg Free Press*

"The story of surviving the horrors of the residential school experience has been told by so many others. But Edmund Metatawabin's *Up Ghost River* is told with such unsettling bravery, in plain, honest language, that this intimate portrait of his childhood resonates longer after the pages are closed. Reading it was an exhausting but important experience for me."
Judy Fong Bates, *Literary Review of Canada*

"Thanks to the efforts of survivors like Edmund the federal government can no longer hide the shocking truth behind this terrible chapter in history, and survivors of St. Anne's and other residential schools may finally receive the justice they rightly deserve. Edmund's effort to document this abuse is as courageous as his dedication to healing himself and others from their experiences."
Nishnawbe Aski Nation (NAN)
Deputy Grand Chief Alvin Fiddler, quoted in *Nation Talk*

"A harrowing personal tale about brutality and healing."
Calgary Herald

"The word 'courageous' is often tossed around without much thought, but in the case of Edmund Metatawabin's residential school memoir, the label fits. . . . While the book's early chapters unearth horrific memories, *Up Ghost River* unfolds into an activist's triumphant story of survival and resistance." *Quill & Quire* (Book of the Year)

"With unsparing honesty, humility and disarming humour, Edmund Metatawabin reveals the darkness at the heart of Canadian history. A painful yet engaging narrative of personal trauma and recovery, this inspiring book also heralds the cultural and spiritual redemption of a people."

Gabor Maté, M.D.,
author of *In the Realm of Hungry Ghosts: Close Encounters with Addiction*

"A harrowing and redemptive story of a man's personal battles with one of Canada's worst practices. Edmund Metatawabin's tale of residential schools and government bureaucracy will leave you angry at the evils of colonization. Yet it will also show you a man's—and a people's—incredible ability to survive and seek justice. There are plenty of ghosts in this book, apportions of shame and responsibility, but Metatawabin's journey and destination on that river will definitely leave you full of hope and richer for it."

Drew Hayden Taylor, author of *Motorcycles & Sweetgrass*

"You know how some books come along and forever change the way you think and feel? *Up Ghost River* is that book for me. . . . This did happen and someone lived it and that's exactly why this book is so important and why everyone should read it. . . . I truly believe that every Canadian should read this book."   *Reeder Reads*

"Moving documentation, recollected tragedy and personal triumph, this book is a necessary first-hand account of being First Nations in contemporary Canada. From the atrocities of residential schools, to the present-day policy challenges, *Up Ghost River* will open your eyes to the all-too-recent history of Canada's First Peoples, through the experiences of a resilient individual and his family."

The Right Honourable Paul Martin,
former Prime Minister of Canada

"*Up Ghost River* is a very difficult story to read, but a necessary one in the reckoning of Canada's abusive and exploitative relationship with its First Nations people. Edmund Metatawabin's measured and honest account shows evidence of remarkable healing, and his story has much in common with the history of colonized indigenous people around the world. Metatawabin's journey is a metaphor for the journey we must all take if we are to heal our relationship to the land at this crucial hour in the environmental fate of the planet. With Alexandra Shimo, Metatawabin writes about his life in a way that is both agonizing and redemptive, personal and political, gut-wrenching and level-headed; it will break your heart."

Christine Pountney, author of *Sweet Jesus*

"[*Up Ghost River*] is a story about losing one's culture and struggling to find it again, a journey of profound healing and importance. . . . The book doesn't just explain that these things happened, it explores the psychological impact of the violence. The book is much more than an emotional story. . . . *Up Ghost River* places the residential schools within a mosaic of racism and oppression, a mosaic which is still being composed. . . . Shocking, detailed and revealing. It is a story of profound courage, suffering, and an ongoing healing process. Despite the often dark and serious concepts discussed, a surprising humour is present as well. Read this book!"   *The Argus*

"A shocking, sadly revealing Canadian story. Cree elder Edmund Metatawabin has the courage to tell how 'white learning' stripped him of his name and systematically brutalized him—including strapping him into a school-built electric chair and electrocuting him—traumatizing him throughout his childhood, youth and adulthood, until he could finally let it all 'pass through' him and find himself as a human being. 'We are still here,' he asserts, and 'our forefathers . . . are still here, all around us, guiding those who listen.' Every Canadian needs to hear this story."

Rudy Wiebe, author of *The Temptations of Big Bear* and *Come Back*

UPGHOST RIVER

A CHIEF'S JOURNEY THROUGH THE
TURBULENT WATERS OF NATIVE HISTORY

EDMUND METATAWABIN
WITH ALEXANDRA SHIMO

VINTAGE CANADA

Published in Canada by Vintage Canada, a division of Penguin Random House Canada
Limited, a Penguin Random House company, in 2015. Originally published in
hardcover in Canada by Alfred A. Knopf Canada, a division of Penguin Random House
Canada Limited, in 2014. Distributed in Canada by Penguin Random House Canada
Limited, Toronto.

Vintage Canada with colophon is a registered trademark.

www.penguinrandomhouse.ca
Page 317 constitutes a continuation of the copyright page.

Library and Archives Canada Cataloguing in Publication

Metatawabin, Edmund, 1947–, author
Up Ghost River : a chief's journey through the turbulent waters of Native history / Edmund
Metatawabin with Alexandra Shimo

ISBN 978-0-307-39988-5
eBook ISBN 978-0-307-39990-8

1. Metatawabin, Edmund, 1947–. 2. Native peoples—Canada—Residential schools.
3. Native peoples—Canada—Social conditions. 4. Cree Indians—Biography.
5. Indian activists—Canada—Biography.
I. Shimo, Alexandra II. Title.

E99.C88M483 2015   971.004'973230092   C2013-908614-5

Text and cover design by Jennifer Lum
Image credit: Metatawabin Productions and Research

Manufactured in Canada

8 10 12 14 15 13 11 9

Penguin
Random
House
VINTAGE CANADA

This book is dedicated to Joan, my partner of forty-four years,
who refused to let my hand go,
and to my children Albalina, Shannin, Jassen and Cedar,
and also to all the residential school survivors.

CONTENTS

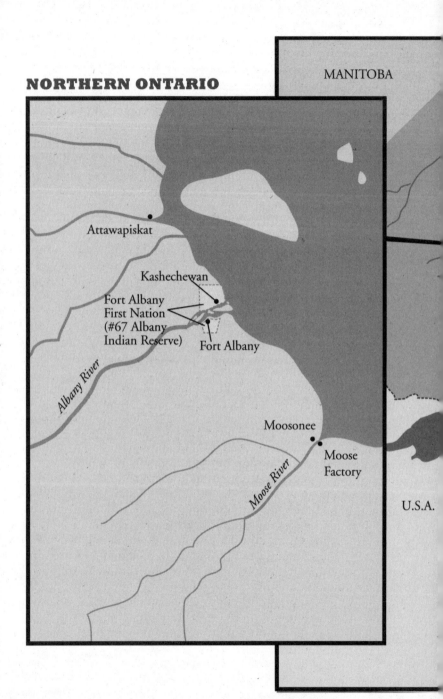

ONTARIO

Peawanuck

James Bay

Attawapiskat

Kashechewan

QUEBEC

Moosonee

ONTARIO

Cochrane

Timmins

Kirkland Lake

Ottawa

Peterborough

Toronto

0	100	200 kilometres
0	100	200 miles

AUTHOR'S NOTE

I have long been a First Nations advocate, but writing a memoir was different entirely. I had previously published a guidebook, *Harvesting: Cree Hunting and Gathering Techniques*, and a novel, *Hanaway,* about a young man trying to discover his Cree culture, but documenting my own story felt painful and fraught. I wanted my story out there as it chronicles an important part of Canadian and First Nations history. Yet I was hampered by gaps in my memory, perhaps because of my unusual childhood or the trauma of what I would later do to my body.

Starting in July 2011, I began to work with author and journalist Alexandra Shimo to try to close those gaps. She interviewed people from my past, and dug up old court transcripts, St. Anne's Residential School records, police interviews and reports through Freedom of Information requests, photos, and newspaper articles to fill in those places where my memory was spotty, checking them against my own recollections. In some places, we changed names and details to protect people's identities. Any dialogue is created as it might have happened, to the best of my memory.

UPGHOST RIVER

INTRODUCTION

On October 18, 2012, the Canadian government tabled a sprawling 457-page bill that generated such opposition among indigenous people that it sparked a worldwide political movement. First Nations viewed Bill C-45, the Jobs and Growth Act, as an attack on our rights and our voices. It made it easier for corporations to build on our traditional land without our consultation or approval, which we viewed as an attack on native sovereignty. And it reduced the legal protections against environmental degradation of our sacred waters, by reducing the number of rivers and other waterways protected under one of Canada's oldest pieces of legislation, the Navigable Waters Protection Act. In response, Idle No More was born.

How you viewed this story depended on where you watched it unfold. I am used to travelling between my isolated northern community and down south, as we like to say, and I am married to a white woman, with four children, so I am accustomed to walking in both worlds. The issue split along well-worn lines: Idle No More's protestors represented the environmentalists vs. big business, the minority vs. the majority, aboriginal rights vs. assimilation, angry natives vs. mainstream Canada. It's a familiar story, but it's only partly true.

For my people in the north, C-45 and the other government bills that were protested under the Idle No More banner were an attack on native sovereignty and environmentalism, but also part of a larger story that continues beyond recent memory. We have been silenced ever since we first met the white man. The Potlatch laws silenced us by preventing us from practising our spirituality, culture and religion. We were put under the extreme stress of shifting from a nomadic to a sedentary lifestyle, and denied spiritual and cultural rituals that had helped us cope, understand who we were and find meaning in the world for thousands of years. We were denied the right to travel or move between reserves without permission from the Indian Agent. We were refused the right to plant crops, banned from cutting down trees or building houses, unless we could get permission from the government minister. When we tried to protest these decisions, the Indian Act prohibited us from hiring lawyers. We were forbidden to appeal any decisions of District Stipendiaries (Indian Agent supervisors), Police Magistrates or Justices of the Peace. The Indian Act silenced us politically by denying us the right to vote, which was only repealed in 1960.[1] We were banned from holding any political meetings.

My own silence began in 1955. It may be a familiar story to you. My childhood was spent in St. Anne's Residential School, which has garnered its own tragic reputation in the national media. There, we were whipped for talking out of turn. Terrible things happened at the residential school—it has a reputation as one of Canada's worst—and the children who tried to voice their concerns were punished. When children were whipped until they bled, they were told not to tell their parents. When kids died at the school, the school authorities ignored the parents' grief and their pleas for answers.

I stayed silent about these experiences until they began to bubble up and could no longer be contained. By then I was married with three children. With an addict's rage, I began to destroy all that I had built: home, family, marriage and career. It would take me several years and many hard lessons to find my feet again. To walk the right road, I had to find the wisdom in indigenous teachings and learn how I could make them relevant to a modern context. I had to start making amends and work toward repairing the harms done to myself and my people.

Once I became chief of Fort Albany, I was able to use these lessons more broadly to help my community. Fort Albany is an isolated, impoverished northern community, near the reserves of Kashechewan and Attawapiskat. Many of the issues that plague those communities— addiction, suicide, family breakdown—have been our fate too. My work has focused on empowering the people who are suffering, especially those who survived St. Anne's Residential School, and their children, as the harms done to one generation become the fate of the next. The media has taken note, and I have represented my people at news conferences in Fort Albany, Ottawa and Toronto. I have won national awards, and some filmmakers have even made a documentary about my work with youth, called *Paquataskamik Is Home*.

When Prime Minister Stephen Harper tabled Bill C-45, these decades of work were threatened. I had already lost my voice once. So too had my people: our silence had become an ever-present companion. I could not let that happen again.

PART ONE

First
there was some other order of things
never spoken
but in dreams of darkest creation.

—Linda Hogan, "The History of Red"

In this dark room,
in this place of fences, strange smells,
and men with yellow eyes
where finally I am caught
and cannot get free,
I close my eyes and am home again.

—Ann Turner, *Sitting Bull Remembers*

ONE

THE BUSH, 300 KILOMETRES NORTH OF FORT ALBANY,
ONTARIO, 1954

I knew something was wrong before I got back to camp. I could hear my family's voices, but I felt it before that. It was like walking into cold mist—you were breathing it in before you'd seen it coming. The feeling hung there, chilling me inside, and I hurried to our mud house, hoping I could make it go away.

Rounding the corner, I saw the fire before I saw Mama. In the fading light, she was standing holding her baby daughter, Rita, gently patting her on the back. Around her the rest of them were squatting—Papa, my four-year-old brother, Alex, and our hunting friends, Charles and Bernadette Tomikatick, and their kids Madeline, thirteen, Gabriel, eleven, and Joseph, nine. Normally Alex and I tried to play with the Tomikatick boys because they were older and knew how to shoot slingshots and carve sticks, but this time they huddled close to the fire same as everyone else.

"This isn't good," Papa said. "She's not eating. Try feeding her again."

"I'm trying," Mama replied. "She's not eating. We should go back to see the doctor."

"We can't go back. It's too far," Papa said.

"She hasn't eaten in two days," Mama said. "And her poo is watery and yellow."

"She'll be fine," he said, but he glanced worriedly at my baby sister.

I went to my place beside Papa, but Mama wanted to go to sleep, and Papa said we needed to make an early start, so we all left the Tomikaticks and the fire and went to our house. Inside, Mama gave me Rita and I put her on the moosehide blankets that covered the floor. Her skin felt funny—sticky and hot to the touch. As I lay her down she woke up and began to cry again. Mama crawled toward her and curled beside her, stroking her hair until Rita finally quieted and fell asleep.

Strange dreams. A grey wolf with yellow eyes, running. I stumbled forward and tried to catch her. I touched her thick winter fur, but she slipped from my grasp. I ran behind but she was faster than me. Then the same sense of dread as I had walking back to camp, the feeling of fog rising up, mist wrapping around me and I can't see and can't breathe.

I opened my eyes to see my family's sleeping bodies. I rolled over to look at Rita. Her eyelashes were completely still. She looked so peaceful. Her jet black hair was damp and her lips flecked by the remnants of Mama's milk. I watched her sleep and felt an overwhelming urge to hold and love her. To feel her soft cheeks against my own.

Carefully, I unpeeled Mama's arm from her tiny body. I stroked her hair and she seemed to move, but I wasn't sure. The ends of her tiny fingernails looked like slices of moon. I kissed her hand. I reached underneath her, picking her up and whispering, "Wake up, little Rita." I scooted to the exit, grabbing some moosehide skins to cover us both. The sun was just starting to rise. Outside, I held her against my chest and walked toward the river, rocking her back and forth. Her body was limp and heavy. And then I looked at her face, and something was different—paler maybe. I felt the first waves of panic.

I quickly walked back to our house, opened the moss-covered door and looked inside. Everyone else was still asleep. What to do with my sister? If I tried to step over the sleeping bodies to lay Rita back down, maybe they would wake and think I had caused her death. But if I didn't, then they would wake in a few hours anyway, and I'd be holding Rita, and then I was back to the beginning: something lifeless in my hands. I stared at my sister and began to whisper, *Please, Gitchi Manitou, the Great Creator. Please. Not now.*

I crept into the house. No one woke as I stepped over the slumbering bodies. I gently picked up Mama's arm. She had golden skin, just like me. I wrapped her arm around Rita. Mama stirred and snuggled her closer. She stayed asleep. I watched them both, hoping Rita's eyes would move. I lay back down and waited for people to wake.

When the air had warmed, Mama opened her eyes and stretched. She relaxed her arm, drawing Rita in closer, and stroked her hair. "My baby girl." She sat up, still holding her. Rita sagged like a doll. Then she looked closely at her face. "Rita?" she said. "Rita?" Then "Keshayno!"

"Mmm . . ." Papa stirred.

"Wake!" Mama shouted.

He stretched and rubbed his eyes. "Yes, Netchi, my loved one."

"It's Rita," Mama said, holding out the baby. Rita's head flopped forward, like a bird with a broken neck.

"No," Papa said. His voice came out strangled. He shook his head back and forth. "No, no, no, no."

Mama began to cry.

Alex sat straight up. "What?" he said. "What is it?" He looked between Mama and Papa, who slumped like a moose after it has been shot. Mama held Rita tightly, grasping her to her chest as if she could squeeze her back to life. Tears welled and rolled down Alex's cheeks. I wanted to cry, too, but there was too much happening in my heart.

We all went outside. It was December. The sky was pale grey and the cold was hard against my cheeks. Snowflakes blanketed the already white ground. We stood outside the house for a while and no one said anything. Mama rocked Rita back and forth.

I heard a noise behind me. Charles Tomikatick was peering out from his mud house. "Everything okay?" he said. He looked between our faces, his eyes saddening as he understood. He ducked back inside to tell the others.

Everyone came out and they took it in turns to wrap their arms around Mama, who was still holding Rita. After a few moments Papa fetched some logs from beside our house and started to build a cooking fire. Normally Mama got the water for morning tea, but she just cradled Rita. Papa made everyone hot bush tea, which is extra sweet. Charles began cutting wood to make a little coffin for Rita.

Mama gazed into the fire. Papa came up behind her and said, "Netchi, we should bury her."

"Not now," she said.

"Yes now."

"Just let me hold her."

"Netchi. She is dead. It is time."

"She'll be okay," Mama replied. "Just let me hold her. Just for a bit." Papa looked between her and Rita and sighed.

Charles finished the coffin and Mama gently laid Rita inside, wrapped in a blanket.

We packed up and Papa fed the five dogs with some meat that Charles gave him. We strapped the coffin tightly to the top of the sled. Alex and I climbed into our seat and we set off, Mama walking beside the sled.

By lunch the dogs were tired, as was everyone in the group. Papa called ahead to the Tomikaticks and they halted their sled. Papa built a fire and Charles came over and gave us some of his pemmican. Once we'd eaten, Papa got up from where he'd been squatting next to the fire.

"It's time," he said to Mama. "We should bury her right here."

"No," she said. "I want a Christian burial."

"There are no churches around, Netchi. Not for miles."

"There's a cemetery at Ghost River."

"That's sixty miles away."

"That's not too far."

"No, Netchi."

"Rita was a Christian. She needs a Christian burial."

"Rita is Cree. She will go to the Spirit World along the Three Day Road."

The Spirit World was different from the Christian one, as far as I could tell. It was home to dead people who looked like me—our Cree ancestors who protected the living. It was both here and far away, Heaven and Earth, a place where the ancestors lived, our brothers and sisters, mothers and fathers, aunts and uncles, *gookums* and *moshoms*, stretching back until the First People, spirits that became human when they touched foot on this land. We were their descendants, made by Gitchi Manitou. When we died, we went to live with our relations in the Spirit World. It was somewhere familiar to me, as comforting as bush tea, whereas Heaven seemed strange. I didn't know much about it, just what I had gleaned from bits of conversation and a painting that Mama had shown me when she took me to church for the first time last summer. Around the painting was a golden frame. The painting showed lots of people standing on clouds, and babies with wings, weird creatures with pale skin and yellow hair, part bird and part white man.

"Ghost River is too far," Papa said. "Let's light the Sacred Fire here." The Sacred Fire would last three days, the length of the wake. A fierce flame, it could not be allowed to go out during that time, for it would guide Rita to the place of death, to be with the spirits of the ancestors and Gitchi Manitou.

"The ground is already frozen," Mama said.

"We can thaw it with a fire. I can be the Ghost Walker." Ghost Walkers could leave this world a little while to guide spirits along the Three Day Road, so they didn't grow confused or lost.

"No," Mama said. "No. That's not right. Rita was a Christian."

"So you'd rather delay Rita's burial than have a good Cree one now?"

Mama pursed her lips but said nothing.

"Fine," Papa said.

We said goodbye to the Tomikaticks and began to head south, toward Ghost River. All day we travelled overland through the snow, with Mama walking behind.

When the sun sank red into the trees, we stopped. Charles had given Papa some extra pemmican but we didn't have a lot and my stomach felt hollow after eating. I was tired, but Papa said we had to "keep going, keep going." Alex sat down in the snow, and then I did the same.

"It's time to get moving again," Papa said, and put us back on the sled. Alex got off again. "Come on!" Papa looked at all of us, shook his head, and began to untie our dogs. We helped Mama build a fire, and Papa found a good sheltered place to put up a tent for our overnight stay. Then he began sawing some logs, building a wooden platform to store our meat and keep it from the wolves and bears. He raised Rita's coffin and put it on the platform next to our food.

I crawled inside the blankets and lay down on the hides, beside Alex. Rita had sometimes slept beside me, and I missed rubbing up against her smooth skin. I shut my eyes and listened to the night. Still and quiet, except for the occasional sound of *scree scree*, the call of the nighthawk. Papa fell asleep quickly and started snoring. I could tell by Mama's breathing that she was still awake. It was faster than Papa's. Unsteady. She didn't fall asleep for a long while.

Where was Rita now? Was her spirit between two worlds, life and death, in the In-Between? Would she hang around, as did some of the dead, still troubled? Would she whisper in my ears? Or come to me in my dreams to make things right? I imagined her coming to me. *Mama*, she said. *Mama, mama*. She couldn't yet say my name, *Edmund*. *It's Ed*, I said. *Mama*, she replied. In my dream, I reached for her, but her spirit slipped through my arms. She faded and was gone.

When we awoke Papa had left. Alex and I fed the dogs and made the cooking fire. The shadows on Ghost River had shortened. Papa came back with a handful of white fur. He skinned the snowshoe hare, and after cutting it up he put it in the saucepan with snow for the broth. We waited until it was cooked, then Mama gave us pieces of meat. Papa put oats into the broth for the dogs.

After breakfast, Papa took Rita down from the platform and opened the casket. I hurried over. She looked the same as before except her skin was greyer and there was frost on her eyelids. Mama wanted to put her in her special baby bag, the *tikinagan*, as if she was still alive, but Papa said no. We needed to help her cross to the Other Side, he said. We need to help her let go.

Papa closed the lid, wiping his eyes and nose. He secured the ropes around the casket and prepared a spot for Alex and me on the sled. He tied on the blankets, food and utensils. Mama would walk behind the sled again.

A lifeless body, but a living spirit. Her spirit slowly slipping from her body into the next world, the place of the ancestors, the realm of the manitous. There she could run with the spirit animals, and greet her great *gookums* and great *moshoms*. She would be surrounded by those who loved her. She would be at peace. She would be free.

We set off. Mama didn't say much as we walked, and sometimes stifled a cry. Papa left her alone, and we walked until our break at midday. We stopped to have something to eat, and to give the dogs some beaver fat. Before we started moving again, I heard him say, "It's not your fault."

"Maybe we could have done something if we were in town. Gone to the *wemistikoshiw* doctor."

"But we weren't."

"He'd help. I know it."

"You don't know that."

"Yes I do."

"Netchi," he said. "Please. Let it go."

"She was my baby, Keshayno. She was our baby girl."

"I know."

At Ghost River trading post, everyone came out to meet us. I think they must have seen us coming on the sled over the snow and ice. It was lucky because my uncle and aunt, Meshen and Emily, must have been passing through, and were there too.

"Oh, Abraham," Meshen said. "I'm so sorry. What happened?"

"She . . ." Papa said. He opened his mouth and shut it again. He swallowed, took a deep breath and nodded.

"It's okay, Abraham. Let's unload her. Emily, take them to the room at the back of Mr. Scott's store. They need to rest."

Next day, the service was at the place with all the crosses. It looked pretty much like the one back home behind the church, except here more grave markers were made of rough wood, whereas ours were all stone. We walked there with Papa and Meshen carrying Rita's coffin. At the front was a holy man, but he looked nothing like the priest, Father Lavois, at home in Fort Albany. He was wearing torn pants instead of a black dress. He swayed from side to side like a duck and sometimes let off loud, smelly farts, which he tried to mask by coughing.

"Where's the priest, Mama?" I asked.

"He's away. This is his helper."

"Why is he special, Mama?"

"Because he is the Creator's helper on Earth. The priest couldn't be here, so he gave that man his powers."

He didn't look like he had special powers. He looked like he had a funny tummy.

After the coffin was lowered into the ground, the stinky man asked my family if they wanted to say any words.

Mama stood up and walked slowly to the front. She looked out at us. I could tell this was hard for her.

"My baby Rita. It's hard. I miss you. We all miss you. You were so happy. Smiling at just a few weeks old. I remember when you first grinned at me. I . . ." She looked down and paused. "I . . ." Her mouth quivered. Tears rolled down her cheeks. Papa walked toward the front, and held her. "I hope you are in Heaven," she mumbled. The holy man asked Papa if he wanted to say a few words. He said no, but asked if he could put some pemmican inside the coffin so Rita would have sustenance during her long journey to the Spirit World. Without food, she could become weak and lose her way. Absolutely not, said the priest's helper. Papa said nothing, but I could tell he was mad. The holy man nodded to a stranger, and he began shovelling dirt onto Rita's grave.

Around sunset, Papa and I left our room in the shopkeeper's house where we were staying and returned to the cemetery by foot. We were supposed to be getting some air—that's what we told Mama. We walked along the main road, our moccasined feet sinking into the fresh snow. Papa jumped the picket fence and grabbed my arm to help me over. While I kept watch, he kneeled at Rita's grave. He stuck his finger into the grave's loose soil, reached into his pocket and pulled out tobacco. He slipped it into the earth. We were supposed to put food onto the casket as well so her spirit could find it, but Papa looked this way and that, and said, "Let's go."

We walked back the way we came. It was dark now, and the cloud covered the moon, making the road hard to follow beneath the snow. When we got back to our room, I saw that Mama was asleep, or at least pretending to be. I curled up next to her and felt her warm breath against my back.

We returned to Fort Albany after the funeral. Mama could not bring herself to return to our trapping camp where we lost Rita. Almost everyone else was still out in the bush, and the empty houses made Fort Albany feel like a ghost town. There were a few people left behind, like those who worked at the school and at the Hudson's Bay store, but they were all a lot older than me, and I missed the Tomikaticks, especially Joseph.

We stayed in our one-room wooden house, and most mornings we had to dig ourselves out from snow. We heated our house with our wood stove. Papa promised that as soon as the ground had thawed he would find some timber and make the house bigger.

One day he came home with two kerosene lanterns. He told us kids to put out all the candles in the house and lie on our moosehide bed. He asked Mama to come and join us, and she said she was in the middle of fixing our moccasins and he should go ahead without her. He sat with us and turned a knob, and the release of gas sounded like a cat hissing and the room became warm with light.

He said, "Last night I had a dream. I was visited by a wolf, a manitou. He said that this year will be good. We will be rewarded as soon as we get back to our trapline."

"When will that be?"

"Soon. Soon. Right, Netchi?" He glanced at Mama. She looked at him but didn't say anything, and carried on with her sewing.

Over the next few weeks Mama mostly stayed home. When I asked her if she could play with me, she said she was tired and that I should go outside and play with Alex. It worried me, and I wondered if Papa had noticed it too, and whether he was going to say anything to her. I knew he wanted to go back to the land to trap, but Mama was too upset. They often discussed these sorts of things at night, after they thought the rest of us had fallen asleep. One night I decided to stay up, to eavesdrop. Once the candle was out, they started whispering to each other in the dark.

"Remember when we first met at the dance?"

"Of course, Keshayno."

"How good you felt in my arms."

Papa loved telling the story about how he met Mama when she was sixteen. He said that as soon as he saw her, he knew that she was the one.

"We danced all night long."

"Keshayno. I'm trying to sleep."

"Then after we were married, we went skinny dipping up the Albany," Papa said.

"Come on, Keshayno."

"I remember your skin was so smooth in the water. It felt like a pebble baked in the sun."

"Keshayno. There are kids around. They can hear you."

"No they can't. We should do that again," Papa said.

"In the snow?"

"In the spring."

"Oh, Keshayno. Things are different now," Mama said.

"But they don't need to be."

"Yes they do."

"What's so different?"

"Everything."

"What?"

"There's Rita . . . and . . ."

"Rita would have wanted this."

"Keshayno. She was a baby. She certainly didn't want her parents swimming naked."

"You know what I mean."

Next morning, Papa made us some hot tea and bannock, and then he went to see the Hudson's Bay Company store manager. He came back and cooked us some lunch—moose meat with onions. We ate on the floor. Papa finished first and cleared his throat.

"I spoke to the manager. It's going to cost me a thousand dollars to get the roofing tile for the extension to the house."

"I see," Mama said.

"That's not good," Papa said.

"No," Mama said.

"I mean, we already have debt at the Hudson's Bay store."

"I know."

"We should probably head out to the bush soon."

"Give me time, Keshayno. We will be fine."

"How do you know?"

"Father Lavois told me." Father Lavois was the head priest in the parish of Fort Albany.

"Him?" he said. "What does he know?"

"He knows."

"You trust his word over a manitou?"

"Yes," she said. "Yes, I do."

TWO

"Can I come? Can I come trapping?" Alex asked. Papa and I were standing by the door of our house. Alex was still sitting on his bed of moosehide and blankets.

"No," Papa said.

"It's not fair! Ed got to go last time."

"He's bigger."

"So?"

"Well, you're not old enough yet."

"Yes I am. I'm five."

Papa shook his head. "This one," he said, gesturing toward Alex. "What a handful. I don't know where he gets it from."

"Probably from you," Mama said. "You used to be like that when you were younger."

It was spring and Papa and I were going trapping. I was already seven, but Papa said I still wasn't big enough, so I watched him as he opened the trap and fastened it to the log that went into the water.

I knew that Papa wanted to put his traps farther afield since the traps he'd set around here hadn't yielded much. I'd tried to talk to him about it and he'd said that it was out of his hands, and when I'd pushed, he had become quiet.

Outside the morning sun bounced on the last ice covering the puddles. Shadows of cloud slithered across worn grass. The first patches of green were sprouting up in the muskeg. We walked silently, until we got to the edge of town.

"Which way is the wind blowing, Ed?"

"West!" I said and pointed.

"Good boy."

Then we came to a depression in the soil that looked like two giant teardrops.

"What do you think made that?" he said.

"That's easy. It's a moose."

"How old is it?"

"I dunno."

"Feel the soil. Is it fresh?"

"Yeah, I guess."

"Look at the grass around the footprint. Is it still flattened? Or has it started to bounce back up?"

"It's already fully up."

"That means the animal was here two or three days ago. If the grass has just started to rise, it's less than a day, and we should follow them. And if the grass is dry, or the soil hard, they are long gone."

"So are we going to follow it?"

"No," he said. "It's already too far away." We walked out to the Albany River, to where Papa had found martens last year. As we got closer, I heard what sounded like a baby crying. Papa started to run, panicked. The trap was supposed to break the marten's neck, but instead the animal was desperate, hissing, squirming, clawing. It smelled of sweat, piss and fear. A bad omen, signalling that Gitchi Manitou was unhappy.

"Shh," he said to the marten, and he made tender sounds like the ones he used to make with Rita. Then he reached into the trap with both hands, there was a snapping sound, and the marten fell slack. A female, from the size. He freed her from the trap and brought her close to his face.

"Life is a gift," he whispered. "Thank you."

"Papa, one day, can I be a hunter like you?"

He shook his head no. I waited for him to explain, but he stayed quiet as he put a piece of meat on the bait pan. Martens don't recognize human scent as easily as animals like foxes and wolves do, but Papa was always extra careful, especially when he had something on his mind. This time he reset the trap with such focus, it was like he was handling a robin's egg. For extra measure, he wiped everything down with a rag.

Alex greeted us at the door. "What you get? What you get?" he said. "A couple of martens," Papa said.

"Anything else?" Mama asked, looking up from her sewing.

"No, I didn't set any more traps."

"Why not?" she said.

"Well for starters, there aren't many animals around here. But I've also noticed the martens and beavers are pretty thin right now. Let's let them recover."

"What about your debt at the store?"

"I'll have to speak to the manager."

"What about the extension to our house you were going to build?"

"I can still do that."

"Keshayno, we're in debt."

"We'll be fine, Netchi. I heard that fur prices are up again."

Over the next few days, Papa scraped the hides and stretched them on a circular frame. He showed me how to scrape the hide with a sharp knife so it could dry better. We hung the frame from a high branch, safe from the dogs.

The day the furs were ready, Papa and I got up before the rest were awake. He helped me button my coat and pants, cooked bannock and tea, and we walked over to the Hudson's Bay store. We climbed the steps and opened the wooden door. A tall man about the same age as Papa was standing at the counter holding what looked like a bulky gun, which he was using to put sticky labels on some bread loaves. Papa had already told me that the manager was also called The Boss and that we all had to be nice to him. Ignoring Papa, the man straightened a price tag on a bag of flour. Above him were shelves stacked with supplies—sugar, Klik canned meat, tomato soup, lard, tea—and on the wall to his right, the more costly goods— ammunition and a number of rifles including a new one just arrived called The Savage 45. Furs were draped from the ceiling and counters, with the most valuable—otter, black fox and wolverine— sheathed in cotton to keep out the dust.

Papa shifted his weight and cleared his throat, and still the man continued pricing. After what seemed like a long while, he turned and slowly began to wipe his hands on his apron.

"Good morning, Abraham," The Boss said in Cree. "What do you think of our weather? Jesus, it's cold."

"It's not so bad. Just the wind."

"It's always so goddamned windy." He looked at my dad. "I had it better in Timmins, you know. Little house in South End, right near the water."

"You have good fortune here."

"I do? S'pose you're right. So what have you got for me?" he said.

Papa pulled out the marten furs. They were the size of lean cats.

"They're beauties, these ones," the man said.

"Yessir."

"Anything else?"

"No sir," Papa replied.

"Do you know the size of your debt?"

"Yessir."

"What is it?"

"Four hundred and twenty dollars and fifteen cents. That's without the roofing tile."

"And how much you think you'll get for a marten?"

"I dunno. I heard prices were up."

"You heard wrong, Abraham."

"Well, how much then?"

"I can give you thirty dollars each."

"Thirty dollars! That's eight dollars less than last week. Why the sudden drop?"

"Toronto isn't buying right now."

"All right, then," Papa said. "Can you give me some sugar and lard?"

"No. There are new rules. The company is asking everyone to pay off their existing debts before getting new supplies."

"I have children," Papa said.

"Yes, I know."

"We are hungry."

"You and everyone else in this town. What am I supposed to do?"

"You are supposed to help us."

"I am just doing my job, Mr. Metatawabin. Company's orders."

"How'd it go?" Mama asked as soon as we opened the door.

"Not bad," Papa replied.

"Did you get the lard?"

"Uh . . . no."

"Why not."

"I forgot."

"You forgot?"

"Yes."

"What about the sugar?"

"No. Not that either."

"So what did you get?"

"Actually I didn't get anything."

"What? Why not?"

"I have too much debt."

"What are you talking about? You said it was under control."

"No, I didn't. I said we have to follow the teachings of the mani-tou. If we do as he says, the Great Creator will provide."

"Provide?! How will the Great Creator take care of us? He's not helping any of us. The animals are getting less and less. We get less money for the furs too."

"We have to be patient. Don't rush things. Let Gitchi Manitou take care of things."

"You and your Gitchi Manitou! What's he going to do? He didn't take care of Rita!"

Mama's mouth looked very big and her voice was getting louder, but there was a breathy, pleading note underneath her anger. Papa was the same as ever, gruff and direct, but he too looked worried that everything would fall down. And so they went back and forth, to and fro, getting even louder. I remembered the story of the fight between the jackfish and the bull moose, the Lord of the Water vs. the God of the Land, who pulled and pushed, the water swelling around them, the currents rising and falling, until the conflict took on a momentum of its own and became part of the landscape, creating the tides and laying down the pattern of things to come.

During the season of *nipin*, when the sun beats down and the black-flies are at their thickest, Mama started going to see Father Lavois more often. He was an influential man, and told her things she held close to her heart. I didn't know the full extent of his powers, but everyone acted as if his words could stop a bullet. Like he had special magic, more potent than the shamans that Papa told me about, and who existed before I was born.

I'd never met a shaman. But I'd heard stories about them through the moccasin telegraph. It was said that they knew how to cure sickness. They had special powers, like being able to fix a broken leg or cool a man who was sweating and hot all over. Some said they could read people's minds. And see into the future. They got some of their knowledge by crossing over the *apeteyo*, the veil that divides the physical and spiritual worlds, to talk to an animal manitou or ancestor, who got their powers from the Great Creator, Gitchi Manitou. He showed them how to see the interconnectedness of all things. To dip below the surface to see the secret forces that ran our lives, the undercurrents, as a wise fisherman would study a river and know how the current would one day shape the river's banks. But the shamans didn't do their ceremonies anymore. They had been banned with the wemistikoshiw laws.

Did Papa miss the shamans? He never said. For Mama, it was like they had never existed. I wondered if it was because she was so busy. Since we had gotten back to the reserve, she went to see Father Lavois every few days. I didn't realize where she was going the first few times. I just awoke one morning and Papa was making bannock instead of Mama.

"Where's Mama?" Alex said.

"Church."

"Can I go?"

"No."

"When's she coming home?" I asked.

"At lunch."

"When's that?"

"Eat your bannock," Papa said.

Mama came home in time to make lunch. We were having moose steak and I helped her cut the meat. Papa was cleaning his gun.

"You need to ask the Hudson's Bay manager if you can work at his store," Mama said.

"Did Father Lavois tell you that?" Papa asked.

"He might have mentioned it," she said.

"I have a job," he said, and he blew a little too hard into the muzzle of his gun.

"Abraham. Yesterday we ate food that the Father gave us."

"Yes."

"I had to ask the priest to feed my family."

"Don't accept it then."

"And have the kids go hungry?"

"They're fine. Aren't you, kids?" I looked between Mama and Papa, feeling caught. Papa looked like he needed me more.

"What about the sickness?" Mama said.

"What sickness?"

"The one that killed the Spences' boys."

"They're at home with Gitchi Manitou. In the land of the ancestors."

"Father Lavois said they wouldn't have died if they hadn't been hungry. Maybe Rita would be here too."

"That's nonsense!"

"The Big Father in Heaven is a powerful protector. He will help you if you agree to be helped," Mama said.

"By coming to church?"

"It's a start."

That night Papa went outside with a cup of his special bear oil. Papa had already told me a little about the amber liquid. He said it was very powerful and the shamans used it a long time ago. Now a few people used it, but only when they were out in the bush and no one was around. It was dangerous if you were caught.

I stood in our doorway and watched him. First he built a fire, then when it was about as big as me, he took the oil and threw it onto the flames so they reached up and hissed yellow and white. He wafted the smoke toward himself and breathed it in. He stared at the fire. The light reddened the palms of his hands, and his body was completely still as if his life force had seeped into the fire.

Why was he doing it now? The thought worried me. It was like he didn't care if anyone saw or if he got into trouble. I wanted to approach him to ask about it but he looked lost, staring deep into the fire.

The next day when I awoke, Papa was already gone. Alex was sleeping and Mama was cooking on our woodstove.

"Wake your brother," Mama said. "Put on your best clothing. We have to see Father Lavois." I wanted to ask why, but Mama had one of those don't-answer-back-do-as-I-say looks. We left before I had finished my tea.

We arrived at the church and Mama told us to wait by the wooden seats. I looked around. I had been to church once last summer and had seen the painting of the bird-men. This time I looked around for the same painting but couldn't find it. There was another drawing framed with a golden square: a man wearing a prickly tuque who was bleeding everywhere. He seemed to be calling out in pain. A group of men was around him, but no one was helping. I wondered what it meant.

A man came toward us, dressed all in black.

"Is this him?" the man asked Mama in Cree. He was looking at me.

"Yes, Father."

"You are doing the right thing," he said.

Then Mama drew some marks on a piece of paper and we went home.

Mama said she would make us all new cups of tea. She kept fussing around us while we were drinking. She asked if Alex and I were hungry, then got up and sat back down. Then she asked us all if we were warm or cold, and I said that I was fine, and Alex did too. I asked her if anything was wrong and she said, "Nothing, nothing." She opened the door, I guess to look for Papa.

When he came home a few hours later, he opened the door wide, rushed in and gave us hugs.

"We have been blessed," he said.

"What are you taking about?" Mama said.

"Alex and Ed, get your shoes and coats!" he said.

"Where are you going?" Mama said.

"I had a vision last night in the fire. A caribou manitou. She led me along the river into the forest."

"You know I don't believe in that stuff," Mama said.

"Let me finish. So this morning when I got up, I retraced the footsteps of my vision. When I got to the forest, I looked down. I didn't see anything. So I shut my eyes and smelled. It was that heavy muskiness that you never forget. I could tell she was near. I opened my eyes, and I began to walk forward. I couldn't see anything at first, but I knew that it would happen. Through the trees was a patch of fur. She was pretty far away, but she had spotted me, so I couldn't get nearer without her bolting. I raised my gun and she didn't even move. Like she knew her fate. She fell with a single shot."

"A caribou around here?" Mama said. Caribou tended to stay away from the reserves and other settlements.

"I know. It's a sign, right?"

"It's . . . I'm not sure. A sign from who?"

"Oh you know, whoever, does it matter? I have something for you," Papa said. "Wait here."

He left the house and came back a few moments later with a metal pail. Inside was something red and wobbly—a caribou heart.

"Netchi. This is for you." He offered it to Mama.

"My favourite. Thank you, Keshayno."

"I told Charles Tomikatick, and he is there now, skinning the animal. I came home so Ed and Alex could see the caribou preparation. I want to show them how to remove the fur and how to extract the tendons for thread. Then we can go to the store manager and—"

Mama interrupted. "Keshayno. I have something to tell you."

"Okay," he said dismissively, turning to Alex and me. "You ready? Let's go."

"Abraham!" Mama said.

"What?"

"Today I went to see Father Lavois."

"What?" he said, focusing on Mama.

"I signed Ed up for residential school."

Papa muffled a cry. "For school? Why, Mary?"

"This life is over. They have to get an education to have a better life. That's what Father Lavois says too."

"What are you talking about? Look!" he said, gesturing at the caribou heart.

"It's just a matter of time."

"We're getting by."

"No, we're hungry and in debt."

"Everyone's in debt," Papa said.

"Exactly."

"Is that what Father Lavois said?"

"Yes," Mama said. "Other stuff too."

"I should never have let you go to church!"

"Abraham, you are not the boss of me!"

"But . . ."

"And it's not just Father Lavois who says the kids must go," Mama said. "It's the Hudson's Bay store manager. It's the nuns. It's everyone."

We walked north across the Albany to where Charles was skinning the caribou. By the time Papa, Alex and I got there, the animal lay on its side in a pool of blood, its brown fur skinned from its belly and hanging like a cape from its neck.

"She's all yours," Charles said. He gave the knife to Papa.

"No thanks," Papa said. Charles raised his eyebrows.

"What's wrong?" he said.

"Nothing."

"Something's up."

"Ed is going to St. Anne's next year."

"Yeah, Bernadette says we have to do the same for Madeline and the boys."

"Women!" Papa said, clenching his fists. Charles waited for him to go on, and after a pause, Papa began speaking in a low voice. "What are you going to do?"

"Dunno. Not much choice. What about you?"

"Too late. Mary already signed the papers with Father Lavois," Papa said.

"I'm sorry," Charles said.

"Me too," Papa said.

"Why are you sorry?" I asked.

Charles said nothing.

"Because you're growing up," Papa said. He turned away from me and began cutting the caribou skin. I knew that wasn't the truth, but since no one was paying attention to me, I squatted down in the grass and watched how the knife divided fur from flesh.

A few days later I awoke before everyone else was up. I brought the goose fat and Papa's gun to his mattress, then lay next to him.

"Ed," he said, waking and rubbing his eyes. "What are you doing?"

"I brought you these," I whispered. "So you can teach me." He looked at me. We both knew that I could clean his gun before I even knew how to build a fire. He sat up and got dressed, then helped me button my shirt and pants. He motioned for me to follow him outside.

The leaves had started to turn, layers of amber masking the dirt roads. We began to walk to the edge of town.

"You're going to school," he said.

"I know," I said. "Why did Charles say he was sorry when you told him?"

"Because he knows that I'm going to miss you." Papa stroked my hair. We were both quiet. "I won't see you for a while."

"How long?"

"You will have to be there all winter."

"Can I come back and visit?"

"No."

"Why not?"

"Because we will be at the family camp."

"Who will look after me?"

"The nuns will be looking after you now."

"I don't want them to look after me. I don't like them."

"You don't even know them."

"They are mean."

"You don't know that."

"Yes, I do. Joseph told me."

"Well, he doesn't know them either."

"I don't understand."

"You need to learn to read and write."

"What if something happens?"

"Nothing will happen," he said.

"I don't believe you," I said.

THREE

The day I was scheduled to leave for St. Anne's, Papa rose early to fetch river water. Normally he scrubbed my hair. This time he wanted me to do it. He showed me how to lather the hard-to-reach parts behind my ears.

We came inside and Mama gave me a plate of dried fish. I nibbled at it but my tummy was too upset to eat all of it. Normally Mama and Papa told me off if I wasted anything but Papa just took my plate and finished it. After breakfast, he and Mama stood around their bed and spoke in hushed tones about what I should pack. Mama wanted me to take the family photo of us all. It was an old one, taken the summer before Rita got sick, so she was there too. I knew it was really special because there were only three photos of Rita, and they were all worn until the paper was soft. But Papa said, "No point, they're just gonna take it from him anyway." They left the photos on their bed and I stood there and looked at them as Papa got dressed.

Alex was already up and dressed. He asked, "Where's he going? Where's he going?" Mama told him that I was going to residential school, but he kept asking, like he didn't understand. When I was packed, I put my hand on Alex's heart and looked him in the eyes, as Papa did when saying goodbye to Mama. Then Mama grabbed me and pulled me into her, and I could smell her scent of bannock and tea.

Papa and I went outside. The sun had broken through the clouds, and I saw that our firewood was wet, so it must have rained in the night. Strange, I hadn't heard it. Papa took my hand and I looked back and saw our chimney spurting smoke. I realized that I wouldn't be there for the final fire before they left for a winter in the bush. It struck me that I wouldn't go with them at all, and I squeezed his hand tighter as we walked to school.

The three-storey school building had always been there, just across the river channel, and I studied its square windows as we approached, wishing I could see inside. For a split second I saw a man through the window. He was wearing a black cloak like Father Lavois, and grabbing the sides of a boy's head. There was a prickly feeling in my chest as I realized he had the boy's ears. The boy had lost his balance, stunned, and then I realized that my imagination was playing tricks on me. This was just a story that Joseph Tomikatick had told me—there was no boy in the window.

We were at the concrete steps. I was trying to hold on to our time together but it was slipping by so fast. Papa was at the top of the steps and knocking on the wooden door.

"Good morning," a nun said to us in Cree. "Come in." We walked into a wide lobby that was nothing like our house. The hall was so bright, with lights shining down from on high and tall windows, and everywhere was white: walls, tablecloths and clocks. No furs or grass on the floor. Instead, hard things—a see-yourself glass, grey stone stairs, and leather-like floors. I saw lots of squares—photo frames, side tables, chair seats—and surfaces that must have taken many hours' scraping to be so smooth. The air was different here, too, and it was not just the smell, which I later discovered was bleach, but the way it moved, like there were lots of invisible things in it, and all the things were too close together.

"I'm Sister Wesley," said the nun. "What's his name?" she said to my father, speaking her mother tongue.

"Edmund Metatawabin."

"And you are Mr. Metatawabin?"

"Uh huh."

She led us to a bench in front of two full coat racks, where two other boys were sitting. One of them was smaller than me, and the other was tall and built. "It's good you came. Sit there, Ed," she said, pointing to a spot next to the slender boy, who was fidgeting with a piece of paper. "Mr. Metatawabin, I'll be right back." She disappeared through a wooden door at the end of the lobby. Papa waited until she was out of earshot before speaking.

"What are your names, boys?"

"Tony," said the taller boy.

"Amocheesh," said the other.

"You boys are a long way from home."

"I'm from Peawanuck," the boy named Amocheesh said.

"I'm from Moosonee," Tony said.

"Hmm . . . your face looks familiar," Papa said to Tony. "Your family traps on the Moose River, right?"

"Yeah, but they are thinking of going farther north, following the caribou."

"That's good. I heard the animals are now near Peawanuck."

"Yeah . . ." Seeing Sister Wesley returning, Tony stopped talking.

"Mr. Metatawabin. You can go."

Papa frowned, glancing at her. I could tell he thought she was rude. He paused, irritated. She waited. When no one said anything, he scooped me up into his arms so I could smell wood smoke and the scents of fall. He gave me a long hug.

"Please not yet," I said. I wanted to cry.

"You will be fine."

"Don't leave me."

"Be strong, Nkosis." I wondered when I would next hear Papa calling me "my son."

Then he left, and I watched my tears dripping onto the floor. I tried not to make much noise, and the droplets seemed small for the river of sadness that was in me. Tony saw me and looked away.

A priest in black came out of the office and stood next to the Cree sister.

"Stop crying," said Sister Wesley. "Let's go." The other boys and I stood. Then we all went up some stairs and the sound of our footsteps bounced off the hard walls. I thought about how the sounds here were different from the bush. There, you can always hear lots of animals breathing, eating and mating; singing and crying; grunting and bellowing; whereas here were the same noises again and again. Step after step, no talking. At the top, I saw metal beds in rows, and a lot of boys, sitting and standing. There were more children than I could count.

"Thisissdalastofdem," said Sister Wesley to the white man. He pointed to us. "Kipkwayettverywonn."

I looked at her, panicked, wondering what she had said. The other boys had been murmuring to each other, but they too froze and stared at her. Then the white man began to speak, with the Cree nun translating.

"Welcome to St. Anne's Residential School," he said. "I am Father Gagnon, the bishop for the region, and your principal. This is Sister Wesley. She will translate for me until you understand English. She is your supervisor. She will care for you before and after the school lessons.

"St. Anne's is the main girls' and boys' school for this region. We take our mission here very seriously. We are here to make you into good Christians and honourable members of Her Majesty's Kingdom. This is a learning environment. That means we expect silence at all times. God speaks to those who listen. Now, the first order of business is the numbering system. For that I need you to get in line from shortest to tallest."

I was not used to lining up or being ranked, so I walked to the back. She grabbed me from where I had placed myself and roughly pulled me toward the front. "Do you think you are that tall?" she said loudly. "You belong here!" Once we were lined up to her satisfaction, she began speaking.

"When I clap twice, it means line up in order of height, just like you are now," she said. Then she walked the line's length, counting. I was small for my age, so was number 4 out of 127.

"These numbers are your new names, so remember them well," she said. I tried the number out silently in my mouth. It felt flat and far away. *This is unfair*, I thought, *even dogs have real names.*

"Many of you have come from homes where the hygiene standards are, how can I put this, a little lax." Sister Wesley was translating for Father Gagnon and as she spoke, she suppressed a smile. "Let's start as we mean to continue. Clean. Everyone take off your clothes. Put them in a pile in the middle of the floor. Then return to the line."

We didn't move. Father Gagnon motioned like he was going to take off Tony's sweater. "Clothes!" Sister Wesley shouted in Cree. "Off!" I didn't want to give up my beaded moosehide moccasins— Mama had made them for me—so I picked at the beads until Sister Wesley pulled them from my hands and tossed them in the pile.

When we were naked, Father Gagnon left the room and Sister Wesley began to walk the length of the line. She shook white powder on our heads and privates if we had hair there. Some of the boys got it into their eyes, and they started to rub them and cry. It smelled bad, like a stinging in my nose. We left the line and hurried one-by-one to the three showers next door, dousing our hair under the warm water. Then we came back to the line, and Sister Wesley handed us each a towel. When everyone was finished, we returned quickly to the dormitory.

"We will now give you the clothes to use for the whole year," Sister Wesley said. "You will be given two sets. If you tear them on purpose you will sew them yourself."

Sister Wesley walked to the cupboard by the wall and began pulling out neatly folded piles of clothes, some denim and some black and white. Each was embroidered with our numbers, according to our height. She also pulled out an undershirt, shorts, bathing trunks, pyjamas and running shoes for each boy. She clapped twice and we got in line again according to height. Then one by one we came forward. My pants didn't quite fit, but I dared not say anything.

It was time for our medical exam. Sister Wesley told us to stay in line, then left the room. In walked a man in a black cassock who introduced himself as Brother Jutras. He sat in a chair and told us to line up in front of him, the smallest boy stopping about four feet from him. I stared at Number Three's back.

"Step forward and pull down your pants," Brother Jutras said when it was my turn. He reached forward and cradled my penis, touching it, examining it carefully, then eventually pulled at the skin to examine the tip. He also felt my balls; his touch immediately made me hard. Somehow I knew it was wrong, and I tried to pull myself away but he held firm. I looked away and waited for him to stop touching me. It took a while. Then he told me to pull up my pants.

Sister Wesley entered. "Time for haircuts," she announced, as she tied on a blue striped apron.

There was silence. Then Tony said, almost inaudibly, "We don't cut our hair."

"Don't you have Indian Agents in Moosonee, Number Twenty-Three?" Long hair had been illegal since before I was born. When I was out in the bush, I saw that a few people still had braids. I asked Papa about it and he said that these people didn't go near the settlements and so they did their best to ignore the white man and the wemistikoshiw ways. I remembered my grandmother saying our hair is a sign of our strength.

Sister Wesley clapped and we lined up. She cut our hair with scissors, then used an electric razor. Our hair tumbled to the floor in tangled clumps, like broken bird's nests. Tony caught my gaze in the mirror, and I jokingly pursed my mouth into the shape of a fish. He smiled.

We heard the clap of Sister Wesley's hands, lined up according to the numbering system, and went downstairs to the dining hall for dinner. I heard utensils scraping plates, and smelled roast beef, potatoes and gravy. I had hardly eaten anything for breakfast, and had no lunch, and my mouth watered. However, lining up with our trays, I realized that the good food was for the nuns; ours was a bowl of watery beans with tiny pieces of meat.

I sat at one of the rows of benches, next to Tony, and dug in. The food tasted like muddy river water. It slid around in my mouth, slipping up my gums and between my teeth. I ate quickly, and afterward, I was still hungry.

"Ed," whispered Tony. "Go 'n' ask for more."

We were supposed to be silent, so I waited until Sister Wesley, who was patrolling the room, had moved to the next table.

"No!" I whispered.

"Come on. They are our people." I looked up from my plate. He was right—the servers behind the counter were all Cree men, younger than Papa. If they'd been raised right, they should share. "Go on," Tony hissed, and he looked at me hard, like it was a test of my bravery.

I looked at them again. They doled out the food onto the plates and barely looked up. I stole a glance toward Sister Wesley, who was at the other end of the hall. I stood up and quickly glanced back at the servers. One of them looked up at me and smiled, as if beckoning. I started making my way to the food line. Once there, I looked over at Tony. He smiled at me and gave me a thumbs-up. I moved up the line and reached for a plate.

"Boy Four!" It was Sister Wesley, who had spotted me from across the room. She moved quickly, almost running. I started to move away from the line, then froze. "You already ate," she said. "Were you trying for extra?"

"Yes," I said, which slipped out before thinking. "I mean no."

"Which? Yes or no?"

"I don't know."

"You don't know. You're greedy, aren't you?"

I said nothing.

"Answer me when I ask you a question," she said.

"Sorry," I said.

"Sorry what?"

"Sorry sorry," I replied. I didn't know what else to say.

"'Sorry, ma'am,' stupid," she said. "Go and get me the whip."

"Where is it?" I said.

"You'll learn soon enough," she said. She glanced around the room and caught sight of an older boy, who left and came back a few minutes later holding a long leather snake.

In the night, I woke up and reached underneath my pyjamas to touch my back. Everything below my neck was on fire. I thought back to the whipping and the pause between strokes, like the felling of a tree, where the rush of movement slices the air. I began to cry. After a few minutes, I heard someone creeping toward me. In the dark, I saw a face: Tony.

"I'm sorry," he whispered. "I didn't know you'd get whipped. Here." He handed me something white. I brought it to my face. It was bread. I broke a bit off, and started to chew. My mouth was dry so it was hard to swallow.

"Where'd you get this?" I asked.

"Stole it."

"I need to go to the bathroom."

"Okay, but don't get caught. You're not allowed."

"Am I supposed to pee my bed?"

"You're not allowed to do that either."

"Oh."

"Just try to go to sleep. You can go to the bathroom in the morning." And then he was gone.

FOUR

The next morning, at 5:30, I awoke to the ringing bell. I felt my pyjamas. They were still dry, and I was relieved. I saw Sister Wesley come into the bedroom. She started walking between the bed rows, slapping the faces of those still sleeping. I really had to go to the bathroom but I was afraid. I got up quickly and looked about. Other boys were making their beds and then standing at the foot, and I copied them.

"Can I go to the toilet?" I whispered to the boy in the bed next door.

"Not till after the inspection."

Once everyone had made their beds, Sister Wesley began to walk along the rows. I had to pee so bad and the morning ritual seemed to take forever. First she checked whether the beds were correctly made, then she pulled down our underpants and looked for any sign of soiling.

Erick, a boy from home, had wet his pants. "You have an accident in the back too?" Sister Wesley said as she spun him around. "Take everything off." He stripped down until naked. "Put your underpants on your head like a hat."

He looked at her, confused.

She motioned for him to pull his wet underpants onto his head. He slowly did as he was told, although he kept holding them until she slapped his hands down. He stayed there naked with them on his head, and she moved to the next bed. Once finished, she clapped her hands again. Everyone rushed to the toilet. I was one of the first, thank Gitchi Manitou. I just made it.

At 6:15 she took us down to chapel. It was smaller than Father Lavois' chapel, with not as many paintings of bleeding men. As I walked in, I caught sight of a big group of girls sitting in pews on the right hand side of the chapel. It was the first time I had seen girls at St. Anne's, and I wondered where they lived. I recognized one of them, Angela, from bumping into her at the Hudson's Bay store. I tried to catch her eye, but she stared at the hymnals in front of her and wouldn't look up.

Once we were seated in the pews, I looked up and saw Father Lavois standing at the lectern.

"What's he doing here?" I asked an older boy.

"He likes doing the service here. He's here a lot," the boy said.

"Innomineepatrisatefillyatespirtussanctee," he said. "Gratia-domineenostreejesukristeeatecarrotsassday." We all stared at him, trying to follow. He sounded the same as the stinky man as Rita's funeral, but I couldn't be sure.

After the service, we filed out of the church to where Sister Wesley was waiting and she took us to breakfast. We lined up outside the kitchen. I got some porridge and sat next to Tony.

"Your turn to get extra," I whispered.

"Yeah. Sorry 'bout that," he said.

"Last time I take your word."

"I didn't know."

"Well you do now."

We continued eating. I didn't like porridge, I decided.

"Hey," Tony said. "You see the way that Father Lavois looked at that tall wemistikoshiw nun at the back of the church?"

"Who?

"I don't know her name. I'll point her out to you."

"How did he look at her?"

"Like a man looks at his wife."

"No way," I said.

"Yup. He was all over her. Check it out next time." Then he grabbed my unfinished bread and filed out of the dining hall to the yard.

The older boys were already there playing tag, ball hockey and soccer. I gazed out across the gravel to the grass and the trees beyond. There was no fence separating school from the freedom outside. But Sister Wesley was watching. It would take a few minutes to get to the trees. If she saw me bolt, I'd be whipped again. I glanced around for Tony, who was playing soccer with the older boys. I joined in too.

When the bell rang, we went to the classroom. I opened the door, and saw a group of us, as many as in a net of baby walleyes, boys and girls, some my age and others slightly older. We walked in, where a different nun was waiting.

"Kumminsitdoun," she said. I looked around for Sister Wesley to translate but she wasn't there. "Sitdounne!!!" the nun shouted. She pointed to an empty desk and chair. I walked to it and sat.

The rest of the lesson continued like that. I didn't understand what was going on but there was no one to translate. Sometimes the nun, Sister Thérèse, stared at me and shouted. I didn't know what to do, so I looked down. She came over and slapped the back of my head. I glanced at up at her, and she glared at me.

"Lookatchmeeweneetalkdouyooo." I stared at her blankly. She hit the back of my head again.

We sat there for what seemed like the length of time it takes the Albany to freeze. My head felt as if it had been set on fire with all the slaps, but somehow I knew I shouldn't cry.

Eventually the bell rang, and we filed out into the yard for playtime. I went to the corner and put my throbbing head in my hands. Around me I could hear laughter as boys played games. The whir of legs seemed to be banging on my head. I could hear strange words, lookatchmeeweneetalkdouyooo and savageboi, repeated over and again. Sister Thérèse's fists seemed to be trapped inside my head. I stayed crouched in the corner until the end of break.

That evening we all went out to dig potatoes in the nearby school fields. As we walked, I tried to see my house but it was obscured by the spruce trees that lined the Albany. I kept silent as we weren't supposed to talk. Amocheesh ignored the rules and began whispering.

"What's that?" he whispered to Tony, pointing to a nearby building made of glass.

"That's where they grow the special food for the priests and nuns," Tony whispered.

"Can we have any?"

"What do you think?" Tony said.

"What do they have?"

"Shhhh!" Tony said, as Sister Wesley turned around.

No one said anything until Sister Wesley had moved down the field. All we could hear were the leaves rustling and shovels digging.

"How's your head?" Tony whispered.

I shrugged. "Fine." It still hurt, but there was no point complaining.

"That woman is so mean."

"I know." I focused on the earth for a while. It was tiring digging the potatoes from the ground—we didn't have enough tools to go around so most of us used our hands. Tony, sensing that I didn't want to talk, began joking around with Joe, another classmate, for a while. When the sun started to set, he turned back to me.

"I saw you looking at that girl in class today," Tony said. "Is she your girlfriend?"

"No," I said blushing. "She lives in Fort Albany. She's a family friend."

"What's her name?"

"Angela."

"Like an *angel*," he said. The last word he said in a funny language, I think it was wemistikoshiw.

"A what?"

"A manitou with wings," he said.

"Manitous don't have wings."

"These ones do. They are special wemistikoshiw manitous. The wemistikoshiw think they live up in the clouds."

"Oh, the bird-men!" I said, remembering the painting. "Angela is a bird-man?"

"No, fart bum. She's a . . ." he paused, as if confused.

"A bird-woman?"

"Yeah. Something like that."

"Quiet," Sister Wesley shouted.

We continued digging potatoes in silence. I looked at Tony and realized he didn't know what he was talking about.

Next day was a Saturday, and it was the first time since arriving that I got to sleep in. We didn't have to get up until seven a.m. and there was no bed-wetting inspection. After breakfast Sister Wesley escorted all the boys in the dorm to the yard. On the way, Tony whispered to me.

"See that kid up there?"

"Which?" I said.

"The tallest one of the juniors." The higher grades, six through eight, were known as seniors. "Number Sixty-Five. Brandon."

"Yeah."

"Beware of him."

"Why?"

"He's older."

"You're lying," I said.

"No."

"Why's he in our year, then?"

"Just because."

Sister Wesley looked back at both of us, so we fell silent for a time.

"So what?" I finally whispered.

"So. He can take you out." He did a mock punch. I looked at Number Sixty-Five. He had paler skin than the rest of the boys and he looked mean. His brown eyes darted about like wasps and his mouth was pulled down like the outline of an arrow. When we got to the yard, some boys huddled in the corner, others began playing tag. Tony wanted to play soccer, and he and another tall boy said they were captains and they began to pick teams. Tony picked me, and I was pleased.

We shouted go, and my classmate got the ball and passed to Tony, who shot wide.

"Who's that?" Amocheesh asked as we waited for the goalie to go and get it.

"Where?" I asked.

"Over there." In the distance, standing at the edge of the playground was a tall, blond-haired man.

"I don't know," I said.

"Oh, him?" Tony said. "That's the new Hudson's Bay store manager. His name is Mike Pasko."

"Why is he standing there watching?" Amocheesh said.

"Who knows," Tony said.

"I don't like it. He's creepy," Amocheesh said.

Our side scored a goal, and then it started to rain and Sister Wesley blew her whistle. I looked out beyond the gravel, where Mike was fiddling with his umbrella.

After playtime, we went upstairs to the showers next to our dorm. We all stood in line. When we were at the top, we collected our special shower trunks to hide our privates. The nuns said that this is because men and boys should be "modest" and no one wants to see your "parts." Sister Wesley left, so we began to talk.

"Fred. You kick like a girl," Tony said.

"Yeah, well you kick like a sick frog," he said.

"That doesn't even make any sense. Frogs don't kick balls."

"So?"

"So think of something better."

"You think of something better!"

"Think of something better to insult myself?"

"Yeah."

"You're dumb."

Tony turned toward me. "I know where they keep the food."

"What food?"

"The stuff that the nuns get."

I thought of what we saw them eating each mealtime: the roast beef, jams and chocolate cakes.

"Where?"

"In the basement."

"Oh," I said. We weren't ever allowed to leave the group without permission and the store cupboard was three floors below.

"We could get some. At night."

"I don't think so," I said. I imagined getting caught and it scared me. I didn't want to be whipped again.

"Don't be a baby."

"I'm not."

"Yes you are.

Let's do it tonight," he said.

"No."

"Crybaby."

"I don't want to."

"Do you want to be my friend or not?"

I shrugged.

"Well that settles it then," Tony said.

After lunch, we didn't have lessons because it was a Saturday. We just went outside to the yard. I didn't feel like running around—I was still hungry as we didn't get much food at lunch—so I stood and watched. Joe and Erick approached, whispering. They pushed past me.

"Hey," I said. "Careful!"

"Sorry," Joe said. He giggled.

"Why're you laughing?" I asked.

"No reason," Erick said.

"We got bread," Joe said. He put his hand in his pocket, pulled out a chunk and shoved it in his mouth, chewed once and swallowed.

"Can I have some?" I asked.

"No," Joe said.

"Where'd you get it?" I said.

"Brother Jutras," Joe said. I had thought that Brother Jutras was some sort of doctor, but it turned out that he was the school's baker.

"He gave that to you?"

"Yeah."

"Why?"

Erick looked uncomfortable and then turned away.

"We didn't have to do anything. Just stand there," Joe said.

"Stand there and do what?"

"Nothing. It didn't even hurt."

"What didn't even hurt?"

"When he touched us."

"Oh," I said. I remembered when he gave me the medical exam. It didn't hurt, but it made me feel uncomfortable. Something about the way he smiled. I wondered whether it was worth the trade-off for bread. I was so hungry. I thought about having fresh bread in my mouth, the way it was warm against my tongue. My mouth watered.

"We're going to go back and get more," Joe said. "He said we could come back whenever we wanted. As long as we trade. Wanna come?"

"Maybe," I said. Was it riskier to go to the basement storeroom to steal, or to go with Joe and Erick to Brother Jutras? I wished there was someone I could ask. Someone who would know. I thought about my papa. He was so far away, and there was no way of speaking to him or hearing his voice.

Maybe it would be better to let Brother Jutras touch me for a slice. After all, Joe said it didn't even hurt. Then I could get bread whenever I wanted.

"Sure," I said. "I'll come."

"We went to the dorm to ask Brother Jutras if it was okay," Joe said. All the brothers and priests slept together in a dorm near the main school building. They tended to stay there on weekends. "Father Lavois said he was asleep." It was after-dinner playtime, and in the fading light, I looked at Joe and Erick to see if they had extra bread. Their hands were empty.

"Oh," I replied. "Are you going back?"

"Father Lavois said not to disturb them," Erick said.

"Maybe we can ask on Monday," Joe said.

"Maybe," Erick replied, and he looked down, then motioned to Joe to leave.

—

While I was waiting, we had a surprise visitor. It was Monday morning. We were sitting in a class with Sister Thérèse who was speaking her wemistikoshiw language. I stared at her and tried to follow what was happening. After a while we heard a knock on the door.

"Kummin!" Sister Thérèse said.

Mr. Pasko walked in.

"Dississmistapasko," Sister Thérèse said. "Heehasastoreintoun." We looked at her blankly.

"Hello, boys," Mike said to us in Cree. "My name is Mike Pasko. I run the Hudson's Bay store."

"*Tanisi*," we replied.

Sister Thérèse began talking again. This time Mike translated.

"Sister Thérèse has to leave for a couple of minutes. But I am going to read you a story." Mike held up a book. "I need children who are good listeners. Does everyone want to show me how good you are at listening?"

We nodded. Mike opened the book and started reading in Cree. It was called *The Ugly Duckling*. When the bird said goodbye to the barnyard, Sister Thérèse left the room. Once the door clicked, he read a few more lines and then closed the book. *He's breaking the rules,* I thought, and it made me nervous.

"What's your name?" he said, pointing at Amocheesh.

"Number Three."

"No, I mean your real name."

Amocheesh hesitated and looked around the room.

"Don't be scared. My name is Mike. What's your real name?"

"Amocheesh," he said, quietly.

"What a great name!"

Amocheesh grinned.

"What's yours?" Mr. Pasko said, pointing to me.

"Edmund."

"You?" he said pointing to a girl named Dayness.

"Dayness Kooses."

"Wonderful." Several boys and girls excitedly raised their hands, as if eager for Mike to comment on their own names.

"Tell me, Amocheesh. Where does your family like to go trapping?"

Amocheesh started to tell Mike, and then asked him if he could have a pen and paper to draw a map. Mike walked to the stationery cupboard. "Why don't we all plot our homes on Amocheesh's map?" In the excitement, we didn't hear Sister Thérèse enter the room.

"Mike!" It was back to English and my heart sank. Sister Thérèse seemed to be angry, but then Mike said something that made her smile. They talked for a few more minutes, then he turned around and waved to us and we waved back, and he left.

That evening we went out again to dig potatoes. Three of us were crouching around a potato plant and guessing what Mike had said to Sister Thérèse to make her smile.

"I think he said, 'Take off your veil. I'll make you a woman,'" Tony said. Everyone laughed.

"How would he do that?" Amocheesh asked.

"You don't know anything," Tony said. I didn't know either, but didn't want to be mocked.

"Yes, I do," Amocheesh said.

"Okay. So how?"

"Shh," said Sister Wesley, stalking toward us. Once she was close enough, she cuffed Tony around the head and told him to shut up.

When she was out of earshot, Tony said to Amocheesh, "Okay, so tell me, big shot."

"You tell me," Amocheesh replied.

"I'm not telling you."

"Why not?"

"Because my papa said I should keep it to myself."

"Your pa didn't tell you."

"Shh," I said. "She's coming."

Sister Wesley stood over us and looked down.

"You're leaving too much dirt on them," she said. "Hold out your hands." Amocheesh, Tony and I held ours out. She slapped us all three times with her wooden stick. It stung, but wasn't as bad as the whip. Amocheesh started to cry. "Stop crying, Number Three," she said. "Stop crying or I'll give you something to cry about." Amocheesh looked at his hands and wept silently. Sister Wesley shook her head and went back to patrolling the rest of the potato fields.

In the weeks leading up to Christmas, I looked for a chance to ask Joe and Erick about whether they had asked Brother Jutras if I could come with them, but we were so busy with the extra work of cleaning the school before the holidays that it was hard to find the time to talk.

The days slipped by in a rush of holiday preparations and excitement, and then it was the last lesson on Friday. When the bell rang, everyone streamed out of the classroom. I said goodbye to Tony, Joe and Amocheesh at the school steps and we parted ways. Like everyone from far away, they stayed at school for the Christmas holidays, and I walked across the bridge home, with about twenty other boys and girls. We walked in silence, as if talking was still forbidden even this far from school.

I kept an eye out for Angela, as I knew she would be returning to Fort Albany too, but didn't see her on the bridge. I saw her several times each day at chapel and in our lessons, but we were never allowed to talk. The times that we were allowed to talk quietly, at playtime and in the school dining room, the girls were taken elsewhere. I wondered what she thought of me. *Did* she think of me? I had smiled at her in our English lessons, and thought she had smiled back. I decided that once we were home I would go and visit.

When I got to my house, I did something I had never done before. I stopped outside the door. It felt different. Like it wasn't my own home. I wondered what had changed: everything looked the same, but felt unfamiliar. The logs by the side of the house looked the same, although now covered in snow, as did the path and the cross out back that Papa had built so Mama could pray for Rita. I couldn't figure out what it was. I knocked on the door.

Papa answered and picked me up in his arms. He carried me into the house. I took in his smell of leaves and wood smoke and buried my face in his hair. My heart felt warm against his.

"My boy," he said, and brushed my hair away from my eyes. I looked at his eyes, as his gaze shifted from worry to love.

"I missed you," I said.

"Me too," he replied. "Too much."

That night we ate all my favourite foods: goose and cranberry jam and bannock. The tastes were sharp and sweet and fatty and rich and it was all so good that I ate and ate until Papa said, "What, don't they feed you at St. Anne's?"

"Yeah, they do," I said. "But not as much. And not like this."

"Hmm," he said, and he glanced at me worriedly, then looked at Mama, although she seemed not to notice as she was still serving everyone.

"Things were better this year," he said. "We caught one hundred animals. Made about four grand, which means we paid off our debt and then some." He glanced at Mama and smiled. She smiled back. "And this one is turning into quite the hunter," he said, pointing to Alex. I looked at Alex. He was only five. He was definitely too young to shoot a gun.

"What do you mean?" I asked.

"He's been helping me track the animals."

"How?"

"Looking for footprints. That sort of stuff."

"I can do that."

"I know you can."

"So why are you letting him do it?"

"Well, Ed. You're not around."

Alex was having a hard time cutting his meat, and Papa turned away from me and began to help him with his knife. Eventually he turned back to me. "There's something we wanted to tell you." He glanced at Mama.

"What?" I said, looking down.

"Mama is pregnant!" Papa said.

"Really?" I said, looking at Mama.

"Yes," she said, and she took Papa's hand.

"When is it coming?"

"In the season of *sekwan*, when the buds open and the geese arrive," Papa said.

"Can I watch the birth?"

"No," he said, frowning. "We'll be out in the bush."

"Let me come with you."

"No," he said. "We already went through this. You have to go back to school."

"I don't want to," I said, quietly.

"Ed!" he said louder.

"Papa, please! It's not fair!"

"That's enough!" he said, and he stared at me until I fell silent. I decided to bring it up later in the holidays. There was no way I was going back.

Just before Christmas, Papa went and chopped down a spruce tree for Mama. We had never had a Christmas tree before, but Father Lavois had told her it was a way to honour the Lord Jesus Christ. We had one at St. Anne's too, although I can't remember the reason why, I think it was something about God liking big dead plants. The tree Papa picked was too big to fit inside the house—it would have filled the entire room—so we planted it in the snow outside.

Then Mama and Alex came outside, and Mama sang one of the English songs she had learned from Father Lavois. Alex tried to join in but he didn't know the words. I knew a few of them. It went "Wewissyouu a Mary Christmas. Wewissyouu a Mary Christmas." And you repeated those words over and over.

After the song, Papa took Alex inside because he was cold. I looked at Mama, who looked happier than I'd seen her in a long time. *Now is my chance*, I thought.

"Mama. I really want to see the new baby being born."

"Ed, you have to go back to school."

"Why?"

"You need to learn to read and write."

"Please. I don't like it there."

"School is always hard."

"But Sister Wesley has a new whip."

"I was whipped at residential school."

"You were?" I knew that she had gone to a residential school in Fort George across James Bay, but what this meant hadn't clicked. I wondered if her school was as bad as mine.

"Yes. The nun caught me throwing stones in the yard. They whipped me so hard I cried for two days. After that, I never did it again."

"So you know," I said. I couldn't believe that she knew how mean the nuns were and still wanted me to return to school. I wanted to curl up into a little ball and cry.

"They taught me discipline."

"Discipline," I said, my voice breaking.

"Yes, discipline."

"Mama. Please. It's worse now."

"I doubt it."

"Why are you making me go back?"

"You have to. It's the law."

"They are so mean!"

"You need to learn to read and write. You need to learn the wemistikoshiw ways."

"They hurt us for no reason."

"That's not true. You must have done something wrong."

"I wanted more food," I said, describing my ill-fated trip to the lunch line on the first day of school.

"You were stealing?" she asked.

"Yes. No." I felt like I was back at St. Anne's.

"We always taught you never to steal."

"It wasn't my fault!"

"Stealing is always wrong."

"I don't want to go back," I said.

Over the rest of the holidays, I tried to bring the topic up again with Mama and Papa but they always said the matter was already decided. Eventually I gave up.

I stayed close to home more than I used to. I liked to play with Papa's things when he was out of the house, they smelled of him. Once when I was wearing his hat, Mama took it away, saying I would get it dirty, but it upset me so much that she relented and let me wear it in the house, and even let me sleep in it.

On the day that I went back to school, Papa, Mama and Alex were scheduled to head for their trapline. Papa made a big breakfast of bannock and rabbit, but I was too anxious to eat it. I waited by the door for Papa to take me.

"Ed," he said. "Your mama isn't feeling well. I'm going to take her to the infirmary. Can you go to school by yourself today? Or do you need me to take you?"

I felt crushed. I really wanted to be with him, even for a few more minutes. I stared at the floor and then looked up at him. He looked between Mama and me worriedly.

"Okay, Papa," I said. I put on my coat and left.

I walked toward the river, looking at the spruce forest on the other side. Once on the bridge, I looked back. I could make out patches of roof between the trees and shrubs that lined the river. All I could think: I love you Mama, Papa and Alex. I already miss you so much.

FIVE

Back at school, Tony came up to me at first break. He was more
energetic than I had seen him in a while.

"Look what I got!" He put his hand into his pocket and showed
me a corner of yellow paper. It looked like a packet of chewing gum.
"One of the older boys gave it to me."

"Can I have some?" I was still debating whether or not to go to
Brother Jutras. Joe had finally said that it was okay as long as I didn't
tell anyone.

"Yeah. Not right now though. Sister Wesley is watching." I looked
around the yard and saw her standing next to the entrance. He was
right. We were quiet for a while, hoping she would pay attention to
the other boys instead.

"How was your break?"

"Good," I said. "We got presents this year." Mama had decided
that we would have Christmas presents as well as the spruce tree. We
had never done that before, but she said she wanted a celebration
worthy of the baby Jesus.

"Presents?"

"Christmas presents."

"Yeah. Some people have started doing that in my town, too."

"Did you get any?"

"Nah. Is Alex coming to St. Anne's this year?"

"No. Next."

"Lucky him," Tony said. "One more year out in the bush."

"Yeah. I know."

Tony hid the gum under his mattress and rationed it out. Sometimes we'd take it in turns to chew the same piece. Tony always got the first chew, and normally I got to go next so the gum still had some flavour. It was risky—I'd heard from some of the older boys that the punishment for chewing gum was to kneel in front of the class with the piece stuck to your nose, while the rest of the class laughed and pointed.

Chewing the gum took my mind off things, and made me forget the pains in my stomach for a while. But they always came back stronger. Tony said it happened to him too, and that's why we should go stealing. I didn't want to, I was too scared. But every day he kept on at me, calling me yellow legs, lazy bones or a wemistikoshiw trapper. I ignored him, but it was hard seeing the nuns eat their chicken or steaks every night and being hungry.

The night I agreed to go with Tony, we kneeled listening to Sister Wesley say her nightly prayers, telling us, as usual, that we were all sinners who would probably go to hell, then got into bed. I rolled over so I could see the dorm door ajar, and the thin line of light radiating from under Sister Wesley's bedroom door down the hall. I waited for her to turn it off. She seemed to be taking a while. I turned toward the window. The blinds were open, and I could see the moon brightening thin patches of cloud. What if we didn't go to the storeroom, but went home? We could sneak downstairs and go out through the front door and run all the way across the bridge. Or better, we could run out to the bush. As I was imagining this, I drifted off to sleep.

"Hey, wait up!" I called out to Tony in the playground the next day. He paused. "Are you mad at me?"

"No." I could tell that he was angry.

"Look. I didn't mean to fall asleep. I thought you were going to wake me."

"I tried."

"So did you get anything?"

"No. Father Gagnon was down on the first floor. I had to hide."

"Oh. Are you going again?"

"Yeah."

"When?"

"Tonight. Are you coming or are you a yellow legs?"

"I'm coming."

Tony was leading me through the dark lobby. I was terrified. We got to the basement stairs, and they were cold. Once we were at the bottom, we stole past the room where they kept boys when they'd been bad. The door was shut and I didn't hear anyone inside. We walked past the store cupboard where they kept potatoes, beets and carrots and opened another door. It looked like the place where they kept canned goods, but I couldn't tell in the dark.

"Here," Tony said. He fumbled about and I saw a flame. We went inside. Tony took down a can and put it in my hands. It was too dark to see what it was.

"This one is corn," he said. The lighter went out so he flicked it again. "Here's some Spam." He handed it to me.

"Get one more," I said. He grabbed another can of Spam.

"Let's go to the toilets," Tony said.

"It's too risky."

"No it's not. The downstairs ones. Then we can eat this in peace," he said. I thought about going upstairs. We would wake everyone up trying to open the cans. Then we'd have to share the food.

"Okay," I said.

"I heard that you got food." Amocheesh came up to Tony and me in the playground a few days later.

"Who told you that?" I asked.

"Just heard it."

"No," I said.

"Liar. I can tell."

"Maybe," Tony said.

"Can you take me with you?"

"No," Tony said.

"Why not?" Amocheesh asked.

"Too risky."

"Please," Amocheesh said.

"No," Tony said.

"But I'm hungry."

"We can't get caught."

"You're mean," he said, and walked off. I waited until he was out of earshot.

"Maybe we should let him come," I said.

"No. He's not fast enough."

"He can run good," I said.

"He's too noisy," he replied. It was true, Amocheesh ran like a duck.

"He can be quiet. Besides, he's hungry."

"Everyone is. You want everyone to come?"

We didn't go back for a few nights. I kept falling asleep while

Sister Wesley's light was still on. I think Tony must have done the same because he didn't bug me about it.

A few weeks later, Sister Wesley was filling in for Sister Thérèse, and she had decided to read from her favourite book. It was a list of all the things that you had to do to be good. The list was very long. She called it catch-the-chism. She read in Cree, and we had to repeat back to her in unison.

"Who was the first to break the law?" She really liked this bit. When she said it, her voice got louder and sometimes bits of spit flew out. I already knew most of the answers, as she sometimes read to us at night as well.

"He who makes his god in the image of the devil by paying homage to the sun, to the stars, to the idols, he who drums, participates in shaking tent ceremonies, evil chanting, evil feasting, evil pipe ceremonies, sweetgrass . . ."

As she spoke, I remembered Papa throwing the bear oil into the fire. That was an evil ceremony, wasn't it? I wondered if he would be scared of Sister Wesley. She was shorter than him, but much meaner. And she had a whip. Sometimes, she didn't stop until there was blood everywhere. It made me feel sick. I tried not to look but then she might whip you for looking away. A bell sounded twice, interrupting my thoughts. We all stood up. It was a bomb drill. Sister Wesley clapped and we got in a line from biggest to smallest.

Outside, we walked away from the air force base that the wemistikoshiws were building north of the school. Sister Wesley said we needed the building to protect us from other wemistikoshiw men who live a long way away, who are called the Soviets.

The base wasn't finished yet, but I'd already seen glimpses of it. The building was made of brick, not like our wooden house, and surrounded by a wooden fence. Inside were wemistikoshiw men and some locals that they liked to boss around.

That night, as I was trying to fall asleep, I heard the sound of metal ripping. I waited, then heard some slurping.

"Is that food?" It sounded like Brandon, the older, scary one.

"No." The voice sounded like Amocheesh's.

"It's food," Brandon said. "I can tell. Bring it here."

"No," Amocheesh said. "It's nothing."

"Shh," said Tony.

"Come here and give it to me," Brandon said.

"No," Amocheesh said.

"Bastard." It was a voice I didn't recognize, coming from a distance away. Some people said that Brandon's dad was actually a wemistikoshiw. We called these children *pakwachwaypaeygan*, or someone born without a father.

"Who said that?" Brandon said into the dark. No one replied. "Who said it?" he asked again, louder and slower this time. "That's it," he said. He got up and walked toward Amocheesh's bed. Then we could hear a scuffle.

"No!" Amocheesh said. "Stop it!"

We heard footsteps coming our way from outside the room. Brandon hurried back to his bed.

The door opened. I saw someone holding what looked like a fat pen, radiating a circle of light. A face lit from below: Sister Wesley.

The next morning I found Amocheesh standing naked by the sink in the bathroom. In his hands were his underpants with a reddish stain on them. It looked like the remnants of tomato sauce. We scrubbed the stain with our fingernails until we heard the bell. Amocheesh put the underwear back on under his pyjama pants and we rushed next door as Sister Wesley began the morning's bed-wetting inspection.

"What is this?" she said, pulling down Amocheesh's pyjamas.

"Nothing."

"Take them off." He did as he was told. She held his underpants under his nose.

"Is it food?"

"No."

"What is it then?"

"I pooed myself."

"You little liar. Stay right there."

She put the underpants inside her pocket, continued with the bed-wetting inspection, then clapped her hands and we all filed out to chapel.

We were out in the yard. A few boys were playing tag. Sister Wesley was patrolling. I walked up to Tony.

"What's going to happen to Amocheesh?"

"I dunno," he said. He looked worried. "Hopefully nothing."

"Do you really believe that?"

"No."

"I heard that they had a new whip. It has metal on the end," I said.

"Yeah. Maybe. Or the electric chair," Tony said.

"The what?" I asked.

"What did you hear?" Brandon had approached with his friends Russell and Jamie. They were both in the year above, where Brandon used to be before he was kept back.

"Nothing," I said.

"This is your fault," Tony said.

"What?!" Brandon said.

I bit my lip. I'd heard that Brandon beat up boys who answered back. Brandon was a head taller than me.

"You poured the tomato sauce on him," Tony said.

"Don't tell tales, Chief Sticky Fingers." He shoved his face in Tony's.

"Get lost," Tony said, and started to walk away. "Come on, Ed," he said. I hurried to catch up. I glanced around. Sister Wesley was watching us—fights happened but they were against the rules—and for once, I was pleased to feel her beady eyes locked onto me.

After lunch we learned that we couldn't go out to the yard because of a special show in the playroom. We streamed inside, lining up around the perimeter, as packed as flies around spoiled meat, with the smaller boys in front. Everyone seemed to be whispering nervously.

"Why are we waiting?" I asked the boy in front of me. He shrugged.

"It's the electric chair!" whispered the boy next to me. Everything else fell away. I stared at the doorway.

Sister Wesley and Brother Goulet walked in carrying a metal chair with wires coming out. Setting it down in the room's centre, Brother Goulet, who doubled as the school electrician, attached two clips to the legs with wires that connected to a wooden box with plastic knobs and a crank. Sister Wesley stood near, checking that everyone could see.

Brother Jutras led a boy into the hall, who hung his head and dragged his feet like a limp bear. His hair was tangled and face so pale that it took me a few seconds to realize it was Amocheesh. "Brotha. Purleease. Purleasease. No." The words sounded garbled and strange, and then I realized that Amocheesh was speaking a new language: English.

Brother Goulet picked up the whip resting on the chair's seat. He sat eight-year-old Amocheesh down and whipped his legs when he tried to stand. Father Gagnon entered the room, and moved to its centre to address us. He started speaking English, with Brother Goulet translating.

"This boy," he said, "committed a big sin. Last night he crept into the St. Anne's storeroom and stole some beans. Then he tried to eat them in bed. When confronted, he lied about it. Luckily Sister Wesley realized the truth." As Father Gagnon spoke, Sister Wesley buckled Amocheesh's arms and legs to the chair.

"Some of you come from homes where it is okay to steal. That is not the case at St. Anne's. Our job is to make you honest and good. To make you upstanding members of Her Majesty's Kingdom. When you take from St. Anne's storeroom or anywhere else, everyone suffers. You shame yourself and you bring shame on the school. Is that clear?"

"Yes," we replied in unison.

Sister Wesley began to crank a handle on the wooden box. Nothing happened.

"Oh, Jesus Christ," Father Gagnon said. Brother Goulet went to get his tools.

While he was gone, Sister Wesley opened the wooden box and fiddled with the wires. Then she said, *"Aha!"* and started to turn the crank.

Amocheesh stiffened and sucked in his breath. She turned the knob. He cried out and started to squirm.

"Don't be a baby," Sister Wesley said. She twisted the knob again, and his whole body tensed. Then he slumped in the chair. Everyone stopped talking. No one laughed. We all waited for him to get up.

Sister Wesley turned the current off. "Get up," she said. Amocheesh didn't move. *They've killed him*, I thought. "Get up," she said.

"Christ," Father Gagnon said. Sister Wesley kicked the boy's foot. It didn't move. Then they unfastened the buckles, and Brother Goulet carried him out of the playroom.

SIX

I noticed Mike Pasko out in the yard. He was throwing his hands in the air and laughing as boys ran around him. I remembered him asking everyone their names and it made me feel warm inside, like I used to feel before St. Anne's. He waved at me.

"Hi," I said, walking over.

"Hi, Ed," Mike said in Cree.

"You remembered my name," I said, and blushed.

"Of course. You feeling okay? You look kinda sick."

"Yeah. I'm . . ." I wondered whether I was allowed to tell him what had happened with Amocheesh. I decided against it, just in case it got back to the nuns. "I've not been feeling well."

"Don't let this place get to you, Ed."

I smiled, then quickly checked to see if anyone was watching. He also glanced to and fro. "Sometimes I take boys away from here," he whispered.

"Where?"

"Special places. Don't tell."

"I won't. Where?"

"Hunting. Or on trips. Whatever they want."

"It's allowed?"

"Of course. It's a big treat."

"Where do you go?"

"Wherever they want."

"What happens there?"

"I can't tell you now."

"Why not?"

"You're too young."

"When will you tell me?"

"Soon enough," he said, and he reached over and ruffled my hair.

It was raining so our break was in the playroom. I was playing Chinese checkers with Joe. Sister Wesley was sick, so Sister Wheesk was on duty. She was from Fort Albany, and taught the older years how to write Cree, so sometimes she was nicer than the rest of the nuns and brothers. I finished the game and went up to her.

"Can I go to the infirmary?" I asked.

"Yes," she said. "But be back here in fifteen minutes."

I hurried down the hallway to the back entrance and out the door, headed for the building next door where they were keeping Amocheesh. I crossed the wooden bridge that spanned the creek, ran up the grass and opened the door of the two-storey brick infirmary, and walked into a waiting room with some chairs. A middle-aged man from my hometown said hello to me in Cree. I nodded to him and sat down and waited. After a few minutes, a woman wearing a white nurse's uniform came into the room.

"Can I help you?" she asked in Cree.

"My friend, Amocheesh. Number Three. He's in there."

"Yes," she said.

"Can I see him?"

"No. He's sleeping."

"Oh," I said.

"Come back in a couple of hours," she said.

"I can't."

"Why not?"

"They won't let me. I need to get permission."

"Well I can't wake him up."

"Can you tell him that I came? It's Ed. Number Four."

"Okay, Number Four. I will." She shut the door.

We didn't have another break from cleaning until that evening. By then, everyone was so tired that they just stood huddled in groups.

"Did you get to see Amocheesh?" Tony asked.

"No. He was sleeping," I replied.

"Sleeping? What an excuse!"

"You think he wasn't sleeping?"

"No."

"Is he going to be okay?"

"Who knows," he said, and bit his lip.

Amocheesh got out of the infirmary at some point that night. I woke up and looked around and he was already folding his sheets for the bed-wetting inspection. I wanted to talk to him and find out if he was okay, but Sister Wesley and the others were particularly strict that day, and we weren't allowed to talk until the afternoon playtime.

"So how was it?" I asked him. "Did they whip you in there?"

"No. Not at all."

"Did they make you do any school work?"

"No. They gave me my own toy."

"Your own toy?" None of us had our own toys. "What did you get?"

"I got a toy horse. It was made of wood."

"Do you still have it?"

"No. I had to leave it there."

"Oh." I wished I could have a toy horse.

"And I could talk whenever I wanted," he said.

"Who did you talk to?"

"The nurses. They were really nice."

"They were?"

"Yeah. And they gave me really nice food. Like a chicken breast. And sauce. Lots of it."

"Like the nuns eat?"

"Yep. Just like the nuns."

"Did you get any chocolate cake?" I asked as Tony approached.

"What you get?" Tony asked.

"Chocolate cake," said Amocheesh.

"No way," he said.

"Yep." My mouth watered and my stomach growled.

"Yeah. I'm going back."

"How's that?" I asked. It was hard to get to the infirmary. You had to be really sick, otherwise they just sent you to the dorm. Even when they beat you till you bled you didn't always get to go.

"I'm going to have an accident," Amocheesh said.

"What sort?" I asked.

"I'm gonna choose," he said.

"That's stupid," Tony said.

"If you're that hungry, maybe you could just go to Brother Jutras," I said.

"No, an accident is better. I heard that Brother Jutras makes your thingy hurt."

"That's not what Joe—" I clapped my hand over my mouth. I hadn't meant to blurt it out.

"What?" Tony asked.

"Maybe it doesn't hurt," I said.

"How do you know?"

"I don't," I lied.

"Did you go?" Tony asked.

"No," I replied.

"Good," he said. "Don't."

I kept waiting for Mr. Pasko to tell me about the special place. In the meantime, Amocheesh wasn't around that much anymore. He was always helping out Father Lavois in chapel. If Father Lavois thought you were really good then you might have your cleaning duties stopped for a few days. We were talking about it when Brandon and his friend Russell approached at the next playtime break.

"I know something you don't know," Brandon said.

"I doubt it," Tony replied.

"What's that supposed to mean?" Brandon took a step forward and glared.

Tony shrugged. "Whatever."

"Oh yeah. Well, get this, smarty-pants. Mr. Shaw is coming," Brandon said.

"Who's that?" I asked.

"The Indian Agent," Brandon replied.

"Oh no," I said.

"What?" Tony said.

"It's good news, dummy," Brandon said.

"I doubt it," Tony said.

"Mr. Shaw already came here," Russell said.

"When?" Tony asked.

"Before you got here," Russell added.

"So?" Tony said.

"So he took all the whips away," Brandon said.

"I don't believe it," Tony said.

"He did!" Russell said.

"You'll see," Brandon said.

I didn't think much of it, until a few weeks later when we heard at breakfast that Mr. Shaw really was coming. Sister Wesley didn't say anything about the whips. Instead, she told us that there was a new cleaning schedule because the school had to be spotless before he arrived.

Over the next few weeks, everyone was very busy preparing for Mr. Shaw. We kept cleaning, scrubbing and mopping, as the weather got hotter. On the day that he was supposed to come, we heard that his flight had been delayed and that he had decided to postpone his trip until after the summer holidays.

It was the last day of the school year. I couldn't stop thinking of what I would do when I got home, and anyone could have seen the twinkle in my eyes. We heard a loud scraping of chairs, and we all stood up. We weren't allowed to run, but we could barely contain ourselves, all pushing toward the door. There was still a risk that Father Gagnon would whip us for being pushy, but somehow this thought slipped from my mind as I left the classroom and hurried toward the front door. I was going home for the summer holidays—three months of freedom.

Outside was so bright. I could smell cut grass, horse manure and a hint of spruce. And then I was running across the wooden bridge, streaming past everyone, the water gushing beneath me. Just beyond the trees I could see glimpses of my house.

I ran up the path all the way to the front door, crying tears of joy. Home.

We were out on the Albany River, Alex, Papa and myself in our wooden canoe. Mama and my new baby sister, Mary-Louise, were at home. It was one of those days where the water and the blue sky seem to merge. Papa had some fishing line and thread in his hands. He was showing me how to tie a lure.

"The most important thing is that it's secure and the lure can move freely," Papa said. "The first thing we need to do is tie a bigger knot in the main line, so tie a granny knot, and then don't pull it tight—make sure it stays slightly open," he said, pointing to the circular knot at the end of the thread.

Alex and I watched and listened intently. Papa expected us to commit the process to memory the first time, just like he had to do when he was growing up.

When he finished, he watched as we did it ourselves. Alex got it right the first time, but I had trouble pushing the line through the final loop. My fingers felt too big for the small hole.

"Don't worry about it, son," Papa said. "Just try again." He watched me until I got it right.

I was carrying a pike home. It was so big that I had to hold it near my face so it didn't drag on the ground. I'd caught it myself. Papa told me that I'm a quick learner and that Mama and Mary-Louise will be really happy about the pike. Alex was carrying a walleye but his was smaller than mine, only the length of his arm. We had left Papa to finish up at the river.

Mama opened the door as we walked up the path.

"My boys," she said, smiling at us. She came out with a chopping board, which she put on the tree stump next to the house, and began gutting the fish. "Wanna help, Ed?" she asked.

"I . . . I don't remember how."

"Sure you do. Come here," she said. I stood in front of her and she leaned her head on my shoulders and took my hands, showing me how to use the knife. "You're getting so big," she said. "You have such strong hands."

—

The days ran together in a blur of fishing and eating and playing slingshots with Alex. I hadn't practised my aim all school year. Since I'd been gone, Alex had gotten better than me and could hit the farthest branches of the treetops.

"So what you learn at school?" Alex asked.

"Lots of things."

"Like what?"

"I'm learning how to write Cree."

"I already know that," Alex said.

"You do not."

"I do."

"Show me." He took a stick and drew a few scribbles in the dirt. I didn't know how to write perfectly but I was pretty sure that what he had scrawled didn't make any sense. "So what's it say, big shot?"

"Uh . . . it says, uh . . . Alex."

"No it doesn't."

"Yes it does."

I took his writing stick and drew some circles with lines through them.

"That says Alex," I lied.

He took the stick and began trying to copy the gibberish. I laughed inside. I couldn't wait to tell Tony.

A few days before I had to go back to St. Anne's, I got a terrible stomach ache. After the second day of being in pain, Mama took me to the infirmary. We were lucky. The doctor who flew in only once per month was in town.

"What's wrong with him?" he asked Mama. She told him my symptoms. He motioned me to sit on a long table and then pulled up my shirt. I expected him to ask me to pull down my pants to feel my penis, like Brother Jutras had, but instead he pulled up my shirt and pressed my stomach in different places.

"Ow," I said. It hurt everywhere he touched. Then he told me to open my mouth and he put a wooden stick inside.

"Okay, Ed, you can get down," he said.

"What's wrong, Dr. Browning?" Mama asked.

"I think it's a case of pre-school nerves."

"What's that?"

"It means that it's all in his head."

"What should we do?"

"Nothing. He'll be fine."

"But he's not eating."

"Just give him some tea."

"He's not drinking much either."

"Don't worry. He'll be fine as soon as he gets back to school," he said. He scribbled some notes on a pad of paper. "Next!" he said, and Mama and I left.

"Come on. Get up!" Mama said. It was the day I was going back to school. Everyone else was already up and dressed.

"I don't feel good," I replied.

"Ed. Please. You'll be late."

"I don't feel good."

"Come on, Ed. You'll be fine," Mama said. "Papa had to go and see Mr. Pasko at the store so I'm helping you today." I slowly pulled on my pants. "Ed, can you hurry, please?"

She went to the trunk where everyone's clothes were kept. Alex began pulling them all out of the trunk.

"Not now, Alex. Please, Ed," Mama said. "Can you hurry?"

—

We crossed over the bridge together—Mama, who was carrying Mary-Louise, Alex and me. I tried to take Mama's hand but there wasn't one spare so eventually I just grabbed onto her coat.

As the school came into view, I felt a rush of fear and the urge to pee. I turned back toward home.

"Come on, Ed!" Mama said.

"I have to go, Mama," I said.

"Go in the school then."

"I don't want to." Brother Goulet was standing in the school's doorway.

"Number Four. Come and get registered," he said in Cree.

"But I have to pee," I said to him.

"After. Come."

I turned to Mama. "Can you wait here until I finish?" She nodded.

Brother Goulet walked me to Father Gagnon's office where a group of boys were already in line. I stood at the back, trying to hold it. Once my name had been checked, I hurried to pee, then rushed back to the front door and looked outside. Mama, Alex and Mary-Louise were gone.

That first day of the new school year we had to shower again with the chemicals. It felt like a hole had opened in my chest and was getting bigger. The hole made me want to bolt so I stared at the floor, trying to hold everything in.

Most of the new boys were bigger than me, but I was a little taller, too, so when we went to line up to get our new numbers and new uniforms, my number was 15 out of 130. I looked at the number on the collar of my shirt. I didn't want it. I just wanted to be Ed. The void in my chest was hurting so much that I felt like I was falling into it. It got worse during Brother Jutras's "medical exam." I didn't look in his eyes when he did it. Just waited and tried not to feel anything. When it was over, and the other boys went to the yard, I went to the toilets and cried. I was feeling very homesick. I'd had enough of school. I hated being slapped and whipped all the time. I wished I could just disappear.

When there were no more tears, I left the toilets and headed for the yard. On the way, I saw Mike Pasko.

"Whoa!" he said in Cree. "You okay, Ed?"

"Yeah."

"You look like you've been crying."

"No. Maybe. I don't know."

He pulled out a handkerchief. "Here." For some reason, this gesture made the pain inside hurt more. I bit my lip. "What happened?"

"It's just . . ." I wasn't sure if I was allowed to tell him about being whipped and Brother Jutras's "exams." My tears began to fall again.

"Come on. If you stop crying, I'll give you a surprise."

"What?"

"I can't tell you. It's a secret."

"What sort of surprise?" I said, wiping my face.

"I can't tell you right now."

"Why not?"

"I have to check if it's allowed."

"What's allowed?"

"So many questions, Ed! Be a good boy and you'll find out."

I didn't see Mr. Pasko for a few weeks. We weren't going out to the yard as much now. We had to stay inside and sit in silence. It was because of the news on the radio. The Cold War was heating up.

I wondered how a Cold War could get warm—wouldn't it be a Hot War instead? My granddad had been in the First World War. He said that he had been sent across an ocean to live in a muddy trench and eat biscuits and dried milk. It didn't sound like a Hot War from the way he described it. It sounded loud, damp and bloody.

As the days went by I waited for my secret to be revealed. I wanted to tell Tony, but I knew that I wasn't allowed. Mr. Pasko had already done one nice thing for us—last Christmas, he had bought us all new hockey sticks so we could play ball hockey outside. He wore red and called himself Santa Claus, and the younger boys got to sit on his lap as he bounced them up and down. I wondered if he would give me a special present, one I didn't have to share with anyone. Or maybe he would let me work in his store. He did that with some of the older boys.

I kept waiting and waiting and then it happened on a Saturday. I was out in the yard playing tag with Joe, Amocheesh and Erick when Sister Wheesk came over.

"Message for you, Fifteen," she said. "Go and see Father Gagnon."

I left the yard and walked to Father Gagnon's office. Mr. Pasko was standing there, talking to Father Gagnon.

"You ready?" he asked.

"Where are we going?"

"It's a surprise. Come with me." We left together through the front door into a bright, cloudless day. I could see the grass and the spruce forest in the distance. I felt free as a moose that has escaped a group of hunters. I ran to his van and he helped me onto the bench seat. He started the van, and the radio came on. It was country and western. Once he was out of the parking lot he started singing along. I smiled, but I didn't know the words so I just nodded in time. We turned off the main road and drove into a narrow track sheltered by thick spruce trees.

"Where are we going?"

"You'll see."

The road twisted, and then the trees fell away and there was grass and the blue of the Albany River. We drove toward the water, and Mr. Pasko stopped the truck before he hit the rocks.

"She's beautiful, isn't she?" he said in Cree, squeezing my leg.

"Yeah. Do you want to get out?"

"Not yet," he said. "I just want to sit here and enjoy it with you."

"Okay."

We watched the river for a while. The sun glittered along the water like raindrops of light. Mr. Pasko hugged me, and it made me feel warm inside.

"You know, this reminds me of my place in Montreal."

"Where's that?"

"Down south."

"Oh."

"It's the most beautiful city in all of Canada. Maybe in all of the world."

"Oh."

"You should see it. You'd like it."

"I don't think my parents would let me."

"Sure they would. Other boys have been there."

"They have?"

"Yup. They got to stay there all summer."

"Did they have fun?"

Mr. Pasko laughed. "Of course. Lots of fun. That's where my boys grow up. Become real men."

I kept looking for Mr. Pasko after that whenever I was out in the yard or between my lessons. I knew he did our grocery deliveries, but I didn't see him. I waited for a few weeks, and then I heard that he was going away for a while. A boy who had graduated from St. Anne's a few years ago was going to manage his store.

I was disappointed. Mr. Pasko had told me not to tell anyone about our outing in case the other boys became jealous. But if he was away, maybe it was okay. The other boys couldn't become jealous because he wasn't here. I told Amocheesh about it over lunch.

"Last week I went with Mike Pasko to the river," I said.

"Really? That's cool. I wanna go sometime. What did you do?"

"We drove down to the water. And we listened to the radio together."

"Did you catch anything?"

"No. We didn't go fishing."

"Really? He took Brandon fishing."

"He did? Brandon?" I couldn't believe it. Why did he·take him? Brandon was mean.

"Yup. He caught a big pike."

"When?"

"I dunno. Maybe a month ago. Everyone was talking about it."

"They were?"

"Yeah. Brandon was bragging big time. He really liked it."

"Why'd he pick him?"

"I dunno. 'Cause he's older, I guess."

I had felt special before, like someone cared about me. Now I felt small and alone again.

SEVEN

I went home for Christmas. It was nice, but different from the previous Christmas. My family got stuck in the bush because the ice was too thin for the dogs to go very fast, so I had to stay at St. Anne's for five extra days. When I finally got home, on the day before Christmas, Mary-Louise had a high fever, so Mama and Papa went back and forth between home and the infirmary. I tried to find a time to talk about everything I had been through, but they were too worried about the baby. Sometimes, I heard Mama on her knees saying things like "Please, Jesus. Please don't take another one."

On the morning that I was scheduled to go back, I got a terrible stomach ache once again. I heard Mama and Papa talking about it.

"Should we take him to the infirmary?" Mama asked Papa.

"What happened last time?"

"The doctor said it was 'pre-school nerves.'"

"What's that mean?"

"He said it was all in his head."

"Did he think it was serious?"

"No."

Papa came up to crouch beside me on my furs. "Are you going to be okay?"

"I don't know, Papa."

"Where does it hurt?" I pointed to my belly. He put his hand on my belly and began to rub. I could feel warmth radiating from his hand to my heart. "Does that feel better?"

"A bit."

"My boy," he said. "You're going to be fine."

At school, Tony came up to me at first break.

"Guess what?" he said.

"What?"

"Mr. Shaw is coming next week!"

"I've heard that before."

"No, this time it's for real. I heard it from Father Lavois."

"What if his flight is delayed?"

"Well, then he'll rearrange."

"We'll see."

"What's wrong?"

"Nothing," I said. A heavy feeling of dread had settled over me since I'd walked in the door.

"Cheer up, brother."

On the day that Mr. Shaw arrived, Sister Wesley went through our bedroom closet where the clothes were kept in numbered cardboard boxes. She took out all the torn and worn uniforms, which she put in bags. In their place, she put new numbered uniforms. When she was finished, she began the bed-wetting inspection. This time, she didn't hit any of the boys, just took any soiled underwear and put it in her bag and told us to find new ones in the closet.

On the way to chapel, Tony caught up with me. He began to talk, even though it was against the rules.

"If I'd known Sister Wesley would do that, I'd have pooed my pants."

I laughed. Maybe Brandon was right: maybe Mr. Shaw was going to make everything better.

At breakfast that day we were served a big portion of scrambled eggs and bacon. I had never eaten bacon before, and at first I found it salty but as I ate, I liked it more. I wanted extra, although I wasn't so dumb as to ask, after what had happened on my first day of school.

At playtime, no one got whipped, even when Nicholas, a new boy who was in my year and from Fort Albany, began to play throwing stones. Normally we were told off when we played the games that we grew up with. The nuns said they were too dangerous. This time, when Nicholas threw a rock at the tree at the edge of the yard, Sister Wesley didn't say a word. So then he threw a stick up into its branches and began trying to knock it down with some stones. Soon Amocheesh and Joe had joined in too. I held back. I still wasn't sure what would happen. I glanced at Sister Wesley, who stared at us all. I wondered why she didn't come over and cuff our ears. Maybe she was waiting for the right moment.

After the bell rang we went to our lesson. Brother Goulet was filling in for our Grade 2 teacher, Sister Camille, and speaking to us in English. I understood some of the words now. He kept looking at the classroom door expectantly. Mr. Shaw still hadn't arrived, so the brother took out a Cree prayer book and we shut our eyes. "Oh merciful God: have mercy on all Jews, Turks, infidels and heretics and also upon all those heathen nations, on whom the light of Thy glorious Gospel hath not yet shone: especially the Indians of this continent." We heard a knock and I opened my eyes.

"Come in," Brother Goulet said in English. A man wearing a grey suit and brown shoes walked in. "This is Indian Agent Shaw," the brother said in Cree. "Say 'Hello, Mr. Shaw,'" he instructed. We had been taught the English phrase "Hello, Mr. Shaw" for the occasion and we repeated the words. I looked around the classroom. Tony was a few desks away. He gestured that he was passing me a piece of paper. I shook my head no.

"He's come all the way from North Bay to see us. Isn't this a wonderful treat, boys?" he said in Cree.

"Yes," we said in English in unison. Tony had ignored me, and finished the note, and now it was making its way across the rows. The girl next to me, Dayness, put her hand on my desk and unveiled a crumpled ball.

"Number Fifteen!" Brother Goulet said in Cree. "What's in your hand?"

"Nothing," I said nervously, in Cree.

"In English?" he said. I had been taught the word but couldn't remember, and I was starting to panic. "It's 'nah-THING,'" Brother Goulet said. He looked at Mr. Shaw knowingly, and explained what had happened.

"Come here and bring it with you," he said in Cree. I got up from my desk and slowly walked to the front. "Open your hand," he said in Cree. I unfurled my fingers. Tony had drawn two stick figures. It was hard to say, but it looked like one was whipping the other. Brother Goulet looked at it, raised his eyebrows and scrunched it into a ball.

"Gharbahje," he said. He turned to me and started speaking in Cree. "Don't let this happen again."

"Sorry, Brother Goulet," I said in Cree. I glanced around the classroom to the spot where they kept the whip. It wasn't there. I waited for him to ask me to go and get it. Instead he motioned his hand like he was flicking away a piece of dust, and I returned to my seat.

—

"You hear?" Joe said. Tony and I were in the playground. "Ed drew a picture making fun of Brother Goulet and he didn't even get in trouble!"

"Course I heard, dummy," Tony said. "It wasn't Ed. It was me."

"You're cool."

"Whatever," he said.

Joe hesitated. "So you wanna play throwing stones?" he asked, gesturing to the boys at the edge of the yard who were trying to hit the stick out of a lone jack pine tree.

"Not now," Tony said. "We're busy." He put his arm around my shoulders and stared at Joe, waiting for him to leave. After a few moments, Joe got the message.

"Let's go to the woods," he said, when Joe was out of earshot.

"No way."

"They won't do anything with Mr. Shaw here."

"Yes they will."

"No they won't. You saw what happened with the picture."

"So."

"You're like a wemistikoshiw trapper. Wuss."

"No, I'm not."

"Yellow legs."

"Stop that."

"Come on then!" Tony said. He glanced at Sister Wesley and began to make his way across the icy yard.

"What are you doing?" I hissed, but I followed him. "She can still see us."

He didn't reply, just kept walking. "This is dumb!" I whispered hoarsely as I followed. He quickened his pace, crossed into the icy fields beyond the yard, and began to make his way toward the forest. I ran quickly, sinking into his snowy footsteps.

"We have to keep going," he said, once we got to the spruce forest.

"Where?"

"We have to go to the bush."

"Why?"

"We can't go back. They'll give us the electric chair. Or put us in the basement." The basement was where they put boys who'd been really bad. It was unlit and didn't have a toilet. It was full of rats. After being locked in there, boys cried at night for weeks.

"What?! Wait! I can't!"

"Yes you can. We need to head northwest. Then we can find my mama and papa."

"But I'm cold."

"We can make a fire when we're farther away."

"We don't have anything to eat."

"We can catch some fish."

"What if we freeze?"

"We won't."

"But they will come and find us. We've left footprints. Then we will be in even more trouble."

"We're already in trouble."

"You said that they wouldn't do anything with Mr. Shaw here."

"Well, maybe. But he'll be gone by tomorrow."

"You lied to me."

"I was giving you courage."

"I don't care. I want to go back."

"We can't. They'll whip us and put us in the electric chair."

"If we keep going, they'll come and find us and it will be worse. They'll whip us and we'll bleed and bleed."

"No . . ." He began speaking but then caught himself. He seemed to slump, as if the fear had turned to defeat.

"It's not fair," he said quietly.

We didn't want to be seen hanging about the school, so we stayed out by the trees until we heard the bell marking the end of lessons. Then we hurried to the school. I was afraid that we would be caught as we crossed the field, and I watched for Sister Wesley as I ran but couldn't find her in the yard. Then I caught sight of Sister Wheesk, who was playing pat-a-cake with some of the boys. We ran to the opposite corner of the playground. As soon as we got to the gravel, we bent over to catch our breaths.

"There you are!" Amocheesh said. "Everyone was looking for you."

"We were just getting some air," Tony said.

"You guys are in such trouble. Everyone thought you'd run away. Sister Camille did the register at the beginning of class."

"What did she say?"

"Nothing, with Mr. Shaw here. She just pretended that you guys were ill. But he'll be gone by tomorrow."

They waited for a few days to punish us. Perhaps they hadn't decided how best to teach us a lesson. Or they thought that Mr. Shaw would come back. Tony and I talked about it during the breaks.

"What are they waiting for?" I wondered.

"How should I know?" he said.

I glanced about. It could happen at any time. I tried to remember what my dad had taught me about being brave. You needed to be as courageous as a mother bear with her cubs, he said. That was one of the Seven Sacred Teachings.[2] You need to stand, unafraid, and fight to the death. But what if they killed me? I bit my lip, trying not to cry.

On the day that we were punished, excitement ran through the room like a snake through dry grass. None of the nuns had announced anything, but it was as if the news travelled through air. The other boys were staring at Tony and me.

It started during the bed-wetting inspection. I tried to remember the Cree story about the courage of the Mother Bear but every time I thought about it, I saw Sister Wesley's face on top of the sow's body. The she-bear creature had angry eyes, and she was nothing like the animal in Papa's teaching.

After breakfast we were supposed to go and play in the playroom, but Sister Wesley took Tony and me into one of the classrooms, which was empty except for Father Gagnon. Father Gagnon began to talk, with Sister Wesley translating.

"Why did you do it?" Father Gagnon asked Tony.

"Do what?"

"You know what I'm talking about! Run away!"

"We didn't run away," Tony said.

"Don't answer me back, Number Fifty-Nine!"

"We needed some air."

"We give you air, Number Fifty-Nine. That's what playtimes are for."

"Sorry," Tony mumbled.

"Is that all you can say? You almost ruined the reputation of this school and that's all you can say? Sorry?"

"Sorry, Father Gagnon."

"What about you, Number Fifteen?"

"I . . ." I paused, wondering how I could dispel his anger.

"It was my idea," Tony said.

"Let him talk," Father Gagnon said.

"I . . ." My mind was completely blank.

"Speak up, Number Fifteen."

"It was his idea," I said eventually. I looked at Tony and his eyes flashed with anger. Father Gagnon turned to Tony.

"You know, I've been watching you for quite some time."

"You have?"

"It's boys like you that put everyone at risk. Like a dead rat in a well."

Tony glared at him.

"What do we do with dead rats?"

Tony said nothing.

"We remove them so everyone can drink." Tony and I looked at each other, uncertain about what the priest was getting at.

Father Gagnon led Tony and me to the playroom, with Sister Wesley and Brother Goulet following. When we got there the other boys were lined up around the walls, as they had been for Amocheesh's electrocution.

"These boys put the reputation of this school at risk," Father Gagnon said, with Sister Wesley translating. "They endangered their own lives and those of everyone in this room. They nearly brought shame to this school. On Monday, they tried to run away. Luckily Sister Camille noticed they were missing and notified us immediately. They were found before they could bring harm to themselves or any of you.

"Let this be a lesson to you all. Running away from St. Anne's is a mortal sin. You will be punished by the Lord and here on Earth. We will find you and we will imprint on your body and soul what you have done wrong. Is that clear?"

No one said anything. The silence was as loud as a waterfall.

Sister Wesley sat Tony down in the electric chair. It had a metal frame, with the seat and back made of plywood. Brother Goulet buckled my friend's arms into the straps, then checked their tightness. Satisfied, he began to turn the handle on the wooden box. Tony cried out. He began to squirm. He bit his lip. Brother Goulet cranked it higher. Tony's body stiffened, fell slack, and tensed again. Brother Goulet turned it off. Tony began to cry. Sister Wesley led him away.

It was my turn. Brother Goulet sat me down. My legs didn't reach the floor. He buckled me in.

"It won't happen again, Brother," I said.

"You bet it won't."

I held the arms of the chair as hard as I could. I looked at Brother Goulet's hand as he turned the handle, and felt a searing jolt of pain running from my hands to my legs. I gasped. I tried to pull my arms free. I couldn't. I could feel my legs waving in front of me. The pain lessened, then intensified like falling through ice.

It stopped.

Then another renewed jolt coursed through my body just as hard as the first time. I wiggled this way and that. My teeth had snapped together. My eyes were closed. I didn't want to see anyone. I knew I was making a fool of myself.

All around me was burning, pulling me under. I let go and everything went black.

I woke up and looked around. No one else was in the dormitory. Everything hurt. Inside me was hot, and I felt like my blood wanted to burst out of my body. I got out of bed and went to the cabinet and pulled out my pants and shirt. They slipped from my fingers. Everything was so heavy. I picked them up again and went back to the mattress and slowly got dressed. I started down the stairs but they felt too steep. I sat down mid-step and watched the dust fluttering to the wooden floor. When I heard the bell, I went down to find everyone.

In the dining hall, everyone stared at me. I ignored them and went to get a bowl of porridge. I managed two bites before I threw up. I stared at the grey-tinged oats mixed with pieces of carrot on top of my bowl. Suddenly Sister Wesley was next to me. She took the bowl from my hands and put it on the floor.

"Eat it," she said. I reached down to pick up the bowl. "No. Eat like a dog." I stared at her, and then she slowly pushed me onto all fours. I put my head into the bowl. The smell made me gag. I tried to eat from the side of the bowl, but couldn't reach the porridge under the vomit. I gagged. The puke was lumpy and tasted vinegary and bitter. I vomited again and fainted.

I heard the wake-up bell and I checked my underpants. Dry. What a relief. I got up and waited for the bed-wetting inspection. Then I went to the closet to get my clothes. I felt woozy. After chapel, I went down to the dining hall. I looked for Tony and Amocheesh but couldn't see them. I stood in line for my porridge. When I got to the front of the line, the server looked at me and shook his head no.

"Porridge?" I asked.

"No. Sister Wesley's orders." I looked around the hall and caught sight of her across the room. She nodded at the server. He reached down and pulled up the bowl from yesterday. Inside was stale porridge with bits of puke floating on top. "You have to finish this before you can have your breakfast."

I couldn't believe what he had said. He glanced across the room to where Sister Wesley was watching us. He shook his head slightly as if he wanted me to know that he thought it unfair, and gave me the bowl.

I took it back to my seat. I looked at it. I wanted to vomit again. I put a spoonful in my mouth. The acrid taste made me gag. Retching, I plugged my nose and ate my first mouthful. On my second mouthful, I vomited again into my mouth. It tasted rotten and I tried not to puke. I swallowed quickly and held my stomach, trying to keep it down. I took a few breaths and bit my lip, trying not to cry. I kept eating.

I was the last one to leave the dining hall. The last mouthful took me a long time. Everyone else had gone, except Sister Wesley.

"Go," she said. "Go to your lessons." She looked at my bowl, then back at me. "Savage boy. You're disgusting."

During my morning lessons, my stomach felt like it was going to explode. The pain pushed out from deep within me. It felt like I had gotten very small, and all that was left was a wall of hurt. I asked if I could go to the infirmary, and was given permission during morning break. Nicholas escorted me. Once we left the school, we began whispering.

"Where's Tony?" I asked.

"Still in the basement."

"How long has he been in there?"

"Since he was electrocuted."

"How long's that?"

"Two days."

"I heard there are rats down there."

Nicholas nodded.

I began thinking about Tony trapped in the dark with rats crawling over him, on his feet and up his legs. I shuddered. "When are they letting him out?"

"I dunno."

"Do you think he will be okay?"

"I dunno."

"Why won't they let him out?"

"Maybe because he was bad."

We reached the infirmary and Nicholas walked me inside. We waited until the nurse came out from the examination room.

"Yes?" she said.

"He's sick," Nicholas said, gesturing at me.

"Come in," she said.

In the infirmary there were a couple of other boys lying down underneath grey blankets.

"What's wrong?" the nun said.

"My stomach hurts."

"When did it start?"

Was I allowed to tell her about being made to eat the vomit? I wasn't sure. I decided to risk it.

"Yesterday. When Sister Wesley made me eat the vomit."

"Another one," she said. She took my temperature and gave me some pills. I went to sleep.

That night, I awoke once all the lights were out. Hardly any light—not even from the windows. I rubbed my eyes and stared. Two yellow eyes. I reached forward and felt a muzzle. A wet nose and warm breath. My stomach stopped hurting, and a warmth spread over me. For the first time in a long while, I felt calm.

Three days later, the pain had stopped and I was free to go. I missed chapel and went straight to breakfast. I lined up for porridge. I didn't want it—the idea of it made me want to retch. My stomach rumbled, and I tried to keep everything down. If I vomited again, it would be much worse. Maybe I would have to eat it from the floor. Sister Wesley had made other kids do that sometimes. It made me feel sick thinking about it, and I swallowed a few times. When I looked up, I saw Tony. I caught his gaze, but felt too sick to wave. He looked away. I didn't understand.

He got his porridge and turned away from our usual table. Where was he going? I really wanted to tell him what happened. He walked to the next table and sat down next to Brandon. Him? Why him? I stared at them. Tony said something I couldn't hear. Brandon laughed. What was he doing? I walked over.

"Hi, Tony," I said.

"Hi," he said. He looked at me like he was examining a shoddy piece of fur.

"Are you okay?" I said.

"Yeah."

"Can I sit here?"

"No."

"Oh," I said. He began whispering something to Brandon. "Are you . . ." I paused.

"Am I what?"

"Are you mad at me?"

"Are you mad at me?" he said in a high-pitched, mocking voice.

"What are you doing?"

"What are you doing?" he said in the same voice. Everyone at the table began to laugh.

"Eh, Number Fifteen! Get lost!" Brandon said.

I walked to the other table and sat down. I ate quickly, wiping the wetness from my eyes.

The next few months drifted by. I remember getting in trouble a lot. For some reason, I kept peeing my pants. I tried to hold it, but it leaked out. In chapel, morning lessons, afternoon lessons, doing farm work. Each time, I didn't say anything, just sat in the wet cold and waited until Sister Wesley found out. Sometimes she beat me. Or she would take me to the playroom where all the punishments happened. We lined up to be whipped.

EIGHT

Somehow I made it to the last day of the school year and I was going home for the summer. I was in the playroom messing about with some other ten-year-old boys, waiting for the final bell. Amocheesh and I were playing cards. Sister Camille appeared in the doorway.

"Message for you, Fifteen," she said in English. I left the cards and walked to Father Gagnon's office. The message was a telegram that my parents were going to be a day late coming back from the bush.

The next morning I walked across the bridge. I hadn't said much to anyone since being electrocuted and then snubbed by Tony. The words would rise up inside of me, but they always came out wrong. Or they came out and they sounded different, like someone had flown inside my body and taken my place. There was another Ed who had taken over my body. He carried on like nothing had happened.

I walked home and sat outside my house. After a couple of hours waiting, Papa came up the path holding Mary-Louise, with Mama and Alex walking behind him.

"Ed!" Alex said, and ran past Papa to meet me.

"Hi, Ed!" Papa said. He and Mama were carrying all their stuff from the canoe.

"Hi," I said.

"Can you help us?" Papa said. I picked up his bag and gun. We walked inside.

"How are you doing, son?" Papa said.

"Fine." I looked about the house. It looked cramped.

"You okay?" Mama asked.

"Yes," I said and shrugged. I leaned against the wall and crossed my arms. Mama and Papa exchanged glances, and then Papa came over and gave me a hug. His touch felt cold.

"I'm sorry we're late, son. We got held up. Simeon Scott in Kapiskau relayed the message to Father Gagnon."

That night Mama cooked foods from my past. There was goose roasted on tamarack, moose meat stew with onions and blueberry jam. It was heavy and rich. I tried to eat but I wasn't very hungry. Mama said I was too thin, so I put it in my mouth and swallowed it down. Afterwards, she asked if I wanted to show her some of the things I had learned in school, but I said I was tired and went to bed early.

Next morning, Papa woke me up before anyone else. "Let's go fishing!" he said. "Come on. Just you and me."

"Okay," I said.

We walked down to the river. Papa looked at me worriedly as we walked.

"You okay?" he said.

"Yeah."

Then he began speaking about a beaver reserve he'd heard about down south, and I tried to listen but his words ran together and wouldn't stay in my brain. Sometimes I thought about being made to eat the vomit. Or I saw Brother Goulet's hand on the handle of the electric chair and felt the pain shooting through my legs. I stared at the grass. Papa was asking me a question. I hadn't heard, so I nodded.

"Ed," he said. "What's gotten into you?"

"Nothing."

He stared at me. When we got down to the water, he showed me some of the new lures that he'd made.

"What do you think, Ed?"

"Whatever."

"What do you mean, 'whatever'?"

"They look broken."

"What are you taking about?"

I shrugged.

"Ed?"

"Can we go home now?"

"We've only just got here!"

"I'm bored. This is boring."

"What's boring?"

"This," I said, pointing at the fishing line. "Everything."

Papa shook his head. "No, we are not going home. I don't care if you think it's boring. Everyone needs to eat. Which means I need to fish."

After we got home, Papa asked me to clean the fish. I took the knife and started to clean the scales but it was annoying, so I stabbed the fish in the eye. I pulled it out and did it again. Papa took the fish out of my hand.

"That's not funny."

"Yes, it is. It's funny, isn't it, Alex?"

Alex smiled and shrugged. "I guess."

"You've spoiled the meat."

"Maybe," I said. I wiped my hands on my pants and sat on the floor.

—

Mama and Papa left, and I stayed home to look after Mary-Louise and Alex. I wanted to practise using Papa's knife to carve some sticks, but then Alex wanted to go outside and I didn't want to.

"Please," he said.

"No."

"Pleeease," he said again.

"I said no."

"I'm going out anyway." I grabbed him, and cuffed him around the ear. It wasn't that hard, but he started to cry.

"Shut up, Alex. You'll get me into trouble." He cried harder. I said, "Shut up. Shut up, stupid. Shut up." Still crying, he hit his fist against my chest. Something inside me snapped. I cuffed him around the head just like they had done to me on my first day at St. Anne's. The blows felt like a release. He wailed and wouldn't shut up as his face turned to panic. Once the anger was gone, I stopped and stared. Alex was crying so hard, he could hardly breathe.

I didn't want him to cry. I wished I hadn't hit him so hard. Now I was going to be in big trouble.

"Sorry," I said. It made him cry harder. I felt trapped. Mama and Papa were coming home any second. I walked toward Mary-Louise, trying to pretend like it had never happened, but she pushed me away, ran to Alex and put her arms around him. He leaned against her and cried until his tears were dry.

When Mama and Papa finally came home, they looked around the room.

"What happened?" Papa asked, leaning down and examining Alex's swollen lips and eye.

"He started it," I said, pointing to Alex.

"Started what?"

"He . . . he . . . he . . . hiuh . . . hit . . . me!" Alex said, between sobs.

"He was rude," I said.

"You do not hit your brother."

"He hit me too," I said.

"I don't care. You are older. You do not hit your brother."

Then Papa went outside to get some water to boil for a warm compress, while Mama took Alex in her arms. Mama and Papa cuddled him and kissed him gently. I wished they were doing that for me. No one had touched me like that for a long time.

No one said much that night. Everyone was still mad at me, I could tell. Papa and Mama kept fussing over Alex, hugging him, asking him questions, holding up their fingers in front of his face, and asking him to count. Mama asked Papa whether they should take him to the infirmary, but Papa thought it wasn't serious enough. At last, we kids lay down on the floor, Mama and Papa went to their bed, and we went to sleep.

The next day, Papa said he wanted to take me for a walk. I knew that he was going to tell me off, so I took a really long time getting dressed.

We walked down to the river.

"Ed. What do you think 'all my relations' means?"

"It means we are all related."

"What does that mean?"

"It means that everyone is family."

"Who's your family?"

"You, Mama, Alex, Mary-Louise, Grandpa and Grandma."

"Yes. Those people are your family. But 'all my relations' isn't just about family. It's about how we were born. How we were created. We were all created by Gitchi Manitou. That means we are all related to each other. We were all made from the same stuff. We are all part of the same family. Humans. The Four-Leggeds, or the animals, and the trees, the Standing Ones. Everything you see around you is part of your family, the people, plants, the trees, and even the rocks. We need all these things to live, and they need us. We are all related. We are all part of the cycle of life. What you see around you must be treated with respect. So that means that we honour the animals when we go out hunting. We thank them for the life that they give us. For giving us their flesh so that we can live. And it means that you are good to your brother when you are looking after him. You do not hit him. You are not rude to him. You treat him like you want to be treated yourself. That's what it is to follow the Red Road."

I half-listened to his words, but who was related anyway? If Papa thought of me that way, then why did he send me to that school? He should have tried to protect me. He should have stood up to Father Lavois. And if everyone was related then why was Sister Wesley so mean? Was she following the Red Road? What about Brother Goulet? Was the electric chair part of this teaching?

I stared at him. He was still talking, opening and closing his mouth, like a fish. His hands were moving too, and it looked like he was slicing the air, like Father Gagnon. Noise was coming out of his lips, but none of it made any sense.

NINE

June 1963

We made it. Twelve kids from my class of thirty graduated from Grade 8. Nine boys and three girls, including Amocheesh, Erick, Nicholas, Fred, Joe, Brandon, and Angela. Some kids were held back, and others, like Tony, had gone back to the bush to be with their parents, who hid them from the priests, Hudson's Bay managers and Indian Agents.

The day of our graduation, the school was a little noisier. At chapel, a few boys sang their own words to the songs. "Christ we never have to be here again, praise be to God," "Come Let Us Be Gone Forever," stuff like that. After the service, Father Lavois stood next to Brother Jutras and they shook our hands on the way out. Some of the boys waited until they were out of the church, then wiped their hands on the grass or on their pants. No one said anything. We didn't need to.

At breakfast, a couple of seniors started a food fight. Sister Wesley ran over and began shouting, but they just laughed as if nothing she could do would harm them anymore. It was like the spell had been broken and we were coming back to life. We all wore dark suits and mortarboards, which was lucky because some of the boys behind me started flicking ink in our last lesson. I looked at my hand on the black cloth. *I'm still here*, I thought. *I didn't die.* For a long time, I had watched my body, as if everything was happening to someone else. I had listened to conversations as if I was in another room, and everything was happening from far away. As I stared at my fingers, I thought, *This is me. I'm here again.* I didn't quite believe it.

My parents had arranged to meet me during the end-of-year concert. I thought about going home before the concert to say hello, but part of me didn't really care that they were back in town: we had grown more distant during the eight years I was at St. Anne's. I didn't write as much anymore. Not that it mattered; my letters didn't contain much except bland descriptions of anything positive I was allowed to explain—the school censors removed the rest—which meant that they were pretty thin.

So after the final bell rang, I hung about the playroom. Brandon was playing checkers. I was still angry at him, but suddenly I realized it didn't matter. *He'll never be mean to me again*, I thought. *I'll never be whipped or be made to eat my own vomit.* I survived the electric chair and the daily bed-wetting exams. There would be no more annual "medical exams" by Brother Jutras. I was alive. Life had to get better now.

I was standing by myself next to my beauty the Albany. It was a sunny day. Ahead was sky-blue water, and above the rocky grey ledges, deep green spruces jutted like spears against the sky. I came here to get away. Our family had continued to grow rapidly since the birth of Mary-Louise, so now we had Chris who was six, Leo who was five, Jane who was four and Denise who was two.

"You all right?" Alex said. He must have approached while I was lost in thought. I shrugged. I felt bad that I hadn't been much of a brother to him while I was at school, but it was hard with all the rules. We weren't allowed to do things like hug. That'd get you a sharp word or slap. And we weren't supposed to talk much either. Not too loudly, and only at playtimes. We had drifted.

"You're leaving," he said. "I'm jealous."

"You'll be out soon enough," I said.

"I'm going to miss you."

"Yeah, well . . ." I said. He looked hurt. "Me too."

"Be good, Ed," Mama said. Mama, Papa and Chris were seeing me off at the Fort Albany airport, which was a one-room wooden shack. Alex was at home minding the rest of my brothers and sisters. Four other St. Anne's students were flying with me—Fred, Erick, Nicholas and Angela—and their parents crowded around them, our elbows touching. The rest of the graduates would meet us in Timmins, and we would take the train together to Cochrane. From there, the girls would go on to their new homes in North Bay. We would take a bus to meet our new foster families in Swastika, then drive to Kirkland Lake.

"Yeah, okay, Mama."

"We love you, Ed," Papa said.

"You too." I picked up my suitcase and walked to the plane. I didn't look back.

We were loading our luggage onto a school bus in Cochrane. It was the first time I had seen something so big and yellow; actually it was the first time I'd seen any vehicle except in newspapers and magazines. In real life they were so fast. They whipped past, or swerved at the last minute. And the roads. They were smooth and hard. No grass or weeds anywhere. Down the street were tall posts with funny metal hats. I racked my brain trying to remember what I knew about them. I turned to Erick, who was had just finished stacking his bag.

"Erick. What are they?"

"What?"

"Those poles."

"Oh yeah. I saw them in a magazine once. They're lamp posts."

No one could stop looking out the window all the way to Swastika. It wasn't just the lamp posts. It was the metal signs sticking out from poles. And the white lines on the roads. And the building where we stopped to fill up the tank. No one knew where the gas came from, but the driver said it was piped in underground. Then we were back on the road again, heading toward the train station. We lined up and were given squares of paper with numbers on them, which Erick said were tickets. Once we got on board, we found seats, and everything whipped past, the grass and the rivers and the trees, which had stopped being still, and were flying faster than a pike slipping through my fingers.

In Swastika, we were herded into church pews with some St. Anne's students from higher years, and other teens I didn't recognize, flown in from northern residential schools.

At the front, a thirty-something man asked for silence and began talking.

"Hello, boys! I'm Douglas Cooper." It was our foster home supervisor. "I'm here to manage the transition from residential to high school. Fortunately, the Indian Affairs Branch of the Department of Citizenship and Immigration is very generous. It pays your foster parents to look after you and feed you. It provides funding for all your school supplies and clothes. It isn't an excessive amount, so please try to be careful. We don't have enough to pay for torn clothes or ripped jeans or other stupidity. And we give each of you a ten-dollar monthly allowance so you have something to spend on candy and movies and the like. Now in return for this generosity, we have set a few ground rules. The first is that there is no smoking or drinking. No going out after school, except for school activities. You are to come straight home as soon as school is out. Weekend curfew is eleven p.m. And please try to be as nice as you can to your foster parents. They try to do their best to be good caretakers."

Mr. Cooper began matching us with foster parents. At my name, a tall man named Joseph Ryan stood up and waved. I scrutinized his face. He had greying hair, black bushy eyebrows and deep creases around his eyes. He seemed kind, like someone who might give you more food, if you asked nicely.

On the way to the Ryans' house, Joseph turned around to the five of us—Fred, Erick, Amocheesh, Nicholas and myself—who were crammed into the station wagon. There would be ten of us staying with him, but we couldn't all squeeze into the car, so we were taking two trips.

"It's three to a room," he said. "That okay?"

"What about one hundred and ten to a room?" Nicholas asked. They crammed us in tight at St. Anne's dormitory, and the rest of us laughed.

"Huh?" Joseph asked.

"Forget it," Nicholas said.

"What's so funny?"

"Nothing, Mr. Ryan. Sorry."

"Why were you all laughing?"

"No reason."

"Tell me."

"It was just . . ." Nicholas looked scared. "We had to share with about a hundred other boys at St. Anne's. That's all."

"Oh I see," Mr. Ryan said. "Okay then." He shook his head. "Good. Here you'll be a lot more comfortable."

The Ryans' house was huge, bigger than any of the houses in Fort Albany—three storeys—with window shutters and a front porch. Mr. Ryan told us to quickly unpack, as dinner would be in an hour.

Everything was so different from St. Anne's. No one deloused us, shaved our heads and confiscated our possessions. No one gave us new uniforms. Instead, Joseph's wife, Irene, asked us our names, and said she would do her best to remember them, and then led us upstairs.

"I made up the beds for you," she said. "Each boy has two drawers each."

An hour later, we came down to a dinner table full of meat and other goodies. It was like the nuns' table. There was roast beef, gravy, mashed potatoes, peas, carrots, and afterwards chocolate mousse. Irene said we could eat as much as we liked, so I heaped more and more onto my plate.

"You're hungry!" Joseph said.

"Yeah." I was full already, but I didn't know how much longer the food was going to last. "Is it okay?"

"Sure!"

"Thank you, Mr. Ryan." I kept eating until my stomach hurt.

We weren't allowed to watch TV or go out during the week, so after dinner we all went to our rooms. Erick opened his drawer and took out a needle that he'd brought with him from home. He wanted to play the pin game. Lots of boys played it at St. Anne's, especially the older years. The rules were pretty easy. You scored a stroke on your arm until it bled. Then you passed the pin to the next person. He did the same. The winner was the person who could cut the most lines. We used to have to wait a few weeks until the scabs healed and then we could play again. I had done it once. It didn't hurt that much. It felt more like a release.

Erick sliced his forearm, then gave the pin to me.

"Your turn," he said.

"I don't want to," I said.

"Do it."

"No. I don't want to."

"Wuss." He looked about the room. "Who's next?" No one said anything. "Chickens. The lot of you." He cut a few more lines on his own arm and put down the pin. I turned away. He was in a dark mood, and I didn't want to be part of it.

TEN

Next morning, Mrs. Ryan gave us a packed lunch and we walked to our new high school: Kirkland Lake Collegiate Vocational Institute. The school was bigger than any building I'd ever seen. Kids stood in groups on the lawn, and everyone was in a hurry. We'd already been given our timetables and each of us looked at the times and room numbers, and then began scrambling trying to find the right door.

I arrived late for my first class. Not that it mattered much. I walked in, apologized and sat down. My teacher, Mrs. Karr, didn't slap me. She didn't go and send another student for her whip. She didn't even shout. She simply pointed to an empty chair, and I went to the back of the class, where the other native students were sitting.

It was lunchtime and we were sitting in the high school cafeteria with about three hundred people. It was packed in there, but luckily, all the St. Anne's students sat together.

"How's your first day at KLCVI?" Fred asked.

"Kirkland Lake Collector of Various Indians!" Nicholas replied. We all laughed. We called it that and it was true—mostly Crees and Ojibways, but there were also natives from all over.

"I don't like it," Amocheesh said.

"You don't like anything," Nicholas said.

"This guy Justin called me a wagon burner," Amocheesh replied.

"Who's he?" Nicholas asked.

"Some guy who pushed me into the lockers. He's a senior."

"We should take 'em, beat 'em up," Erick said.

"Beat up who?" Nicholas said.

"Everyone in the whole school," Erick said.

"That's dumb," Nicholas said.

"You're dumb," Erick said.

"Geesh. Why you always so down on everything?"

"I'm not."

"And they made me take off all my clothes in the shower," Amocheesh continued complaining. Once he got going, it was hard to make him stop. Still, I agreed with him. I didn't like being naked in the shower. It wasn't like at St. Anne's. There, we had always worn bathing trunks, so we would stay "modest." It was one of the few rules that I liked. The clothing made me feel safer. Some of the brothers liked to watch us undress, and at least with the trunks you felt less exposed. They might catch a flash as you removed your towel, but if you were quick, they wouldn't see much.

"What did you do? Did you have to take off everything?" Fred asked.

"I didn't do anything at first. But then the gym teacher got mad."

"It's so unfair," Erick said. "I hate it. I hate this place."

"It's not so bad," Nicholas said. "I heard that some of the older years bought booze."

"So?" Erick said.

"So we could too," Nicholas said.

"Where from?" Fred asked.

"The LCBO."

"That's not allowed," Amocheesh replied.

"What's gotten into him?" Nicholas said, gesturing toward Amocheesh.

"We'll get into trouble if we go and buy booze," I replied. Nicholas had to watch it: Irene and Joseph weren't as mean as Sister Wesley, but there would be trouble if we broke the rules, and who knew what would happen. The rest of my friends continued talking, and I felt caught in memories, of being whipped on my first day of school, of being electrocuted, and of being slapped when Sister Wesley found out I had wet my pants. I was stuck and unsure how to get out. After a while I tried to distract myself. "Hey, I hear that Irene is making mac and cheese tonight."

"I love her mac and cheese. It's so creamy!" Fred said.

"She going to make it with wine?" Nicholas asked.

"Geesh. You're obsessed," I replied.

That night, Irene made her special mac and cheese. With cream, not wine. We all ate as much as we could, it was so good. In the middle of dinner, Irene said someone had left a phone message.

"Where from?" Fred asked. We never got any phone messages. No one on the reserve had a phone except for Father Lavois, and his was a radio phone that was hard to hear, and only for emergencies.

"A man called Mike Pasko."

"What does he want?" Fred asked.

"He just called to say hello. He said he knows you," Irene said.

"Knows me?" Fred said.

"Knows all of you," Irene replied.

"He does," I replied.

"How?" I explained to her that he was the Hudson's Bay manager, and he was really friendly. He took boys fishing sometimes and let them work at his store. In our final year, he had brought us all hockey skates, and gave skating lessons on the lake behind the school.

"Oh how sweet!" she said.

"Did he say anything else?" I asked.

"No. Not much. He said he might stop by if he was passing through."

"Stop here?" Amocheesh asked.

"That's what he said."

"Maybe he'll take me to the movies," Amocheesh said.

"Or me," I said.

We didn't hear from Mr. Pasko for a while after that. I didn't mind—there was a lot going on. I was training to be on the track team, and had meets most nights. And I was trying to change my schedule. They had put us all in the technical stream of KLCVI because the teachers said it was easier for Indians to get jobs doing something practical. I needed a job, but hoped to do more than just work with my hands. I wanted to be a teacher or something like that. I told Nicholas about it over lunch.

"Why don't you stick to what you're good at?" he said. "You're already too behind to get into the academic stream. I'm focusing on carpentry."

"Well, maybe I don't want to be a carpenter."

"Jesus was a carpenter."

"Yeah, and look what happened to him!" We both laughed.

"All right. So what do you want to be?"

"I dunno. A teacher, I think."

"How are you going to do that?"

"I'm going to study really hard."

"At KLCVI."

"Yeah."

"And what does the V stand for?"

"Vocational."

"Exactly."

"So?"

"If you wanted to be a teacher, you should have gone to a regular high school."

"What?" I couldn't believe it. I had tried so hard at St. Anne's. I was one of the few people who made it through. I had put up with it all because I thought it would give me more options, so I could teach or work in an office. After eight years, I had graduated, but it hadn't made any difference. I was stuck being a carpenter. What had been the point?

"Don't look so down, brother," Nicholas said. "A carpenter isn't so bad. At least you'll have a job."

That night, Nicholas tried to cheer me up. He came into our bedroom when I was reading.

"It's not so bad," he said.

"Speak for yourself."

"You'll do it one day."

"Do what?"

"Teach? Write? Whatever you want."

"How do you know that?"

"Because you try really hard."

"Look. You're right. Being a teacher is a dumb dream. We're Indians. In a vocational school. That's just our lot."

"I have an idea that will cheer you up."

"What?"

"I've arranged for one of the older guys from St. Anne's to get us some booze."

"Big deal."

"Come on. It'll be fun. We can drink it on the school field." There was an elementary school in front of the Ryans' house. "Besides, Erick's already in."

"Why did you ask him?" Erick was always so negative; it put a downer on everything.

"He asked."

"What if we get caught? Won't they send us back to St. Anne's?"

"Why would they do that?"

"For being troublemakers."

"No way. Things are different around here. You'll see."

It was a Saturday night when we went out to buy booze. I felt sick, but Nicholas and Erick had already decided on the date and arranged it with our buyer, the twenty-two-year-old brother of a wemistikoshiw high school senior, who agreed to do it for a commission of two dollars. We waited behind the store. He came out and handed us the wine in brown paper bags.

"Got the money?" he said. We handed him ten dollars.

"Just don't get caught. And if you do, remember, it wasn't me."

We had bought the cheapest stuff in the store, but it didn't matter. We hurried to the field. Nicholas popped the bottle with an opener he'd nicked from the Ryans. He took a swig, then passed it to Erick, who passed it to me. It tasted like vinegar.

"I don't feel good," I said.

"You're such a baby," Erick said.

I really needed to go to the bathroom and get some water, so I left them there and ran across the street to the Ryans'. Nicholas promised me they wouldn't finish it all while I was gone.

"Where have you been?" Mrs. Ryan asked, when I opened the front door.

"Just out."

"Have you seen Nicholas or Erick?"

"No," I said.

"Amocheesh told me some of you were hanging out on the field." I wondered if he had ratted us out.

"Maybe."

"Maybe?"

"Maybe I saw them there. I don't know." Mrs. Ryan gave me a sharp look.

"Joseph has gone out looking for them."

"Oh."

"Are you okay? You don't look so good."

"Yes, I'm fine, Mrs. Ryan. I just need to lie down."

I went to the bathroom and kneeled in front of the toilet seat. I dry-retched, but nothing came up. Would they be whipped? Electrocuted? What was going to happen to them? My mind spun.

At the sound of voices, I came downstairs. Joseph had them by the forearms, one on either side. They were giggling.

"Jesus Christ," Joseph said. "I'm going to have to tell Mr. Cooper about this. And in the meantime, you're both grounded."

"Grounded?" Nicholas asked. "What's that?"

"It means you have to stay home!" We all looked at him, waiting for him to tell us another punishment.

"That's it?" Erick asked.

"Yes, that's it!" Joseph exclaimed. "You'll be cooped up here for a month!" We stared at him, waiting to hear the bad part.

"Stop staring! I have half a mind to ground all of you. Go upstairs! I don't know what's gotten into you all."

—

The annoying thing about having Erick and Nicholas at home was that it was harder for me to study. I had decided that I would probably never make it as a teacher, but I still wanted to graduate high school, maybe even complete Grade 13.

Every time I went up to my room, they were there. It was like they were suddenly my best friends.

"Hey, Ed. You got a girlfriend yet?" Nicholas asked. Erick smirked.

"No." I blushed. There was a native girl, from Matachewan Reserve, named Connie, whom I sometimes saw when I was at track. I liked her but I didn't know whether she liked me.

"What about that girl Connie? Didn't she wave to you at track the other day?"

"Maybe."

"Ed has a ghurl-freeend!" Nicholas sang. Erick joined in.

"Shut up, you guys," I said.

"I heard that wemistikoshiw girls kiss like this," Nicholas said and he stuck out his tongue, like he was trying to shove it down someone's throat.

"Wemistikoshiw girls are disgusting," Erick said.

"Whatever," Nicholas said.

"I'd never do that," Erick added.

"Yes you would. You'd do it right now." He jumped on top of Erick and began to wrestle him on the bed.

"Be quiet, you guys!" I cried. "Or I'll tell Mrs. Ryan."

"Goody two-shoes," Nicholas said. He got off Erick and stood up. "Hey, I heard Mr. Pasko is coming to town."

"Whatever," I said.

"No, it's true."

"What would he do here?"

"He's going to take us all to a hockey game."

"What?" I said. "All ten of us?"

"No, three of us," Erick said.

"Why only three?"

"He only has four tickets."

"Well, how will he choose?"

"I don't know. Ask Mrs. Ryan."

I asked her about it over dinner. She confirmed: Mr. Pasko was coming to town and had four tickets to the Toronto Maple Leafs.

"Isn't that expensive?" I asked Mrs. Ryan.

"He says he's got it covered. Foster Hewitt donated the tickets."

"He knows Foster Hewitt?"

We were allowed to watch *Hockey Night in Canada* on Saturday nights and Foster Hewitt was the broadcaster.

"No. I think he just said it was a gift to some poor native children," she said.

Mrs. Ryan had decided that we would draw straws. Except for Nicholas and Erick. They couldn't go because they were still grounded. After dinner we made a circle around Mr. Ryan and picked our fate. I couldn't believe it. Me, Amocheesh and Fred would be going to Toronto for our first ever professional hockey game.

A month later, Mike showed up on Saturday morning at six. He had rented a van because the drive was long—eight hours—and after the game, we might have to pull over and sleep in the back.

As we got in, the other boys stood in the upstairs window and waved goodbye. None of them had ever been to Toronto before. I could tell they were all jealous.

I called "shotgun" and got to sit in the front seat. I was tired, but Mr. Pasko wanted to talk.

"So how are you boys getting along?" he asked.

"It's cool."

"Irene and Joseph, right? They seem nice."

"They are."

"They feeding you well?"

"Oh yeah. We get lots of nice food." I told him about Mrs. Ryan's mac and cheese.

"And what about after school? Do you have a girlfriend?"

"No. Not yet. I'm really busy." I told him about studying hard and training to be on the track team for 400 and 800 metres.

"I didn't know you were a runner. You any good?"

"My gym teacher, Mr. Preston, says I am."

"You'll have to show me sometime."

Toronto was even bigger than Kirkland Lake. Everywhere there were these wires overhead, crisscrossing the sky. There were people rushing about and cars honking their horns. The buildings were stacked on top of each other, reaching into the sky. On some of them were flashing lights and fluttering flags, the Canadian and British.

The hockey game was at Maple Leaf Gardens. The building took up a whole city block. Inside, excitement crackled in the icy air, and it smelled of beer, sweat and adrenaline. We took our seats and waited while some of the referees skated around the rink, examining the ice. We were sitting in the Maple Leaf section, but opposite, I could see some fans in red and white, the colours of the Detroit Red Wings.

Once the game started, the players whizzed around the ice and slammed into the boards. We even got to see a brawl. Everyone stood up in the bleachers and shouted, "Fight! Fight!" The Maple Leafs' goalie, Johnny Bower, dropped his stick and started punching one of the Wings' defencemen. Both men took off their gloves and then the referee slowly glided over and pushed them apart.

During the break Mr. Pasko got us some hot dogs and Cokes.

"There's yours," he said, and he handed me a hot dog and an extra large fries.

"Uh . . . Mr. Pasko. I only have money for a small," I said, embarrassed.

"Don't worry. I got it covered."

"Thanks, Mr. Pasko."

"You're welcome." Pause. "So what's your time like? You know, for the four hundred metres."

"Sixty seconds. But I'm hoping to get it to fifty-five."

"I was about that time at your age."

"You were?"

"Yes. Do you want anything else? A drink? I'm getting a beer."

"I'm not allowed."

"Mr. and Mrs. Ryan keep you on a tight leash, do they?"

"Sometimes."

"So, what are you up to this summer?"

"I'm not sure. I should go back home."

"And do what?"

"Fish. I don't know."

"Not much work in Fort Albany."

"Yeah, I know."

"You could always work for me."

"Where? Fort Albany?"

"No. In Montreal."

"Uh, that's far."

"Other boys have done it."

"Yeah, I know."

"You could make lots of money and you'd have free room and board. I have a beautiful house."

"Uh . . . I'd have to ask my parents."

"Of course! Have them contact me if you like. I can provide references."

"Thanks, Mr. Pasko."

"It's Mike, Ed. We're friends, right?"

"Right."

ELEVEN

I wasn't allowed to stay with the Ryans during the summer, and so had written to my folks to ask if I could stay with Mike. I didn't hear back, so took the train home with the other St. Anne's graduates. I didn't intend to stay long, just until I had their permission and could get out of there.

"It's a great idea," Mama said, when I asked them over dinner. "You'll get to see another city. Get a real job. Meet new people."

"Who's going to help me around here?" Papa said.

"Alex can help you."

"It's a long way."

"Come on, Keshayno. It will be good for him."

I packed a suitcase and flew to Moosonee, and then took the train to meet Mike in Cochrane. He was standing on the platform, smiling. He was wearing a beige blazer and leather brogues, and I remember thinking that he never looked like that in Fort Albany. I wondered if he had dressed up for me, or whether everyone dressed like that in Montreal. I probably didn't have the right clothes.

Mike picked up the suitcase that I had borrowed from Mrs. Ryan and put one arm around my shoulder.

"How was your trip?"

"Good," I said. "Not too long."

"I'm glad you took the early train. We've got a long drive ahead of us."

"That's good," I said nervously.

"Wait till you see my car," he said. "She's a beaut." We walked out into the parking lot and I looked around. "Can you drive, Ed?"

"Not yet."

"If you're helpful, maybe I'll give you a lesson this summer."

"Thank you, Mike."

"Good boy," he said, and he squeezed me closer.

We got to his car, a brown Edsel, and he helped me into the front seat. He got in and turned on the radio.

"Check this out." He took my hand and put it on the speakers. "Feel those vibrations. They are Delco slimline. Forty watts, eight ohm. Sexy buggers. Doesn't get better than that."

"Cool," I said, although I had no idea what he was talking about. He kept holding my hand.

"This car is a chick magnet. You should see how babes check you out."

We drove through field-flanked flat towns with French names: Grand-Remous, Mont-Laurier, Rivière-Rouge. "See, Ed?" as we cruised through Labelle, looking for somewhere to eat. "Check out that girl over there!" Ahead was a teenager wearing a long flowing skirt. "She was all over you. She wants you."

It didn't seem true, but I laughed anyway.

The journey to his house took twelve hours. We listened to lots of music with men singing and playing the guitar. I knew it was rock and roll, but didn't know any of the band names, and Mike told me it was the Beatles and the Stones. We stopped at a diner on the way for fries. I didn't have any money, but Mike said not to worry, I could pay him back as soon as I started work. When the sun slipped behind the Earth, we stopped again, at another diner, and had shepherd's pie and carrots.

We didn't make it into Montreal until after midnight so I didn't see much of the city except streets that were as wide as rivers, and signs all jumbled on top of each other and pointing this way and that. It was night but there were lights shining everywhere from buildings taller than trees in the forest back home.

We drove to a street that was narrower than the others with the buildings closer together. He parked and we walked toward a two-storey house with a long metal staircase, decorated with beautiful twirls of metal, like vines crawling up the bannister. We walked up to the second floor, huffing and puffing with our luggage. I wanted to look around, and asked if I could turn the house lights on.

"Let's leave them off. I'm tired," Mike said.

"Okay," I said. The house was dark, but I could see the shadows of furniture from the streetlamps outside.

"It's a one-bedroom, so we'll have to share."

"Oh," I said.

"Don't worry. That's where all the boys sleep."

"Oh."

"Come here." He took my hand and led me down the hallway. When we were in the bedroom, he let go.

"Just change here. It's dark anyway."

I quickly took off all my clothes, except my T-shirt and underpants. I could hear him doing the same behind me. I groped forward and got into the bed, pulling up the covers and shutting my eyes. He got into bed and snuggled into me. I felt a hard thing pushing into my backside. I moved toward the edge of the bed. He snuggled closer. The hard thing pushed into my backside. I moved again.

"Stop moving," he ordered. He inched closer and forced me to be still. "You asked me to come and get you. To help you," he whispered.

"I . . ."

"Lie still," he said.

His hands gripped my shoulders. I could feel him pushing through the fabric. I couldn't see what he was doing, but I could feel his breath on the back of my neck, smelling like the old meat and carrots we had for dinner, along with his musky cologne. In out, in out, the hot breath on the back of my neck. Then he let go of my shoulder and reached around, inside my underpants. With his touch, I couldn't help it, but I was immediately hard. He exhaled a long breath on the back of my neck. Then he started rocking back and forth again, hips in time with his hand, and I thought *He's not that strong, I could probably fight him off.* I had these thoughts even as I lay still. My underpants were between his penis and my skin, and I thought that he was going to pull those down too and I kept waiting for it to happen, but instead the cotton was pushed up inside me. It hurt, but I didn't say anything. I just stared at the bedside lamp and counted each time the thing entered into me. When I got to 28, I began to hold my breath and the numbers went on in my head, faster and faster. At 147, he shuddered, and thrust inside of me, the pain searing my backside and washing over my body.

It was over.

I didn't move. He went to sleep soon after that.

At some point I must have fallen asleep, because I awoke to the sight of him dressing. I didn't want to do anything but sleep, but I also wanted to go home. I waited until he was dressed before I spoke.

"Mike. I don't feel well. Do you think you could give me the money to go home?"

"I will," he said.

"When?"

"Soon."

"How soon?"

"Soon enough."

Then he changed the subject and told me that I was free to eat cereal for breakfast, and pointed toward the kitchen. He left for work shortly afterwards. I tried to go back to sleep.

He came home that evening and heated up a couple of TV dinners in the oven, and we watched some TV. He told me about his work, and how the price of furs had fallen, and that the Hudson's Bay Company was scaling back.

"Probably can't take you on at Headquarters. At least, not right now. Maybe later if things pick up."

"Oh," I said. "What will I tell my parents about my job?"

"Tell them the truth. There are no jobs."

"I promised my dad that I would be working."

"Understandable. Well, as I said, things might pick up."

"When?"

"So many questions, Ed! I'm doing my best."

"I said that I'd be making twenty dollars per week."

"Well, that was a lie, wasn't it?" Mike had never told me the amount I'd earn, but I had made up a figure I thought would impress my folks.

"I . . . I guess."

"Relax, Ed." He came over and sat down at the edge of the bed, brushing my hair away from my face. "Don't worry. I can always give you some pocket money at the end of the summer." His touch felt clammy but I didn't move. "We'll work something out, I promise."

That night I moved to the edge of the bed, but he still found me. It took longer. I counted to 205. Afterwards, I stared at the lamp and vowed to go home the next day.

In the morning I didn't ask for money, just pretended to be asleep. Once he had left the house, I dressed quickly and went outside. There was no one on his street, so I walked until I found a main road. It was full of honking cars. There were lots of people in a hurry. They pushed past me and said Egg-soosey-ma. I wondered what it meant. The air was muggy and it felt grimy in my throat. Finally I found a man who was standing motionless, looking at his watch.

"Can you tell me where the train station is?" He looked at me and shook his head and walked away. Next I asked a lady wearing a fancy coat and walking a fluffy dog. She pointed toward the end of the street. I smiled at her and started walking.

It took about an hour to get to the end of the street. I didn't have a watch, but I used the sun. When I got to the final set of traffic lights, my mouth was dry and I still couldn't find the train station. I looked about for a place where I could drink for free. There weren't even any puddles. I sat down on the sidewalk and cried until there were no tears left. I was still thirsty so I licked them. I sat on the sidewalk for what must have been a few hours, watching the sun turn blood red. Mike would be home by now. I was suddenly worried that he would be angry. I hurried all the way back that long street and rang the bell. He answered.

"Where have you been?" he said. His brow was furrowed.

"Out."

"Doing what?"

"Just walking."

"Did you . . . meet anyone?"

"No."

"You're late."

"Sorry, Mr. Pasko." His eyebrows arched.

"I was worried about you. Come in."

A TV dinner was on the dining room table. Meat with brown sauce, peas and potatoes. I ate very slowly, and watched him watch the TV.

"You coming?" he said, getting up as if to go to bed.

"In a minute."

"Don't take too long."

"Okay, Mr. Pasko."

"Call me Mike."

The days continued like that. I watched him as I had watched Sister Wesley slapping the boys awake. They did with you what they wanted to because that was how it was and how it had been from the beginning. Sometimes, it seemed to be happening to someone else. I floated above the bedroom and I watched him moving closer, heard him grunting, and I waited until it was all over.

Other days, the panic prickling my throat and chest woke me up. *Not now*, I thought. *Please, not now. Please. Please.* I lay very still and screwed up my eyes and waited as he woke up, brushed his teeth, ate breakfast and left. Then I stayed in bed, as if paralyzed. *Get up. Get up, you idiot.*

I pulled my clothes on and dragged myself to the bathroom. I ate a handful of breakfast cereal and left the house. I put one foot in front of the other, past the other houses with vines spreading along the walls, conquering the brick. I was going. Where? The train station. I just needed to get to the train station.

I didn't have any money. I'd never find the station. No one would understand once I got there. I would stop, shaking with fear, then will my feet to step forward. Sometimes it worked. Other times, I just sat down and didn't move for the rest of the afternoon.

Had I been born in a different body with a different history, I might have gone to the police. I could have reported him and stopped it. Maybe he would have gone to jail. I knew from the radio news that that's what the wemistikoshiw did. But I wasn't wemistikoshiw. Our stories were different. In Fort Albany the police flew in to tell us about laws that we didn't realize existed. We were guilty. We had broken The Law. The Potlatch Ban, the Indian Act, the Constitution Act, the Land Act. You had broken the laws of Her Majesty's Kingdom. Did we understand? My great-granddad, John Metatawabin, was taken away by the RCMP for "Indian cultural activities."[3] We were never sure which ones finally sent the police over the edge; whether it was his braids down his back or the rumours that he did shaking tent ceremonies out in the forest in the dead of night. Who knows? Both were illegal under the Potlatch laws. The police flew in, arrested him, took him away on a float plane and that was the last we saw of him. He couldn't speak English or write, so we never heard from him, nor found out what had happened to him. My guess is that he died in prison.

One morning when the summer was almost over, I woke up and went to the toilet. I washed the stains from my underpants and put them back on, still wet. I looked in the mirror. My face looked like it was covered in boils: a smear of red and pus. I went back to bed and waited for Mike to awake. He got up and asked if I wanted any tea. Then he noticed the pimples.

"What's on your face?"

My hands reached up instinctively, touching them. "I don't know," I said.

"Jesus. It's everywhere."

He didn't touch me again. He drove me back to Kirkland Lake a few days later.

Students at St. Anne's Residential School, ca. 1954.

Three women with a child in a tikinagan (between the two women on the right), ca. 1945. They are de-branching and loading logs to a sled, which a horse would then haul to the sawmill. The Roman Catholic Church Mission hired local women to do the heavy work, including harvesting trees, working the mill, clearing the land, and doing farm work. They worked Monday to Friday, from dawn to nightfall, and were paid a small daily wage (using O.M.I. coinage), along with half a loaf of homemade bread and a 20 oz. can of beans.

Crossing Yellow Creek, over a bridge during spring high water, ca. 1950. The bridge connected St. Anne's Residential School to the village of Fort Albany, where there were services such as the Hudson's Bay store, post office and Holy Angels Catholic Church. Yellow Creek fed into the Albany River to the west.

My parents, Abraham and Mary Metatawabin, on their wedding day in 1947.

Our old family home in Fort Albany, 1956.

Me at age four in Fort Albany. I would go to St. Anne's nearly four years later.

Local Cree women who worked at St. Anne's Residential School. At the far right is my mom, Mary Metatawabin.

Father Lavois and the St. Anne's girl students on a weekend canoeing trip, ca. 1953. A popular destination was a camp across the lake, where they would have picnics and campfires.

The St. Anne's mission boat was used to bring food, household and hunting supplies from Moosonee to Fort Albany. During the holidays, it took students from the nearby communities to and from school.

St. Anne's Residential School, ca. 1954 (top), and again in 1962/63 (right). The school was destroyed by fire in 2002.

Children digging potatoes in the field. By the 1950s the Catholic mission had expansive fields of potatoes, carrots and other hardy vegetables. In the greenhouse they grew strawberries, blueberries and tomatoes—none of which we ever tasted.

Boys in uniform at St. Anne's Residential School.

Graduating class at St. Anne's Residential School, ca. 1963. I'm on the left, in the second row from the top. Sister Anne is in front of me, Sister Gloria is at far right, and Brother Lauzon and Father Leguerrier, Bishop of Moosonee, are in front-row centre.

Fort Albany, Ontario, ca. 1955, looking north, and showing Holy Angels Catholic Church.

Me in spring 1964 at Kirkland Lake Collegiate Vocational Institute, Ontario. That summer I went to Montreal with Mike Pasko.

Christmas at the Ryans' foster home, Kirkland Lake, Ontario, ca. 1963. I'm at bottom left.

My family on a trip from Edmonton, Alberta, to Fort Albany, Ontario, in fall 1983. Once in Ontario, we travelled by freighter canoe on the Albany River, a distance of 400 km. The trip took ten days to complete, moving through a variety of terrain. From left: Shannin, Albalina, me, Jassen. Joan took the picture.

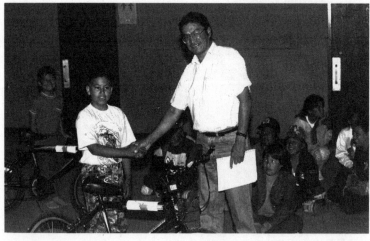

As Chief of Fort Albany, Ontario, awarding bikes for good attendance and performance in school, 1991.

Yours truly completing the Canadian International Marathon in Toronto in 2001. All those years of track paid off.

The crew of the annual Paquataskamik rafting trip. Each summer we bring youth on a multi-day expedition down the Albany River, moving 40 km each day. The trip brings youth together with elders, and teaches them about the natural environment (Paquataskamik), cultural wisdom and working together as a community. From left to right, starting at top: Bernard Sutherland, Captain Edmund Metatawabin, Corey Reuben, Andrea Iahtail, Austin Nakogee, Malesh Kataquapit, Geronimo Spence

(partially hidden), Kendall Nakogee, Anastash Paul-Martin, Shelton Metatawabin, Elder Joseph Sutherland, Braiden Metatawabin, Andrew Iahtail, Corey Reuben, Karen and Jassen Metatawabin.

The Paquataskamik raft with crew aboard.

Working together to build the Paquataskamik raft.

With John Edwards at the sawmill I operate in Fort Albany. The sawmill employs four people in the summer months and two during the winter.

The log home that Joan and I built together in Fort Albany.

PART TWO

Indian secrets can be disclosed suddenly, like a storm.

Indian men, of course, are storms. They should destroy the lives

of any white women who choose to love them.

—Sherman Alexie, from the poem "How to Write the Great

American Indian Novel"

TWELVE

FORT ALBANY, ONTARIO, 1968

It was windy that day, windy enough that people were running about and tying down the tarps on their canoes. A couple of younger guys like me were hunched in their doorways, trying to light up. Days like these, I like to play a little game: roll the spark wheel and bet. If she took, I'd go down to the water. And if not, I'd go back inside my parents' home, tiptoe around my younger brothers sleeping on the floor, and go back to bed.

That's me, there. The small guy puffing with all he's got next to the Albany. The spark took all right. I'm there dragging down until the last breath, until my fingers and lips are burnt.

Why come back here? Well, Kirkland Lake wasn't home. Oh, it had felt sorta like home with the Ryans, but they only kept us for one school year. After them, we moved to the Tekaucs', the Russians. They kept to themselves. They watched TV in the living room, where us boys weren't allowed. Who knew what was going on most of the time. *Zatknis!* That's what I remember. We had no idea what it meant. We made jokes about it among ourselves and laughed bitterly, smoking forbidden cigarettes outside.

After that it was the Staymores, the O'Neils, the Hugheses. I went back to high school and forgot about Connie. She wasn't worth it. Too much trouble. Her and all the other girls. They wanted something I didn't have. Always on my case. Instead, I'd made the school track team for the 400 and 800 metres. I was short with thin legs but I loved the feeling of taking off, leaving everything behind. Just keep moving. I liked to bolt, whether it was from my crowded house or classroom.

Just before I graduated high school, a letter came from Ma to tell me that the community had appointed Pa chief. The village had met and talked for hours, then decided that he was the best person for the job. Thought he'd be the best person to preserve some of our sacred traditions. In his acceptance speech, he warned about some of the wemistikoshiw customs, like TV, french fries and bingo, coming to native communities and how we had to be careful.

Though I had always enjoyed TV at the Ryans' and my other foster homes, Pa had already been to a couple of reserves where they had TVs, and he said things weren't the same. People just sat there, watching the wemistikoshiw world blasted into their living rooms. They stopped going out on the land, and stayed all day on the couch. Stopped yakking over dinner to sit there and point at the coloured screen. Westerns, hockey, cooking shows, it didn't matter. Shiny box took their words.

We used to be great talkers. Stories a mile high and then some. Like my granddad who, during the great famine that we had at the start of the twentieth century, caught three moose and brought them back to town for everyone to share. Trophy stories, we called them. You couldn't take them too seriously. I mean, who really cared who brought back the big prize? The moose meat was gonna be shared around anyway. For me, it wasn't what I caught but that I felt my feet in the earth, watched the light flickering across the river's depths.

That I saw the water and the wind move together, like in some crazy electric dance. I can feel it right now. The loosening of all those knots in my stomach. Easing of the tension around my neck. Unclenching of my fists. We have a Cree word for this letting go, for the loosening that happens when you are out on the land. We call it *kayamenta*. The closest English translation is probably "tranquility."

I was standing there, trying to light up my second cigarette when I saw her. A figure with flyaway hair, walking a ways downstream. She was white but she moved like she was native, as if trying not to leave a footprint, to leave the land beautiful and untouched. She was quiet too, just watching and taking everything in.

She looked up then and saw me watching her.

"You're Ed Metatawabin," she said and her green eyes caught the fall light.

"Yes. Have we met before?"

"No, but I'm friends with your friend John. And you know teachers, we like to talk."

"What did John say about me?"

"He said you're a very good teacher. You teach adults ESL, right?"

"Yes." It had been a struggle, and a lot of hard work, but I had finally succeeded with my childhood dream of becoming a teacher. I didn't want to return to St. Anne's Residential School so I had approached the nearest reserve of Kashechewan, an hour away by boat. I had told their chief of my ambition, and he told me there was an opening and to apply for the job. I didn't have the wemistikoshiw certificates, but round here, I was more qualified than most as I was the only one from my year to complete Grade 13.

She stuck out her hand. "I'm Joan Barnes. I teach kindergarten at St. Anne's." I shuddered involuntarily. "It's not that bad!" she said.

"Sorry, that's not it. It's cold for this time of year."

"Tell me about it. You should get a warmer coat."

Was she flirting with me? I never got much dating experience in high school and it was hard to say.

"Yes," I said, racking my brain for a question that would keep her talking. "Where are you from?"

"Wilberforce," she said. "It's about an hour from Peterborough."

"You're a long way from home."

"Yup. Well, I tried the Arctic, but there weren't any jobs up there."

"The Arctic? What's in the Arctic?"

"I don't know. Polar bears. Eskimos. It sounded romantic, I guess. I grew up on Farley Mowat."

In the north, we called Farley Mowat "Mr. Hardly-Know-It" for all the stuff that he made up. But it wasn't the type of thing that you'd say to someone you've just met, especially someone this beautiful.

"He's a poet," I said. "A good writer."

"I know," she said, and grinned.

And then we both stood there, smiling at each other awkwardly, until she gave a half-wave and went back the way she came, treading lightly.

It was a Friday, and I got off work early and decided to go and see the woman with the green eyes.

St. Anne's was a place that I usually tried to avoid. Some of my brothers and sisters boarded here: Mary-Louise (twelve), Chris (eleven), Leo (ten), Jane (nine) and Denise (seven). I heard that it had gotten a little better since I was at school—they'd gotten rid of the whips and the electric chair. The smell of the place had not, and each scent—the bleach and baked beans—brought back another memory.

My plan was to meet Joan at her classroom, and walk her home. I stood outside her classroom, and shifted my weight between my feet as I waited for the final bell.

When it sounded, the door opened and the kids were running around my legs. My little brother Mike, five, who was in kindergarten but lived at home, saw me and grabbed my arms, almost pulling the flowers I had picked for Joan out of my hands. Suddenly I felt embarrassed about this wemistikoshiw custom. I hadn't dated much, especially a white woman—my body made me feel awkward. It was a sick feeling that began with Brother Jutras's medical exams and grew worse after my summer in Montreal.

"Hey, Mike," I said. "Can you go and give a message to Leo for me? Tell him that Ma says hello." It was a lame excuse, and he gave me a look that suggested he knew I was trying to get rid of him, but after a couple of urgent hints, he agreed.

"Oh! Hi, Ed," Joan said, coming to the door. "Do you want to come in? I'm just getting my bags." I watched her put her books into her rucksack and basket. So many of them. As she straightened, I handed her the bunch of bluebells.

"Oh, they're beautiful."

"I was going to give you dandelions, but I was told that you're not supposed to."

"Says who?"

"Isn't a dandelion a weed?"

"It is, but I like them."

"Me too. In Cree, there's no word for weed. All plants are useful."

"I like that."

"Yeah, me too. Can I carry your books? Where are you going?"

"Sure. Just home. I'd invite you in, but we have to get permission to bring strangers home." Joan lived at the "teacherage," a row of houses next to St. Anne's. Natives weren't allowed in there. The higher-ups were worried about what they called "half-breed"[4] children, which, like all their insults, made us sound more animal than human.

"That's okay. Maybe I could just come to your door." I was living with my parents and three of my brothers: six of us in a two-bedroom house. Alex had gone to high school, and the others boarded at St. Anne's. Even when they weren't home for holidays, it was still crowded. I didn't want to take her home to that. Too many elbows and hair in your face. So we slowly walked back to her house and she told me that this was her first job and it was nothing like what they had taught her in teacher's college. Most of the kids spoke Cree at home, and whispered to each other in Cree, and she didn't know what was going on. I thought about all the times as a kid when I hadn't known what was going on, and the times when the nuns whispered to each other in English and I had sat waiting for punishment. Then I looked at her. I didn't normally talk to girls. They made my tongue feel thick and heavy. But Joan listened so carefully, it made me want to feel different.

"You wanna, uh . . . I'm free tomorrow evening. You want me to teach you some Cree?" The words came tumbling out before I had a chance to change my mind.

"Sure! I really need it!" she said, and smiled.

"Look up," I said when Joan came to her front door. I backed up a few steps—I had homebrew on my breath to help me with my nerves, and didn't want her to notice. "The moon is translucent tonight, isn't she?"

"That's how you greet me?"

"I know, I know. Look up." A flash of movement, and the flapping of black wings against fading blue sky. A flock of Canada geese. "Do you know what we call this month? *Obimahamowi peesim*. It's when the geese fly south. Their rhythms are so important around here."

"Obi-maha-mowi-peesim. I like that. It's poetic."

"You're poetic."

"And you're a flirt. Is this my lesson?"

"No, let's go for a walk."

We walked through the reserve toward the Albany as she tried to wrap her tongue around Cree's soft vowels and different grammar. She said it was like learning a combination of Arabic and Latin. I asked her if she could speak either and she said no, but after she was done here, she wanted to go to a place far away and exotic.

"Like where?" I asked.

"I don't know. Egypt. I'd love to go to Cairo. Or Marrakesh."

"Mar-rah-kash. That sounds like *mamaskatch*!"

"What's that mean?"

"It means unbelievable or incredible. *You're* incredible." I wasn't normally this forward, but the homebrew had given me a spurt of confidence.

"Uh . . . thanks, Ed."

"Can we do this again?"

"Of course. We'll see each other around."

"No, I mean, can we do *this* again?"

"Have another lesson?"

"This! Me here. You there." I pointed to the space between us. "Walking."

"What a flirt!"

I grinned.

"Yeah, do you mind?"

"No. I like it."

I spent a sleepless night trying to think of ways to impress her, this tall woman who seemed to have everything. When dawn broke, I decided to make her a wood sculpture of a wolf, and I climbed over my brothers' sleeping bodies to work outside. After a few hours, the temperature had warmed and I could see the first puffs of smoke as the town came to life.

Ever since I could remember, a wolf had guided me. My manitou. The animal represented the first of our Seven Sacred Teachings, a lesson on humility. She embodied the virtue, by living for the pack and walking with her head down. Her instruction was the most important, and Papa had taught me to remember it with the dawn of each day. To see the sun rise in the east, and know that you are a small part of her larger power, a speck on this great Earth, is a humbling daily practice. I wanted Joan to start to see the world like this, so I carved my feelings in wood.

"Oh my God, it's beautiful," she said when I brought over my gift a few days later.

"She's my guide," I said.

"This sculpture?"

"Her wolf spirit. A manitou."

"What's that?"

"Sometimes we natives have animal spirits to guide us when we need help. Just something that we do. It goes way back."

"Really? I thought that was just in the movies."

"No, it's deeper than that. Animals are our teachers. Their spirits live with our ancestors and the Great Creator Gitchi Manitou in the Spirit World. Each of them offers a Sacred Teaching about how to be in the world."

"What did the wolf teach you?"

"Lots of things. To try to be there for my friends. To put my head down and keep going."

"Keep going where?"

"Wherever you need to be. Right here." I blushed and she smiled.

"It's funny," she said. "When I was a kid I used to have my own spirit. Not really a spirit, but an imaginary friend. Her name was Jodi. When I was thirteen I told my best friend about her."

"What happened?"

"I was a bit old for an imaginary friend. At least she thought so. She told the whole school. I never lived it down. "

"Kids can be really mean."

"Tell me about it. After that I used to spend more time at home. I started writing and reading lots."

"You did?" I said. "Me too."

"When?" she said.

"After I got to high school in Kirkland Lake. I started reading more. I wanted to make it to the academic stream. And I was lucky. The Ryans had lots of books."

"The who?"

"The Ryans. They were my first foster family. They were . . . like . . . parents to me." I looked at her hands. I saw a flash of a man's fingers reaching toward me, and felt a rush of panic.

"You okay?"

"Yeah. Fine. Just thinking of something that happened a long time ago."

"What?" I looked at her hands again. It was only Joan. Such slender, gentle hands. "Nothing."

"You seem upset."

"It's nothing. Where was I?"

"We were talking about our childhoods."

"Sorry."

"Don't worry about it."

"I . . . sometimes I get . . ." I wasn't sure what to call my lapses into my past ". . . distracted."

"That's okay. I get it."

"Can I take you out on the Albany sometime?"

"I'd like that."

Over the next few days, Joan didn't have time for our river trip, as she was filling in for a colleague who was sick, so I decided on a different tactic. To spend more time with Joan, I needed to befriend her roommate, Donna, so she would look the other way when I came by the house. I already knew what the wemistikoshiw missed most. They all talked about it once they got off work: booze. It was more precious than caribou heart on our supposedly dry reserve.

Was our reserve ever dry? Booze was illegal on the reserves until 1951. One of Ottawa's many laws. Then the federal government decided that the laws weren't doing any good, so they legalized it on the reserves. Our local band council decided that the loosening of the laws didn't help our community, so they brought in their own anti-booze rule.

Not that any of the regulations made much difference. We ignored them. Just made homebrew instead. Pa had the best recipe in the whole of James Bay. He never had enough because he shared it around with other families, so I had to be careful how much I took. Too much and I had to dilute the brewing bucket with water. Too much water and there would be trouble.

"Here. A present." Standing at Joan's door, I handed her a metal flask full of homebrew. She peered outside, to see if anyone was watching. No one was on her street.

"You wanna come in?" she said, pulling me inside and shutting the door.

"Is Donna here?"

"No, she's out, thankfully."

"The gift is for you and Donna."

"What is it?"

"Try it."

She took a small sip. "God, it's strong. Ah. It burns the throat."

"Does the trick, though."

"Where did you get this?"

"My dad made it."

"Really? Isn't it banned?"

"Yeah. But they banned a lot of things. Best to ignore the rules."

"Ha. It reminds me of when we used to drink behind the sheds in the schoolyard."

"You did that?"

"Sure. We all did. Until my dad found out."

"How'd he find out?"

"He went through my bag one morning. I didn't realize until afterwards. And then he just came into the school. Marched right through the playground and confronted us all. Everyone got into big trouble."

"Oh. What happened to you?"

"I was suspended for two weeks. After that, my parents thought it was best if I went to a new school to get away from 'bad influences.'"

"I'm a bad influence," I said. I took out my cigarettes and lit one.

"I know," she said. "Can I have one?"

"I didn't know you smoked," I said, and gave her the packet.

"I don't normally." I lit her up.

"I had my first cigarette at twelve," I said. "We smuggled them into St. Anne's."

"Tell me about that."

"About what?"

"St. Anne's"

"I went to school. I stayed for eight years. Then I came out."

"What happened in the middle?"

"Lots of things."

"Are you going to tell me?"

"There's not much more to say."

"You mean there's nothing about your time there that you want to tell me?"

What happened? Everything happened. Nothing happened. The wemistikoshiw had so many intrusive questions. What did she want me to say?

"Can we talk about it later?" I said. We heard a key in her front door. It was Donna.

"You should go," Joan said, looking at the door.

"Can I come back?"

"Sure. But let me work on Donna first. She's not much of a drinker. We'll have to be discreet."

Donna didn't want to break the rules, either on drinking homebrew or letting me into the house, so Joan and I decided to spend time together out on the land. Over the next few weeks, I taught her to shoot and how to gut fish. I tried to teach her how to skin a rabbit but she didn't take to that one too well, said the blood made her feel sick.

"The thing about being sick is the taste. You never forget what it feels like to eat it."

"What do you mean?"

"I was thinking about school."

"What happened?"

"Oh you know. They whipped us and . . ." I thought about being forced to eat my own vomit. The memory rushed through me, and I could almost taste digested porridge and carrots in my mouth. "And stuff."

"Whipped you?"

"Yeah, it happened a lot."

"At St. Anne's? Where I work?"

"Yeah, but it's different now. At least, I hope it is," I said.

"We're certainly not allowed to whip anyone."

"Yeah. Well. Times have changed."

"Were you ever whipped?"

"Yep." I took out my flask of homebrew. "You want some?"

"No thanks. What for?"

"For talking. For running in the school. For asking for more food. For not understanding what was going on. Lots of stuff."

"God, that's so awful. Why did they do it?"

"I don't know. It was their job, I guess."

"It was their job to whip the boys?"

"Kill the Indian, Save the Child."

"What?"

"That's just what we heard sometimes. The school policy."⁵

"What does it mean? I don't understand."

"Get rid of the Indian inside of you."

"How do they do that?"

I sighed. "They just . . ." I remembered standing in the line and being given a number, then stripping naked and being deloused. I felt trapped by a wave of sadness, and I wished it would all go away—I just wanted this moment to be about me and Joan. "They just . . . I don't know."

She smiled sadly, and took my hand.

We didn't have cars in Fort Albany, so Joan had bought a new Ski-Doo from the Northern Store. Cost her three months' salary, and she'd only had it a few days but already said it was worth it. Like me, she loved the feeling when everything fell away in the speed of the moment. You opened up the throttle and the wilderness rushed toward you and life fell behind.

It was a Saturday, just after the first snowfall, and Donna was away. I had come over to Joan's house to help her adjust the muffler. Afterwards, we went to her bathroom to wash up.

"You look beautiful this morning," I said. Being out on the land with her on her Ski-Doo had made me feel free and given me a rare boost of confidence.

"I do?" She put out her hands, which were covered in brown smears of oil. I took them in mine. She had smudges of oil on her face too, and I loved the way that black brought the creaminess of her skin into focus.

"Your green eyes make me feel like I'm standing at the Albany, looking straight down."

"How's that?"

"Well, they change constantly. They change with the light and the shadow, and how you're feeling."

"So how do I feel right now?"

"Well, you're a little embarrassed about the oil on your face." She laughed. "And that I'm standing in your messy bathroom."

"You're good!" she said.

"And you're wondering if you remembered to make your bed. You know, just in case."

She blushed. "No I wasn't."

"So can I see?"

"What?"

"Your bed."

"You're terrible!" Her eyes laughed, and we kissed.

"Ma, can you make something special for dinner on Wednesday?"

Ma was in the kitchen cooking scrambled eggs with moose meat for breakfast. Pa was showing Marcel and Danny how to clean a gun.

"What's happening Wednesday?" Ma said.

"A friend is coming over."

"Who?"

"No one. Just someone I like," I said, smiling coyly.

"A girl?! What's gotten into you?"

"Nothing. I just like her."

"What's she like?"

"Well, she's uh . . . she has green eyes."

"She's wemistikoshiw?" Ma said. Pa stopped what he was doing with the boys, and he and Ma exchanged looks.

"Uh, yes."

"Who is she?" Ma asked. "Do I know her?"

"She teaches Mike. She has straight hair, parted down the middle."

"Oh, her! Yes. She's good. A real lady."

I had been nervous about bringing a wemistikoshiw home, but suddenly the tension fell away, just like it did when I stood beside my beauty the Albany.

Joan was at our door. She stuck out her hand. Pa shook it.

"Now you wanna see how we greet each other?" he said.

"Sure!"

"Put out your fist."

He fist-pumped her, then they rubbed elbows.

"Oh, my grandma's going to love that," Joan said.

"Your grandma?" Pa said.

"Yeah, she loves hearing stories about up north. She says I've been given the key to a different world."

"Your *gookum* said that?" Pa said.

"Gookum?" Joan asked.

"That's Cree for grandmother," Ma said.

"Oh yeah. She's great. I really miss her up here."

Pa smiled and looked at me. "This one," he said, and gestured toward Joan. "She's a keeper."

—

We were at Joan's house, lying on her bed, listening to the wind. It was hammering loud on her metal roof.

"Is it ever going to let up?" she asked.

"I like it. It sounds like drumming."

"It makes me afraid that the whole roof is going to come off."

"We have a story about that. About how the wind destroyed the house of a bad man."

"Oh, great."

"No, it's a good story. He was cruel. He got too greedy. He went out and killed a bunch of birds just for the fun of it. So the wind took revenge."

"So how is this a good story?"

"Because it shows us to respect life."

"I see," she said, bemusedly. "Where did you learn all this stuff?"

"My dad, mostly."

"He doesn't talk much."

"Yeah, that's just his way. We sometimes call the wemistikoshiw the 'noisy ones.'"

"The noisy ones?" She sounded incredulous and lightly punched my arm.

"Maybe I shouldn't have said that."

"Which ones in particular?"

"Not *one* of you. *All* of you."

"So you damn us all with that praise."

"*I* don't say that."

"I bet you don't," she said, and threw a pillow at me.

"Joan?"

"Yes."

"Shall I show you how Pa tells Ma that he loves her?" I put my hand on my heart, then placed it on hers. "So you can feel it through my fingers."

"Does this mean what I think it means?"

"Yes," I said.

"I love you too, Ed."

We slipped into an easy rhythm, meeting every day after work to escape to the land. The days ran together into months, until we got the news. I came home by boat from teaching in Kashechewan and went straight to her house as usual. She came to the door in her pyjamas, which was unlike her.

"Oh God, Ed."

"What is it?"

"I went to the nursing station yesterday. I'm pregnant."

I smiled. "You serious?"

"Of course I'm serious."

"I'm a lucky guy. We have been blessed."

"What do I do?"

"Let's have the baby."

"What are you talking about?"

"We'll give the world a gift. The gift of life."

"This was supposed to be my adventure!" she yelled.

"A baby is a great adventure."

"Ed, you don't understand. I'm twenty. I don't have any job security and I'm not married."

"Those are all good reasons to have it."

"For God's sake. What are you talking about?"

"I'll marry you," I said.

"What a proposal!"

"Sorry. That came out wrong. Joan, I love you. Since the first day I met you, I wanted you to be my wife."

"Ed! That's not the point!"

"Well, what is the point?"

"You don't even have a ring!"

I reached into my pocket. I had an old chocolate wrapper and I began to curl it into a loop.

"Joan, will you marry me?"

Her anger broke and she laughed. "Are you serious? With this?" She held up the chocolate wrapper.

"Why not?"

"How am I going to show this to my family?"

"Tell them it's a sacred Cree tradition."

"My dad is never going to fall for that."

"Well, don't tell him until we get a real one. We'll get a gold one in Timmins next holidays."

"Joan told me you're engaged," Ma said. Joan and I were at my parents' house a couple of days later, where there were ten of us tightly packed around a kitchen table full of elbows and clattering dishes. I looked at Joan, trying to figure out whether she'd told them she was pregnant, too. I hoped not. Ever since Rita's death, Ma took the Catholic teachings very seriously, and I didn't want Joan to have to go to confession and go through the embarrassment of the Sacrament of Reconciliation.

"It slipped out over school lunch," Joan said, and looked at me apologetically.

"Does this mean she'll be an Indian?" Ma asked.

"Yeah. Status card and everything," I replied.

"What's my Indian name?" Joan asked.

"Green Eyes," Pa said.

"Really?"

"He's messing around," I replied.

"I like Green Eyes," she said.

"And she showed me her ring," Ma said. "Lucky this isn't a Give Away ceremony, Ed. You show up with a chocolate wrapper, and everyone would think you're too cheap." At the Give Away ceremonies, Crees were famously generous with their gifts to the person being honoured.

"We'll get something better at Christmas," I said.

"You could borrow mine."

"Thanks, Ma. I think Joan wants her own."

"We're proud of you, Ed," Ma said. "As soon as I heard, I went straight over and told Father Daneau." Father Daneau was new to Fort Albany, and he and Father Lavois were working alongside each other as the community priests.

"Ah, Ma. I wish you hadn't done that. We weren't planning to get married at the church." I was angry, but like Pa, I masked my real feelings.

"What are you talking about? You're Catholic. Joan is Catholic. You're having it in the church."

The last time I was in church was a few months earlier. I hadn't wanted to go—hadn't gone since St. Anne's—but Ma kept on at me. We fought about it and she seemed to retreat, at least for a while. Then something in her hardened, and she decided that I was near eternal damnation, and my soul was corrupt, the usual garbage.

Good luck saying no to Ma. If you've ever tried to argue with someone who has raised ten kids and was carrying river water home before she could run, you know that you might as well argue with a moose. I blame the priests—we natives tried to let everyone have his or her own opinion, let a man have his freedom, mind and land, but Ma had grown more Catholic.

The service was uneventful until the Eucharist. I didn't pay much attention until after the girls had received Communion. A group of younger boys knelt before the priest. They shut their eyes and opened their mouths. Their tongues lolled expectantly. My hands started to shake. I felt faint, said "excuse me" to Ma, and went out for a smoke.

Damned if they'd get me kneeling before the Holy Father. I was angrier now that I was alone. I was not going to hold my tongue out like a dog.

"What happened, Ed?" Ma came out of the building when the service was over.

"Needed to pee."

"You were shaking."

"I had to pee bad."

"Is something wrong?"

"Just leave it, Ma."

"Ed. I'm worried about you."

"I said leave it."

Ma and I argued about the wedding location over the next few weeks. To be honest, it felt like trying to change the Canada goose migration route—lots of pointless, honking noise, and you followed them around and around before they took notice and fired at you with putrid green and white.

If you're hunting, you can't just march right up to your prey. They'd hear, or at least smell you. I decided to approach the discussion by staying downwind. That meant coming at the problem from an angle, so I worked on Joan. "Let's not have our wedding at the church," I said one night when I was visiting her. I hadn't yet explained why— I was planning on telling her after the wedding and the birth, when things were more settled. No need to worry her when she was pregnant.

"Where do you want to have it?" Joan asked.

I shrugged. "What about in the open air? We could have a tent." There wasn't much free space in Fort Albany.

"What if it rains? And how will we afford a giant tent?"

"We can save up."

"It seems like a needless expense."

"Joan, you're always telling me that you think the Catholic Church has a lot to answer for."

"It does. But this is our wedding."

Ma found out about my suggestion to Joan and didn't stay upwind. She went right to her target, straight as an arrow.

Our wedding took place at Holy Angels Catholic Church, a stone's throw from St. Anne's.

I had trouble dressing. I felt sweaty and jumpy, and didn't want anyone to see me, at least not right away. I kept thinking about the night before, when I had my first meeting with Joan's parents, Lloyd and Patricia Barnes. It hadn't gone according to plan. Sure, the meal at my parents' house with my nine brothers and sisters had seemed nice enough—Patty said she loved the huckleberry jam that Ma had made—but I still couldn't tell if her parents liked me. I asked Joan about it after the meal.

"No, you're wrong," she said. "They liked you."

"Did they say anything?"

"Not much, no," she said.

"And they didn't mind that you're marrying an Indian?"

"Well. They were surprised. It was all a surprise, Ed. But they like you now."

I stared at her. I sensed that there was more to it than that, especially given Alex's reaction. He had accused me of marrying out—of betraying my race by choosing someone white, and whiter than white, a blonde. I had told him that this was bigger than politics, and then I had stopped fighting about it and gone silent. It was a relief that someone would choose me after what had happened. That I could still have sex. All the pieces could come apart if I didn't stay with it.

Keep focused. That's what I had to do now. The buttons on my shirt wouldn't go into the damned holes. And my shoes—goddammit, why were laces so slippery? Late and sweaty, I finished up and hurried to the church. I walked around the building and opened the side door a crack, peering at the expectant faces. *Where's Ma? Is Joan here? Is Mike coming? Oh God, that's him. Oh no, it's not. Is he here? Maybe he'd gotten word of my wedding and had flown in from Montreal.* My hands shook. I clenched them and counted silently. Open close. One. Open close. Two. My throat tightened. The fear spread downwards, as if there were a hot boulder pressing onto my chest. Breathing troubles. My mind filled with a dense flurry of voices. The floor and ceiling uneven, and swerving to meet each other. Too much was happening in that church. I backed away.

The sky was cloudy and grey, the ground covered in melting ice and snow. The church was a few yards from the spruce forest. I made my way there, the wet and cold seeping through my leather shoes. The muskeg was uneven and slippery, and I walked carefully so I didn't trip.

It was quiet in the forest. I stood next to the spruce trees or, as we call them, the Standing Ones. I felt their cold bark and breathed them in. They were the roots of life. Standing tall and providing food and shelter. Breathing, steadily and silently. I watched and listened to their silence. The icy air cut through the voices in my head, and when I looked up through the jagged branches I saw a faint sliver of light.

I glanced at my wrist. My watch wasn't there: I had forgotten it. How long had I been away? Ten minutes? Twenty? An hour? I hurried back the way I came.

I thought I'd slip in through the side door. I stood outside and listened through the wood. I could hear the sound of competing voices. A few deep breaths, the door ajar, and a sea of faces. Some people were still sitting, but many were standing and talking urgently. I saw my pa at the other end of the church and began to walk over. As people noticed me, they fell silent and stared.

Midway, I saw Ma and Alex walking toward me from the back of the church. I switched direction and began to walk toward them. I could hear my footsteps on the wooden floor.

"Where have you been?"

"Why are your pants wet?"

"What happened to your shoes?"

"Alex went to look for you."

"We were waiting. Everyone was waiting."

They stared at me with their worried eyes. Each anxious face made me feel worse.

"Please," I said. "Where is Joan? I want to see Joan."

"No, Ed," Ma said. "It's bad luck."

"Please," I said, and pushed past her.

She was in the vestry, sitting in a chair, looking down. A loose strand of hair had escaped her veil and hung in her eyes. She was rubbing her thumbs together frantically like she was trying to remove a spot from her skin.

"I thought you walked out on me," she said, and as she looked up, I saw her mascara was smudged.

"I went to see the Standing Ones."

"The what?"

"The trees. I needed their wisdom."

"On your wedding day?"

"I wanted to make sure everything was right."

She shook her head. "I don't understand you."

"I'm sorry. I needed things to be right."

"Couldn't you have gone before?"

"I didn't realize it would take so long."

"You embarrassed me."

"I know. Can you forgive me?"

"Everyone was waiting."

"I know. Please, Joan."

"How can I trust you?"

"I just felt nervous, that's all."

"Why are you so nervous? Are you afraid of making the commitment?"

"No, that's not it! There's a lot going on."

"What's going on? The only thing that's happening is our wedding."

"I panicked."

"Why?"

"I don't know."

"Ed, is there something that you're not telling me?"

"No . . . I . . . I'm scared I guess."

"That's it?"

"Yeah, that's it."

"Let's not have any secrets from each other. I'm scared too, you know."

"You are?"

"Of course."

"Why are you scared?"

"Because this is a big commitment."

I wanted to hold her in my arms. "Please forgive me, Joan."

She shook her head and was silent for a while. Then she stood and we went into the church together.

THIRTEEN

It was against the St. Anne's regulations for me to live with Joan, especially now that it was obvious we had broken the laws on fraternizing. Joan was officially an Indian, at least in the eyes of the law, which meant that she had to live in native housing.

We moved in with my parents. It was packed. Monday to Saturday, it was Joan, Ma, Pa, Marcel (five), Danny (four) and me in our two-bedroom house. On Sundays, Mary-Louise, Chris, Leo, Jane, Denise and Mike came home too. And on holidays, well, forget it. It was all thirteen of us packed into that tiny house. I was used to it growing up, but Joan found it hard, almost inhumane.

I tried to please her by bringing home lots of fresh rabbit and fish. That's what my pa had done for my ma when they were out in the bush and she was pregnant.

"Where were you?" Joan asked. I had decided to wake up early on Sunday morning and go fishing.

"Thought I'd catch our lunch at the Albany. Here, I brought you something." I held up a walleye we could share for supper.

"Ed. Didn't you think of bringing me with you?"

"You were busy."

"Looking after your brothers and sisters."

"Joan, they can take care of themselves."

"No, they can't. Danny is four. Marcel is five. Mike is six. They are way too young."

"Well get Denise, Jane or Leo to look after them."

"They need an adult." All wemistikoshiw lived in constant fear that their children might harm themselves. We tried to let them learn by example, and they did their best to watch over their every move.

"Joan. They are Cree children. They can run free."

"This isn't the bush, you know."

"What's that supposed to mean?"

"Well they aren't growing up on the land anymore. They could get run over by an ATV. Or stick their fingers in an electrical socket. Or burn themselves on the stove."

"They are used to all of that stuff."

"Ed. They spend their childhood inside. They don't grow up making their own toys and building their own fires. Life is different now. They need to be watched constantly."

"Joan. I have nine brothers and sisters. There's no way we can watch them all at every moment of the day."

"Well, it would be easier if you weren't off fishing by yourself." I sighed. I had wanted to help, but it had blown up in my face. I was so frustrated. I needed a drink.

"Fine," I said.

That night, I went to the living room chest where Pa normally kept his homebrew. I wanted to down the lot, but of course I couldn't. And Pa would know if I diluted it too much. Then he'd get angry and shout, and cooped up inside, that felt like blows raining on my head.

Why was Joan so hard on me? Didn't she see I was trying my best? I had tried to do what was right, and now she was mad. I was just trying to please her. I'd thought she was different than the rest. No such luck.

"What are you doing?" Marcel was sleeping on a mat by the homebrew chest and had woken up.

"Nothing. Go back to sleep."

"That's Papa's," he said, pointing to the bucket of homebrew I had in my hand.

"I know."

"That's not allowed."

"I know. Go back to sleep."

My daughter was born early. That's why things got hairy. If she had been on time, we would have bought our plane tickets and flown out to Moosonee and been hanging about in the hospital by the time Joan went into labour. No one on the reserve had a phone, except for Father Daneau, so I hurried to the airport, a wooden hut a five-minute walk away.

The pilot had radioed ahead and an ambulance was waiting at the runway when we arrived in Moosonee. Joan was sweating and shaking and wanted to be sick all the time, but nothing came up. I told her how as a boy, I had seen a midwife or *keshayyahow* deliver Rita out in the bush. How the old woman had boiled red willow in a big pot and how she'd given it to Ma to drink and after she had, Ma stopped moaning so much, and how when we landed, the nurse would make Joan drink something to ease the pain. How the *keshayyahow* brushed Ma's hair away from her face, just as I was doing now with Joan. How she had helped Ma to relax by breathing deeply, just as Joan was finding her own rhythm of breath.

"I know you are going to be fine. I can feel it. In here." I put my hand on her belly. She touched my hand.

"What does it feel like?" she asked softly.

"It feels like strength."

The doctor wheeled Joan into the birthing room. When I tried to follow he told me to wait outside to ensure patient hygiene, but by then I'd had enough of wemistikoshiw men telling me what to do. I forced myself past him into the birthing room and got myself a mask. Then I washed my hands and put on latex gloves. The doctor watched me doing this, and then shrugged and started fastening Joan's feet into the metal stirrups.

Joan was pushing and saying, "I can't, I can't," and I said, "Yes, you can." She squeezed my hand until my knuckles felt broken, and I told her to focus on her breath. Then the doctor said, "Almost there," and Joan looked like her eyes might pop out of their sockets. We heard an *Uh-oh*, and I looked down and saw that my wife's womb seemed to have swallowed the doctor's whole arm. "What is it?" Joan asked and tried to see beyond the bulge of her stomach. The doctor turned to the nurse and said, "Let's get it out quick. Get me 141 D," and she went to the drawer and got what looked like a giant pair of blunt scissors. Joan looked like she'd just been shot. "Relax, sweetie," the doctor said. Joan moaned in pain.

"You are like Oh-Ma-Ma, the first pregnant woman," I said. It was an ancient Cree legend that I'd heard from friends at St. Anne's Residential School.

"She . . . was . . . in . . . pain . . . too?"

"Yes, the whole world was inside of her. She had to push really hard."

Joan grabbed hold of me with both hands, and screamed as if she wanted the Earth to open. The doctor wiggled the scissor things, and I saw the first glimpse of hair, black like mine. Then we saw half of a squished elongated face, smeared with blood. Some floppy shoulders came next. "It's a girl!" the nurse said.

The rest of my daughter came quickly after that, tumbling out like the Spirit Gods from Oh-Ma-Ma. Then the nurse picked up the tiny thing covered in red and white gunk with bruise marks all over her face. The baby opened her toothless mouth and screamed with a volume that was surprising for one so small. I looked at her perfect nose and tiny fingers and toes and what flashed in my mind was the vision of an eagle, hovering above our heads. With a shift in the wind, she curled and dove.

We named her Albalina. It is a name that everyone likes as soon as you say it. I read it in a story in one of those *Life* magazines, about a native man who was travelling along the Amazon River with his wife, Albalina. I had promised myself that if I ever had a girl, I would name her Albalina. I thought about the strong, tanned woman negotiating one of the world's longest rivers, living from the riches of the waters, just as I imagined Albalina would one day paddle along and feast on the bounty of the Albany.

She had skin the colour of an Arctic fox in the summer, lighter than me, darker than her Ma. She was a strong baby who could scream like a raccoon in heat. We brought her home, and everyone came by to give us gifts. It was a wemistikoshiw custom, but one that felt natural, maybe because it was similar to our traditional gift Give Aways. Joan held Albalina, lying on our bed, and the gifts— moosehide booties and a few bibs—piled onto her legs.

"How much longer, do you think?" Joan asked me this question every few weeks. She's already found our living situation tight, but with a crying baby, it was near impossible.

"I'll ask at the band office again," I said.

"You asked a few weeks ago. Do you think it will make any difference?" Normally, the waitlist for housing was seven years.

Sometimes they made exceptions for people who were particularly cramped, but our living situation wasn't any worse than anyone else's.

"I'm sorry, Joan. I'll ask again, but you're right. I doubt it will make much difference."

"What are we going to do?"

"Maybe . . . uh . . . maybe we could spend more time outside?"

"We already do that!"

"I don't know!" This came out louder than I expected. Her shoulders slumped. She looked like she was about to tear up.

"Please, Joan." I hugged her. "Please don't cry. I'll make it better. I promise."

I tried to think of all the things that made Joan happy. Like photography. Her first camera, a Brownie, had been given to her by her grandmother, and it had become a passion. I found the number of a photography store in Timmins from the teacher friend of mine, John, who had first mentioned me to Joan, and went to Father Daneau's house to call the store. I asked whether they had a camera within my price range. As usual, I could only afford the cheapest option. A few weeks later, I surprised her with the gift.

"Thanks, Ed," she said, smiling briefly.

I couldn't tell if it made her happy or not. Did it matter that it didn't have an FD lens? Or a faster shutter speed? It seemed like the wemistikoshiw had this game where only the most expensive object was worth having, which meant almost no one could afford it.

Things were changing on the reserve. Every year you noticed something different—someone had bought themselves a new television or a cassette deck, and then everyone heard about it through the moccasin telegraph and went over to take a look. Maybe I was paranoid, but all this stuff made me uneasy. Especially the houses that the government was building. Most people lived in one-room places in the summer and spent the rest of the year on the land. We were free that way, maybe too independent. But it was hard to say no to a free house, especially one with lino floors and insulation. The free houses were the next step in changing our way of life: we put down our guns and paddles and came indoors.

My dad warned me about following the ways of the wemistikoshiw too closely. He used to tell me that a lot during the summers I came home from high school. He said it was dangerous to get stuck craving their electric things and plastic objects. He said the Cree chief Big Bear had given a similar warning to his own people. Each time my dad said it, I nodded. *Okay, Pa. I get it.* But things were different now. I mean, you could talk about the days when the Cree used moss as diapers until you were blue in the face, but if you showed up somewhere with moss between your daughter's legs, you might as well have put poison ivy down there for some of the looks you'd get.

Our baby sucked up money faster than an ATV with a gas leak, especially now that Joan was no longer working. I began to rack my brain for other ways that we could make some extra money. I asked my old friend, Fred, what he thought when he came by to help me fix my canoe. He currently worked at the Hudson's Bay store, but was soon moving to Timmins to take a job in mining.

"How about you come with me?" Fred said. "It's not so bad. Three weeks on, one week off. It's where the money is at."

I thought about the photos of mines that I had seen in magazines at the Ryans' house. Dark and cramped. Like the basement at St. Anne's. I'd once been sent there to collect a forgotten toilet pail. There was no light other than my torch and it smelled of piss and poo. I couldn't see the rats, but I could hear rustling. I shone my light in the corners and saw a flash of movement. Something grey and furry from the corner of my eye. I stepped forward and my foot slipped on something wet. I dropped the flashlight, stunned. It hit the floor and went out. Crawling on the floor, searching for the light, my hands in dust and stickiness. That stuff never leaves you. Tony had gone in there for two days after we had tried to run away, and afterwards, he wasn't the same.

"That would be a step backwards," I told Fred. "I'm already teaching ESL."

"Suit yourself. But I bet Joan would be happier down south."

I looked at him hard, then relented. "I guess. She's going a bit stir crazy on the reserve."

"So what about it? We could hang out together. Just like old times."

"I was thinking more . . . well, I already teach in Kash. I want to do that down south."

"Down south, I think you need university for that."

"I know, I know. Or working for a school. Something like that."

"I tried to get an office job. Almost got it."

"What happened?"

"Well, I didn't realize. You know how things are. I saw this cool photo of my hero, Russell Means."

Russell Means was one of the leaders of the Occupation of Alcatraz which, in 1969, as part of the Red Power movement, had taken over the island in San Francisco Bay. Ever since the sit-in had begun, long hair and braids had become more popular on the reserves.

"And?"

"So I showed up in my braids. I told her I got the idea from Mr. Means. The boss looked like she was interviewing the devil."

We both laughed. "What happened?"

"Oh, you know. She sat there and nodded a lot. Didn't say nothing, but I knew."

"Did you try again?"

"Nah. What would have been the point?"

—

Joan had heard about a special on oranges and had me go to the Hudson's Bay store to check. I returned empty-handed—the oranges were sold out—but it didn't seem to matter; Joan was happier than I had seen in a while.

"Dad is wiring us some money," she said.

"When did this happen?"

"Father Daneau just dropped by with the message. Don't worry. We don't have to pay it back right away."

"Right," I said and sat down. I had heard that before. *Don't worry, you don't have to pay it back until later.* Mike had said those words on the way to Montreal.

"Tell him we don't want the money."

"No, I'm not doing that."

"I said tell him," I growled.

"Why should I? He offered. We certainly need it."

"I am not accepting money from a white man."

"I hate it when you say those sorts of things."

"What sorts of things?"

"He's not a white man! He's my dad!"

I didn't feel comfortable accepting a white man's money, so we didn't get a loan from her pa. Instead, I managed to earn a few extra dollars by getting a job with the band council, picking up garbage. It wasn't so bad. The work was pretty easy, but it meant I came home stinky, which Joan didn't like. A few weeks later, while we were making dinner together, she presented another solution.

"I think you should go to university."

"No thanks."

"I know what you're worried about—that you'll be too far behind. But I've found this course that's different, in Indian-Eskimo studies. It's the first of its kind in North America. It's at Trent University in

Peterborough, near my hometown. You can learn about all the things that matter to you. Gitchi Manitou, the Sacred Teachings."

"It's not for me," I said.

"Why?"

"I already know about that stuff."

"Exactly."

"So why spend three years learning about it?"

"Because we live with ten other people, Ed. In a two-bedroom house."

"Only on Sundays."

"What's going to happen when they all come home for summer?"

"I . . . maybe . . ." I hung my head, ashamed. "Maybe I could ask at the band office again."

"You know that's not going to help."

She was right, as usual. I stared at the potatoes I had been peeling. I felt trapped and wondered how I'd gotten myself into this mess. I had tried so hard to do all the right things: finish St. Anne's, graduate from high school, get a good job, and yet I was still stuck. Worse, I had dragged Joan into the chaos.

"And we are short on money, Ed. Albalina needs diapers. Baby food. A stroller."

"Yes, I know!" I said a little too loudly.

"And you can't keep picking up garbage."

"Why not?"

"You said it yourself. The band only has money to pay you for eight weeks."

"We'll get by."

FOURTEEN

We moved to Peterborough the same way that all Indians move down south: empty-handed, like we were fleeing. Of course we weren't entirely free from luggage, but we couldn't take much on the plane, especially with Albalina. I didn't mind so much—every object is a memory, of when it is bought and how it is used, and it's better not to be weighed down by all that stuff.

In Peterborough there were newspapers and TVs everywhere. I mean, you could walk into practically any store, and there were papers. We didn't have that up north.

When we arrived, the story headlining most newspapers was about an Indian, Joseph Drybones, who had been found to be drunk in a Yellowknife bar. It was against the law for an Indian to drink off reserve, and he was arrested and charged with contravening section 94(b) of the Indian Act. He represented himself and pled guilty, and was sentenced to either a ten-dollar fine or three days in jail. Then he got himself a lawyer who appealed, arguing that because Drybones only spoke Dene, he hadn't understood what was going on, didn't realize he was pleading guilty, and therefore his plea was invalid. The judge gave him a new trial. This one went better—his lawyer claimed that, all appearances to the contrary, Drybones wasn't a real Indian.

For us, being Indian was a matter of language, culture, race and history, but legally, it was a different matter. It was defined by an official list of names held by the Department of Indian Affairs. Since Drybones had mistakenly been left off the official list, he didn't have legal status. Therefore, his lawyer argued, the law shouldn't apply to him. And even if he was legally an Indian, the law was unfair from the start, as it discriminated against Indians because of their race. The case bounced around the legal system, to ever higher courts, until finally the Supreme Court weighed in. They decided that Indians should have the same drinking rights as everyone else, at least when they were off reserve.

I had mixed feelings about the case. I had been drinking more since Joan and I had married, living in that tiny house, all thirteen of us, with Albalina screaming with teething pains. The only thing that held me back was that it was more difficult to get drunk in Fort Albany. If you went to the bootlegger, you had to pay through the nose and homebrew was always limited because of the time it took to make it. I was priced out of the market, especially with a kid. Now I was down south, where you could walk into a liquor store and, thanks to Joseph Drybones, buy anything you wanted for just a few dollars. It was progress, I guess, as we were finally getting some of the same rights as the wemistikoshiw, but it meant that temptation was always in reach.

Like all native students, I'd come a month early with Joan for catch-up courses. We bought a secondhand car with a small loan, and the money that I'd saved picking up garbage, and moved into a one-bed apartment on Bolivar Street, on Peterborough's west side. Most of the houses on the street were detached two-storeys, but with the money for tuition and a $1,000 monthly student allowance given to us by the band, we found one subdivided into apartments, a stone's throw away from where the rest of the native students were living. I was twenty-two years old, and it was the first time that we had our own place. It felt like I'd made it.

Joan went out and reconnected with a couple of her high school friends, like Svetlana, who'd relocated to Peterborough. She and her parents had made it out of the Soviet Union by sneaking from Russia through Romania and paying some criminal a lot of money for fake passports. By the time they arrived in Canada in the early 1950s, they were stick thin and had nothing but a handful of rubles stuffed into their pockets.

I soon realized that Svetlana didn't think much of natives. She had been nice to me and translated the phrase that the Tekaucs used to repeat, *Zatknis!* It meant *Shut up!* She, Joan and I laughed about it for a while. But after that we butted heads.

"I don't know why they are still complaining," she said. She was sitting in our living room, having some after-dinner wine. A native guy who she worked with (she didn't know anything about his nation other than he was "Indian") at General Electric had been complaining about the storm we'd had the night before, and made an offhand remark about how it compared to the government flooding thousands of acres of Anishinaabe land, displacing his people without any compensation, that had happened with the building of the Trent-Severn Waterway.[6]

"Always history, history, history," she said. "That stuff is in the past. They need to get over it."

"*They?*"

"You know what I mean," Svetlana said. Joan and I exchanged glances.

"*They* haven't been compensated yet," I replied.

"Stuff happens. Look at the Purges," she said. "My grandparents had friends who were taken away. They say something wrong and, *pft*, that's it. Seven years for you. Nine years for you. The KGB have ears everywhere."

"That doesn't make it right, does it?" I said.

"What is right? History? No. Everywhere is history. That's why I like Canada. Come here. Start again." I thought about my past. About my great-granddad being taken away under the Potlatch laws. About going to St. Anne's. About going to Montreal with Mike. Maybe she was right. Maybe that stuff was better dead and buried.

We were sitting in a lecture hall on the first day, myself and the other native students. A guy named Harvey McCue, from Georgina Island First Nation, Ontario, a professor in the Indian-Eskimo Studies Program, was explaining what was required to make it through a university degree.

"University is different from high school. How so?" Harvey asked. Simone, nineteen, put up her hand. I didn't know too much about her—just that her parents were from Skwah First Nation out in Chilliwack, B.C., but she had grown up in Vancouver. "There's more work," she said.

"Some people say that," Harvey said. "You definitely have to spend a lot of time hunched over your books. More than in high school. But at university, everyone has a choice. To work or not is up to you. There's no one telling you what to do. To get your work done, you have to be self-motivated. What else?"

"More parties!" This was shouted out by Clayton, a twenty-year-old who'd spent his childhood in North Spirit Lake First Nation before being shipped off to St. Margaret's Indian Residential School. Everyone laughed.

"Yes, there are more parties at university. If you wanted, you could party every night. But we expect more of you. Going to university is a great honour. If you don't take it seriously, you won't graduate. You won't be able to get your work done if you are partying every night." Clayton was sitting a few seats away and started scribbling a note. He handed it to me.

This guy is so serious.

I know! I wrote back.

He should lighten up, he wrote. *And try my hangover cure.* I smiled.

"If you have a problem," Harvey said, "come and see me any time. That's what I'm here for. To help you stay out of trouble."

Joan was driving me home from school. She had been teaching me to drive, but I hadn't yet passed my test. Albalina was asleep in the backseat.

"So, how did it go?"

"Harvey said we should come and see him if we get into trouble."

"What sort of trouble?"

"Oh you know. Partying. That sort of thing."

"I can't imagine Harvey partying." She had met him at the meet-and-greet on the first day of orientation. I agreed—he seemed like a straight shooter.

"Yeah, well. He's supposed to help us navigate between the two worlds. White and native."

"You'd be good at that."

"Me?"

"Sure. You navigated me, didn't you?"

"Still am."

I was at our apartment. Albalina was asleep and Joan was watching TV. I had a difficult assignment. As part of Native Studies 100, we were looking at the reserve system. Joan popped her head into the living room where I was working.

"Do you really think you should be drinking while you're studying?"

"I've almost finished. And it helps me relax." I was top of my class by Grade 13 at KLCVI. Here, I was behind. It was stressful, especially as I was already married with a kid.

"Ed. I'm worried about you."

"Look. I know my limits."

"Do you? I heard you, you know, last night. Going through the drinks cabinet."

"I had insomnia. Booze helps me get to sleep."

"At four in the morning."

"Yes. It was still dark outside."

"That's not the point, is it?"

"What is the point, Joan?"

"The point is that you drink almost every night."

"I told you. It helps me relax and puts me to sleep. And I'm not drunk by the next morning. But if it's upsetting you, I'll cut down."

"Promise?"

"I promise."

A few months later I was sitting in the university library reading a newspaper editorial by the Cree writer Harold Cardinal, which was part of our politics course. Everyone talked about Cardinal on campus. He had written a book the year before called *The Unjust Society*,[7] which argued that Canada had a long history of trying to wipe out Indians through assimilation and the residential schools. After that book came out, Cardinal was everywhere, writing newspaper columns on the treaties, the reserve unemployment rates, native sovereignty, and it was all biting, deep and smart.

I read his words about assimilation over again and thought about what they meant to me. Did they mean Ma carrying Rita to a Christian cemetery rather than burying her out in the bush? Or Pa taking me to St. Anne's? Or me going to Montreal with Mike Pasko? The concept made me feel trapped. It was like our future had already been written, that we were following a script that was out of our hands.

I looked down at the newspaper. God, I needed a drink. I always did when I thought about this stuff. Reminded me of St. Anne's and Mike Pasko. Fuck, I shouldn't. I'd already promised Joan that I'd cut down. Simone popped her head through the library door.

"A bunch of us are going to the Commoner." It was the local student bar. "Wanna come?"

"No, I better not." I had promised Joan.

"Come on. It'll do you some good." She was right about that one. I certainly needed a drink. "Don't be a stickler."

I looked at the article again and felt the hot anger spreading across my chest. It would be good to burn it off. Booze would do that.

"Meet you there in fifteen."

"Where were you?" Joan asked that night, opening our apartment door.

"We were celebrating."

"Celebrating what?"

"Our assimilation off the reserves!"

"What are you talking about?"

"We are now part of the White Man's World!"

"Ed. Are you drunk?"

"Nah. It was just a couple."

"It doesn't look like it!"

"Why are you always on my case?"

"Because you promised you would cut down and you haven't. You still drink almost every night."

"I'm shorry," I slurred.

"Sorry?! I don't care about sorry. I care about you being sober."

"Relax, Joan."

"Don't tell me to relax. It's you that's making me anxious."

"Come on. Don't be like that."

"I'm going out," she said.

"Where?"

"Just out."

When she returned, I had sobered up. I told her that she was right and that I needed to lay off the booze.

"How can I believe you?"

"I promise."

"You said that last time."

"I know. But this time, I mean it."

"How can I trust you?"

"I've been better, haven't I?"

"You stopped for a little while. But now it's the same again. You drink almost every night. I can smell it on you in the mornings."

"Joan. I'm sober by morning. Besides, I had a rough day. There was this article in the newspaper about the treaties. I told people about it at the bar. Everyone was so mad. They all said, 'that happened to me too.' There were all these broken promises. And then we started to play this drinking game: whose reserve had it worse. If you couldn't think of anything that the wemistikoshiw had done to make your life miserable, you had to drink."

"Oh great."

"Come on, it was just some fun."

"Why do you have to focus on the negative?"

"We were just having a laugh."

"You were out having a laugh while I was at home worried sick, wondering where you are."

"I should have called."

"No, you shouldn't have *gone*. You promised that you'd stop drinking when you had insomnia. You promised me that you'd stop drinking when you were studying. This stuff scares me. We don't have the money for you to go out drinking with your school buddies. You know that."

"Look, I was out with my friends. I got carried away. It's no biggie."

"Yes. It is a biggie. You promised."

"Yes, you're right. I got carried away."

"Ed. It isn't fair. You were supposed to focus on your studies so you can get a better job, not carry on like a teenager." I hung my head.

"You're right."

"Damned right, I'm right."

"Look, I'll make it up to you."

"How?"

"Whatever you want."

"What I want is you to come home after lectures, or whatever, and help me with Albalina."

"Yes, of course," I said.

Over the next few months, I stayed on the straight and narrow. I did my homework, and came home and helped Joan with Albalina. Started to catch up, and my marks went up, not by a mile—Cs to Bs—but by enough. We celebrated (with orange juice) all those things that make life worth living—Albalina taking her first steps, Joan's youngest brother meeting his niece for the first time, Joan selling her first photograph. Joan said she didn't mind—it was healthier. I was happy, happier than I'd been in years.

—

"Ed? Is that you?"

We were back in Peterborough, after spending the summer in Fort Albany, so that I could do year two of university. I shut the front door and went into the living room. Joan was watching TV with Albalina curled up in her lap. I sat next to her. It was *The Brady Bunch*. They should make that show up north with twenty kids, I thought. We watched in silence for a few minutes.

"Ed, there's something I need to tell you."

"Yep," I said, staring at the TV.

"I'm pregnant."

"You are? Oh good," I said. I was still thinking about the story arc of Fort Albany's Brady Bunch, so it took me a few moments to come back to the present. "Great," I added, trying to muster more enthusiasm. We had just returned from three months living with my parents, as we couldn't afford to stay in Peterborough, and had to relearn what everyone on the reserve spends years perfecting—the gentle art of waiting. You wake up and you wait for the outhouse, get in line to use the river water, wait for your turn to use the stove and kettle, wait to use the household's only frying pan. And that's before you've gotten dressed. We'd learned about the economics of over-crowding in our courses at Trent, which somehow made the whole thing worse, like my childhood was a problem to be fixed. And if anything, the issue was getting worse, not better. I imagined myself returning home with two kids in tow, and living with Ma and Pa, and my nine brothers and sisters. That would make fifteen of us in that tiny house.

"Great? Is it really?" Joan said.

"Yes," I said, trying to reassure her and myself. I pulled her closer, protectively, and kissed her shoulder.

"Are we going to be okay?"

"Yeah. Ya. Of course."

"Of course?"

"What do you mean?"

"I'm not working, and how can I know that your drinking isn't a bigger problem than you're letting on?"

"Come on, Joan. Everything is under control."

The last time I had gotten really drunk was at the Commoner, but she kept bringing it up, as if I could turn back the clock.

"Ed, this is serious."

"I know."

"You can't just keep having one more, one more."

"Joan, please."

"Please what?"

"Please stop reminding me that I made a mistake. Mistakes," I corrected myself.

"Ed, this is a new life we're talking about."

"And you are a great mom."

"But what about us?"

"We'll be fine. I promise."

June 1, 1972. My boy was born in Peterborough. Joan had been too pregnant to fly back to Fort Albany so we'd stayed on. He was a biggie, nine pounds, nine ounces. He was bald with bright black eyes. We had already chosen the name, Shannin. Joan's maternal family was from Cork, Ireland, so we chose a name that means "wise river." Now we had two river children to guide us.

"He looks just like you," Joan said. "If you were bald."

"He does?"

"Yes."

"Is that a good thing?"

I remembered back to the way that I'd been shunted between different foster homes in high school. And being behind in all my courses after leaving the reserve. If he was growing up in a wemistikoshiw world, maybe it was better if he looked more like them.

"Yes, of course!" she said. "Come here." She offered me the hand that wasn't holding onto Shannin and I took it. "My boys," she said.

I spent three years at Trent University, but didn't graduate. Joan got pregnant with our third child in my final year, and with the demands of taking care of her and our kids, and trying to catch up after the poor schooling on the reserve, well, I didn't make it. My supervisor, Don, was nice about it. Said I could finish my degree remotely and no one would even need to know. Still, the failure made my face burn.

We moved back to Fort Albany. It was too expensive to fly our stuff up north, so we sold it or gave it away. The days passed in a rush of lists and goodbyes and then we were on a plane.

Ma and Pa greeted us at the airport with such excitement, as if we hadn't seen them for two centuries rather than a few months. Ma was so happy to see the kids, and then Albalina wanted down and Joan, heavily pregnant, ran after her, and Pa took Shannin, while I helped Joan.

And then we were home, back at Ma and Pa's house. I looked around and saw that they'd made a touching effort. On the kitchen table were all my favourite dishes: bannock, potato soup, moose snout, moose steaks and duck, and blackberry jam. Then, as if by telepathy, everyone began arriving at the front door: Alex, Mary-Louise, Chris, Leo, Jane, Denise, Mike, Marcel and Danny. Everyone was hugging us and we were eating and laughing.

"Did you hear that they've put a new satellite in Timmins?" Ma said. "Suzanne and Terri have both gotten their first TVs."

"John Wayne," I said.

"Huh?" Ma said.

"Bet they are watching John Wayne," I said.

"I doubt it. There's only one channel. CBC. Most of the time they watch the news."

We were still waiting for a new house, so every day I tried to take Joan to my beauty the Albany. There's an old Cree legend that you can see your future in the river's water. Pa told me about it before I went into the residential school. It doesn't happen right away. You have to spend a few days on the river. Gradually your mind empties. Slows down. Connects to the rhythms of the Earth. *Kayamenta*. If you're lucky, you might have a vision or some deep insight.

"Whatyadoing?" Joan asked. We were sitting together on the blanket next to the river. Shannin and Albalina were both asleep, and in that rare moment of calm I had been staring at the water under the lazy light of June. I told her about the legend.

"So can you see your future?"

"No. I don't expect to. We've only just got here. You have to spend a while letting go."

"Here, let me have a go," she said. She looked at the water for a few minutes. "No, nothing. Just water. And weeds."

"Take your time," I said, and I wiped her hair away from her brow. She gazed at the water and I watched her green eyes dance. My God, she was beautiful.

"Watching the water is so relaxing," she said after a while.

"I know," I said.

"This reminds me of the time you took me out on your boat. Do you remember that?"

"Which time?"

"The time when you first said the words 'I love you.'"

"I thought that was when we were at your house, listening to the storm."

"Oh yes. You're right. The boat was the second time you said those words. I remember now. When you said it on the boat, I remember the water and the wind, and watching the way you navigated. I thought, this is the man I want to spend my life with."

"You did?" I stroked her arm.

"Ed?"

"Yes."

"My water just broke."

"It's a boy, over!" Joan said. We were in her hospital room in Moose Factory where we had flown after that beautiful day by the Albany. Joan was talking to Ma, who was on the radio phone. She paused. "Yes. We'll be home in two days. Over." Pause. "Yes. His name is Jassen. Over."

I looked down at my newborn son. Jassen, from the Greek, meaning "healer." He was lighter than Shannin, nine pounds five ounces, with alert brown eyes. He smelled so good, like breast milk and raw earth. I thought about what Pa had told me about newborn babies. He said that they were untouched by the pain and corruption of the world. That as they become aware of the world, we must teach them to open their eyes wide, to be unafraid of those around them.

Did Jassen know what was happening in my world? Would he be touched by my pain? I brought him close to my chest. No. I would never let that happen. I would teach him to open his eyes wide. To feel without being afraid. And with these lessons, he would stand tall.

A few months later, I got a message, via radio phone, from my old supervisor. Don was calling with a job offer. They were looking for someone to take care of the Native Studies students.

"You know what it's like for students coming off the rez," he said. I thought back to my time at university. How hard it had been to go from a dry reserve to a place where booze was everywhere. How I had to figure out how to be a parent while catching up with school. How we were always worried about money. How the band sometimes "forgot" to pay our tuition.

"Yes, I do."

"We need someone who's going to be involved."

"What do you mean?"

"Well. We've had criticisms that the students are too far behind academically. Or have drinking problems. We need someone to manage that."

"Manage that?"

"Help them stay on track. I thought that since you had personal experience . . ." He knew that I'd shown up drunk to a few classes when I first got to Trent. "You pulled yourself together, though. I need someone who can help them along a similar journey."

"Thanks for thinking of me," I said. "But I'm not sure I'm qualified." I didn't really feel I had been on any sort of journey.

"You're exactly what we want. Aboriginal teacher. Good listener. Thoughtful. Smart. University graduate."

"But I didn't graduate."

"Well, it took you a while. But you got there in the end. Your paper on cultural schizophrenia was excellent." While in Fort Albany, I had written an academic paper to finally get my degree.

"What makes you think I'm the right person for the job?"

"You'll be great."

FIFTEEN

If you are driving to Peterborough from the northwest, along the Trans-Canada Highway, the first thing you notice is that the city has no rough spots. It's not like Timmins or Kirkland Lake. Everything looks like it should be in a movie set about some old-fashioned town. Even the street names are taken from somewhere else: Edinburgh, Dublin, London. It's like the wemistikoshiws arrived and got so homesick they dug up old photographs, and tried to make models of their past.

Our move down south was different this time. For starters, we were able to rent a three-bedroom house downtown on one of those streets where people have giant firs and spruces tucked onto their front lawns, and there's still space for a garage. We had the whole house this time, so there was enough room for Joan, me, Albalina, Shannin and Jassen, and still we could have family members come and stay.

I was working at one of the best universities in Canada, doing something I loved: helping my people adjust to the demands of being down south. We got another car, nothing fancy, a blue Plymouth, and I could drive myself to work for the first time. It was a beautiful drive, along the Otonabee River, which starts sprawling and relaxed, meandering over marshland, and then rushes into white water as the channel narrows.

We were living the wemistikoshiw dream.

"Can you believe this guy?" Donnie said. Donnie was twenty-four, and one of my students in the Native Studies program. He had drifted between reserves, although he was initially from Manitoulin Island, Ontario. He gestured toward Don, who was at the front of the auditorium, delivering the same speech that Harvey had given to me when I started at Trent.

"What about him?" I said.

"Lecturing us about parties."

I thought back to my time at Trent, and blushed.

"And he's a white guy teaching Native Studies. He's acting like he knows everything. Telling us what to do."

"He's not so bad."

"You the same then?"

"Me? God no."

"You sure? I hear you have a white wife. And a wemistikoshiw job."

"Yeah, well." Pause. "I got lucky, that's all."

"So why did you marry out?"

"I . . ." Pause. "We fell in love." He stared at me like he'd seen something he didn't like. "Come on," I said. "It's not like that. I'm not an apple. I've seen some shit. I know what you're going through. Really I do. Let me show you my old student hangout. It's a great bar called the Commoner. I'll buy you a drink."

"You're late," Joan said, when I walked into our kitchen, where she was cooking dinner.

"Sorry. I was making friends."

"Making friends at the bar?"

"Yeah, with one of my students."

"You're supposed to counsel them, not go drinking with them."

"Joan. Please. I know what I'm doing." I hated when she lectured me like this. It made me feel like I was seven and listening to Sister Wesley screaming in my ear. "I'm doing my job."

Her eyes narrowed. "By going to the bar. Ed. We can't go through all this again."

"I know."

"We have three kids now."

"I know. We're very lucky."

"Please let's just keep what we have."

"We will. We will. Trust me."

It was eleven p.m. when I got the call from my boss, Don. Everyone else in the house was asleep.

"Yes?" I said groggily into the bedroom phone.

"Sorry to bother you but it's about two of the students, Sekwan and Donnie." Donnie had gotten together with Sekwan a few weeks before. She was twenty-three and from Enoch Cree Nation. "They said they were in trouble. They asked for you. Can you go?" The drive between my place and Catharine Parr Traill College, which housed both native and wemistikoshiw undergraduates, took less than five minutes. I rang the bell. Sekwan let me in.

"Jesus. You okay?" Her left eye was puffy and half sealed shut, and her lip was cut.

"Fine." She turned her back and I followed her down the hallway.

In the student den, a broken beer bottle was smashed on the table, the liquid spilling onto the floor. Donnie was slumped in a chair, hanging his hands in the sink, holding ice to his knuckles.

"You needn't have come," Sekwan said. "We're fine now."

"We should take you to a doctor," I said.

"It's nothing," she said. I glanced at Donnie. I was so angry, I wanted to hit him.

"Can we talk?" I asked.

"Go ahead," she said. "Donnie. Get out." He looked at her forlornly, and left. Once he was out of earshot, I offered her a cigarette. She took it.

"We should go to the doctor. You should get that checked out," I said pointing to her eye.

"Ed. It's nothing. Stop making a fuss."

"I can't believe Donnie would do this. Are you going to press charges?"

"No."

"Do you want him to get away with it?"

She shrugged.

"Do you want to talk about it?"

"It was just a fight."

"You shouldn't let him hit you. You should go to the police."

"The cops," she said, and then began laughing bitterly. I stared at her hard, angry that she was just giving in. Then I laughed bitterly too. The Cree word for police, *okipwakhayso*, means "the people who take you away." As in never seen again. Just like my great-granddad, John Metatawabin.

"No outsiders," she said. "We Indians should stick to our own."

"Yeah, well," I said. Then I remembered that I'd had the same reaction when Mike Pasko had raped me.

She turned away, like she wanted me to leave.

"I think the university is going to want to investigate," I said.

"Not if you don't tell them."

"They are going to ask."

"Then make something up," she said, and got out her keys to open the apartment door.

"I . . ."

"We'll be fine. I love him, you know."

I stared at her. Then sadness overtook me and I had to get out of there. Why did they have to fight? I thought back to coming home from St. Anne's for the summer, and pounding Alex until he could hardly breathe. Was that our destiny? Why couldn't we break the cycle? It was embarrassing, shameful.

I got in my car and drove to the nearest bar.

Joan was awake when I crawled into bed.

"Where have you been?"

"I had to go and counsel some students," I said.

"At this hour?"

"Yeah. They got into a fight."

"Couldn't it wait until morning?"

"No."

"I can smell booze on you."

"It was just a couple."

"Just a couple! Do you know how many times I've heard that?"

"Please Joan. I had a bad day."

"Are you having an affair?"

"No!"

"You're telling me that they suddenly needed your advice at eleven p.m."

"Yes. Don called. It's complicated."

"What's so complicated?"

Everything is complicated, I thought. "Joan. Please. Can I just go to sleep?"

"No, tell me."

"I'm tired. Let me sleep."

"Are you drunk?"

"No. I just had a couple."

"Jesus, Ed. You're unbelievable."

"Come on, Joan."

"Don't *come on, Joan* me."

"Please. I've had a hard time."

"Fine." She got up, taking her pillow, and went to sleep on the couch.

When things were calmer, Joan decided to invite her parents over. She said it was important, and I had to be there. I asked what it was about and she wouldn't say. Still I knew something was up because she had asked Svetlana to take the kids to her house.

Her parents, Lloyd and Patty, still lived in Wilberforce, an hour away, but I hadn't seen much of them since the wedding. She accused me of avoiding them, and although I denied it vehemently, part of me knew that she was right. They loved their daughter, and I suspected I hadn't lived up to their expectations. Even when sober.

They arrived at ten o'clock on the dot. Joan had gotten up early to make them a special brunch with eggs, ham and fresh orange juice. I opened the door.

"Ed," Lloyd said. He put out his hand. He seemed uncomfortable.

"Lloyd," I said. Pattie followed him in and I kissed her on the cheek.

I didn't drink much over breakfast—just a couple, in between courses. It was to take the edge off things; them staring at me, the weight of disdain. Of course, I was careful. I went to the bathroom, where I had stashed my Cree Helper. Vodka is the best for times like this; it doesn't even smell. I looked at them when I came out. They didn't even notice. After breakfast, we all went to the lounge.

"Ed. We're concerned about you," Lloyd said.

"What about me?" I wondered what they'd heard.

"Well, Joan says that you're out at all hours of the night . . . and that you come back drunk."

"I might have done that once or twice. I was helping my students."

"They need your help drinking?"

"No, Mr. Barnes. They need my help coping after the reserve."

"At the bars?"

"It's not like that, Mr. Barnes."

"Yes, I'm afraid it is, Ed."

"No it's not," I said. "I was just trying to help Sekwan and Donnie. They were in trouble."

Why was he on my case? Always on my goddamned case. Made me so mad I needed a drink. "Look, why don't we settle down. Let's have some Irish coffees. Joan's are the best."

"You serious?"

"Absolutely."

"We're talking about your alcoholism, and you're offering us an Irish coffee?"

"Jesus Christ! Relax already!"

"Fucking drunk," he muttered under his breath.

"What did you say?"

"Nothing."

"What da fuck did you say?"

"I said you're a fucking drunk. You remind me of those bums you see in Toronto!"

He was calling me a drunk Indian. I couldn't believe it. I got up. *I'm going to punch out his lights*, I thought. He pushed me back down. I got up again.

"Stop it!" Joan shouted. "Stop it!" and she started to cry.

SIXTEEN

Joan wanted me to get some professional help. I tried to explain to her that I didn't need it. I agreed with her that I needed to grow up and take responsibility, but there weren't any native therapists in Peterborough. I didn't want to explain my problems to a wemis-tikoshiw man who didn't know about the Seven Sacred Teachings or the Red Road. I didn't need another white man calling me a drunk. And even if we found a native therapist, how were we supposed to pay? We were already stretched to the limit.

I said, "I'll try harder, I promise."

"At what, Ed?

"Everything. Whatever you want."

"You don't understand."

I was sitting on our bed and she was standing, and with these words she slumped down, as if someone had suddenly removed her spine. She put her head in her hands. I felt overcome by love and remorse, and wanted to scoop her up in my arms.

"I do understand. I made a mistake with your parents and I'm sorry."

"That's not it."

"I love you," I said.

"I know," she said.

"Joan. Please."

"Maybe that's not enough."

"What do you mean?"

"I'm scared," she said.

What happens when your wife is scared? You do your best, I guess. Pick up the kids from school and kindergarten. Wash the dishes. Help her with the laundry. Try to make love. Christ, I don't know. Just try to stop your head from spinning. Work hard to stop the voices. They're always there anyway. Always telling you what you've done wrong. Try to focus, that's all. And you wait. Wait for the news. You know it's coming. The moment of reckoning. In my case, it came on a Tuesday afternoon. It began with a conversation with Don. He called me into his office. Said he had some bad news.

"Really?" I waited for him to tell me that I was a disappointment to my race and the department and was fired.

"Yeah. It's about Sekwan."

"Sekwan?"

It was my fault. I knew it.

"Yeah. She's in hospital. She has a cut hand. She has to get stitches. We think Donnie might be involved, but she isn't saying anything. What happened on that night that I sent you over? You said you had it covered."

"I . . . uh . . . not much." I felt caught. Was it worse to betray Sekwan's trust or to refuse to cooperate? I sensed that Sekwan wasn't going to say anything, no matter what I said.

"So, nothing happened," Don said.

"I . . . not much."

"What do you mean 'not much'?"

"Nothing. Nothing happened."

"The university will want to investigate this new incident."

"Okay."

"If there's something you aren't telling me, it will come out, and then, well, I can't protect you, Ed."

"Okay." I didn't know what to say.

"You can go."

I left Don's office, and cancelled the rest of my student appointments, too upset and confused to be of much help to anyone. Maybe I should have told Don that Donnie had hit her but she wouldn't press charges. If I had told him, then maybe Sekwan would have left Donnie and nothing more would have happened. Did that make me responsible? What if she went back to Donnie? What if something else happened? Would I be accountable? Would I lose my job? What would happen to Joan and my children? They would be so ashamed of me. Jesus, they already disliked me. I felt sick with shame. I should have done more to help Sekwan. I had let her down.

I went to the Commoner bar. After a few drinks, a girl came up to me.

"Hi, Counsellor," she said.

"It's Ed," I said, barely looking up.

"I know," she said.

"Course you know." My vision was a bit blurry, but I recognized her as Sarah, a nineteen-year-old from Curve Lake First Nation. "What will you have?" I asked.

"A gin and tonic." I ordered two and a vodka shot for myself. I looked at her. "Rough day?" she asked.

"Yep."

"What happened?"

"I . . ." I hung my head. "I let people down."

"Who'd you let down?"

"Everyone. Sekwan. Don. My wife. My family. Everyone."

"Why?"

I laughed, bitterly. "Because I'm bad news."

"Bad news, how?"

"Jesus, you don't let up, do you?" She looked hurt. "Sorry, I didn't mean that. Have a drink. It will do you some good." As she drank, I watched her face. She was so pretty. Funny I never noticed such things when I was sober. "Let's not talk about me. It's boring. Tell me about your day." She started talking, telling me about getting a B in Native Studies 100. I half listened as she talked. It was easy to get lost in her voice. It flowed like sweet wine. Her brown eyes looked like she was offering me something tender. What was it? A helping hand? Hope? I smiled. She had the same look as Joan before we married.

"Are you even listening?" she asked, finishing.

"Absolutely." I repeated back most of what she had just said.

"For someone drunk, that wasn't bad." I smiled. A song came on about feeling the warmth of a woman's body, and I began singing to the chorus. She laughed.

"Flirt," she said.

"Do you dance?" I asked.

"Me?"

"Yeah, you."

"Sometimes."

"You wanna dance with me?"

"With you?"

"Sure. Why not?"

I woke up with a splitting headache. I wasn't sure how or what time I'd gotten home. I looked at the clock. Ten a.m. Shit. Everyone already out of the house. School, daycare, and university courses for

Joan. I remembered Don talking to me about Sekwan. Feeling ashamed. The bar. The girl with the hopeful eyes. It was slowly coming back. Her friend had a camera. We had kissed and posed together. Oh no. *Takye*. Shit. I had to get a hold of that camera and stop her developing those photos.

I drove to school and hurried to my office. In the hallway, I bumped into Nancy, Dr. Couture's assistant. Dr. Couture was the chairman of the Native Studies program and Don's boss.

"Can I have a word, Ed?"

"Sorry, Nancy. Can it wait?"

"No." She pulled me into a storeroom that was stacked floor to ceiling with books. It was cramped and we stood face to face. "You know, there's a rumour going around about you."

"Really?" I said. I was falling. I felt sick. "What sort of rumour?"

"Something to do with a girl. A student of yours. And some photos."

"Did you see them?"

"You mean there *are* photos?"

"Yes. No . . . I . . ." Shit, this would ruin everything. I had to stop it before Joan found out.

I had some counselling appointments that afternoon, but I put a notice on my door that said I had to cancel unexpectedly. Then I went to look for Sarah. I needed to destroy the photos and stop her telling anyone. I asked around and heard that she had gone back to her reserve early.

I debated driving there. If I went, would that look like sexual harassment? She was my student. She lived on the reserve with her parents and extended family. But if I didn't go, then surely she'd tell more people and I'd lose my job. Who was I kidding? If Nancy already knew, that meant that Dr. Couture knew, which meant I had already lost my job. Joan would want to know the reason why I had been sacked, which led me back to the photos.

How had this happened? There had been only one person who had truly loved me. One person who had accepted me for who I was, who wasn't afraid to touch my shameful, broken body. Joan had believed in me and trusted me. She had loved and accepted me. She had come to Peterborough to help me get my degree, and we'd started a family. She had supported me in my first job off the reserve. I had let her down. Time and again. So many broken promises. I hung my head in my hands. I was a disgrace. Less than worthless.

I went to the bar.

I got home a few hours later. There was a note on the kitchen table.

Don phoned. He told me everything. Have moved out. Please don't call.

I read the note a few times. I looked in the closets—she had taken only about one third of her clothes. Somehow I found this comforting.

I waited an hour and had some coffee to sober up. It wasn't perfect, but good enough. I just needed to speak to Joan and make everything better.

Lloyd answered the door. I could tell from his tight lips that she had told him at least some of what was going on.

"Can I speak to her?" I said.

"You have some nerve, coming here."

"Please."

"Why should I let you in?"

"I just need to say goodbye."

"You should have thought of that before."

"Please. Just for a few minutes."

He let me in.

In the bedroom, Joan was propped up with some pillows, with Albalina and Shannin on either side. Jassen was sleeping in a fold-out cot.

"What are you doing here?" Joan said.

"I needed to see you."

"How could you?"

"I made a mistake."

"That's what you call it?"

"I wasn't thinking."

"Oh my God, Ed. You don't get it, do you?"

"Joan. Please. I'm sorry. I'll change."

"Get out," she said.

"Joan, please."

"GET OUT!"

Next morning, I drove to the university and walked to Don's office.

"I'm sorry, Don."

"You have a problem."

"I know."

"I'm putting you on leave."

"Thank you."

He shook his head.

"Are you getting help?"

"I will," I said.

"I already called around. There's an in-treatment centre that has a good record at treating native people." He handed me a Post-it with a phone number.

"I've talked to the rest of the staff. They should have some spots free in a few weeks."

"I don't deserve this," I said.

"Who knows what we deserve."

"I'm sorry," I repeated.

"I wish things had worked out differently," he said.

"Me too."

SEVENTEEN

It was one of those January mornings when the sun seems too tired to get up. I took the bus to the airport. Then I stood around and stared at the flashing lights on the departure board for my flight to Calgary. I was finding it difficult to keep down the contents of my stomach, so I went to the water fountain, washed my face and drank deeply.

We flew over the prairies and landed in Calgary, and I took a taxi to the edge of town.

The centre was a bunch of brick buildings that had been converted from a boy's school. A few steps from the entrance I had one final swig of vodka from my water bottle. What would Joan think? She'd given up on me. She'd tried so goddamned hard, and she'd finally quit. I thought about how crushed she'd looked when I'd gone to see her that last time. The memory hurt enough to warrant another swig, but there was none left.

There was a payphone out front and I thought about calling her. She wouldn't want to hear from me. What if I called but didn't say who it was? I could hear her calming voice without having to explain myself. No, that was just creepy.

I slipped the empty bottle into my pocket, pushed through the door and into a large room with a reception desk, where I was directed to what looked like a doctor's waiting room. A woman wearing a green coat sat behind a high circular desk, and facing her was a row of chairs.

"Can I help you?"

"I'm here to check in."

"What's your name?"

"Edmund Metatawabin."

"Can you spell the last name?"

I spelled it.

"Have you ever been here before?"

"No."

She gave me a form. "Just answer what you can. If you can't answer any questions, don't worry, the doctor will go through it with you later."

I filled in part of the form. I left blank the part about how much I drank per day. It depended on the day. And many days, I wasn't sure.

Then a man in a white coat came in. He looked barely older than me.

"Is he next?" he said to the woman in the green coat, pointing toward me. She nodded.

"Come through," he said.

I followed him into a big lounge that looked like a student den with lots of chairs and pillows, and a handful of people milling about watching TV. The doctor opened a door to his left that led into a smaller room with an examining table and some cupboards, and beckoned me inside.

"Edmund. How do I say the last name?"

"Meta-TAH-wabin."

"I see you've filled in most of your questionnaire. That's good."

"Thanks."

"Do you mind if we get some vitals?"

"Some what?"

"Blood pressure, heart rate, that sort of thing."

"No. Go ahead."

The doctor took out a cuff and fastened it around my arm.

I looked at him. He was focused on the cuff. I remembered back to the examinations with Brother Jutras. Every year, same thing. And all those boys that he'd bought off with a piece of bread. My face felt hot as the anger rose. I looked down at the floor. When the feeling had passed, I looked up.

"Alcohol addiction, is it?" The doctor began to pump a tiny rubber balloon. The cuff tightened.

"Yes, sir." He let the balloon fall and the cuff loosened around my arm. He made some notes on my questionnaire.

"You can call me Dr. Wozechowski."

"Yes, Dr. Wozechowski."

"When did you last have a drink?"

"This morning."

"What was it?"

"Cree Helper."

"Sorry?"

"That's just what I call it. Vodka."

He took out a stethoscope. "How much?"

"Just a few shots."

"How many?"

"Five." He wrote it down.

"How much do you normally drink?"

"A bottle during the day. More when I get home."

"How much more?"

"Depends."

"Depends on what?"

"On how much money I have."

"Do you know the symptoms of alcohol withdrawal?"

"No."

"Mood swings, sweats, nausea, depression, fatigue, the shakes. Some people hallucinate. If you get in trouble, go and see the nurse. She can provide medication to calm things down."

"Thank you, Dr. Wozechowski."

He picked up the phone and dialed. "He's done," he said. A lady in a white coat came into the room. She led me through the lounge and down a lobby to my bedroom. It had two narrow beds and two bedside tables with lights and some shelves. Someone else had already checked in. A man, from the look of the clothes.

"You can unpack here. Most people like to hang out in the lounge. We went through it on the way here. There's also a pool room but we've temporarily misplaced the key. Should find it soon. Dinner is at seven."

I unpacked and walked into the lounge. There were a wemistikoshiw and a black guy watching hockey, and another native guy sitting by himself on a plaid couch, smoking. "I'm Maurice," said the smoker, and put out a hand. I walked over and shook it. "Wanna smoke?" He offered me the packet. I took one.

"I'm from Wahta Mohawk First Nation. You?" I told him. "What are you here for?"

"Alcohol."

"Yeah. Me too."

"How long you been here?"

"Oh, just a few days. You?"

"Just got here."

"You're in for a treat."

"Anything I should look out for?"

"Stay away from the heroin and crack users. They are something else. When they arrive, man are they crazy. They get mad. Throw things. Shout. Shit like that."

"Huh." I couldn't believe anyone had it worse than me.

After dinner, I really wanted to hear Joan's voice. I looked at my watch. Eight p.m. She usually went out on Monday evenings to Svetlana's place. If I called and she wasn't home, I could hear her on the answering machine without disturbing or hurting her. I went back to the waiting room.

"Can I use your phone?" I asked the woman in the green coat.

"No phone privileges until after the first week."

"I just want to call my wife," I said.

"Was it the phone or privilege part that you didn't understand?"

"Can you just tell me why?"

"It's about figuring out your own identity before you bring in other people."

I looked at her. I didn't understand the wemistikoshiw concept of identity. It was like the world was full of lonely people, living in their tiny bubbles, and only reaching out when they had a need. My Cree identity began with Joan, Albalina, Shannin and Jassen and then widened to Ma and Pa, my brothers and sisters, aunts and uncles. It stretched back to my *gookums* and my *moshoms* through to the ancestors, who guided us in times of trouble. And beyond them it encompassed the Four-Leggeds and the Standing Ones and the Earth itself and the River of Life. All my relations. *Ni chi shannock.*

"My identity is other people," I said.

"Listen, mister. I don't make the rules."

"Please," I said.

"You'll learn more about boundaries and identity as you go along. For now, just go and make friends. I'm sure your wife is fine."

By the time I returned to my room, my roommate was there. He introduced himself as an alcoholic opera singer and then told me he was very famous and made me promise I would never reveal his name. (It's Daniel, in case you are interested.) Then he got into bed and immediately fell asleep. He began to snore loudly like a leopard frog, a slow clicking sound that opened into a *reeaahhh-uh-uh-uh*. I tried to sleep through his snoring. His barrel chest eased the air out very slowly, and I wondered if I'd have to listen to this every night.

After an hour or two, I went to the bathroom and got some toilet paper and stuffed it into my ears. I lay down on the bed. I had a bad headache. I was sweating and shaking. I thought about the other withdrawal symptoms that had been explained to me. There was a thin bar of light under the window that faded and then later there were lots of shadows but I couldn't tell if the lights were from some cars outside the centre or if my eyes were playing tricks on me. I felt locked in, just like at St. Anne's. I got up and walked around the room. I lay back down. I got up and rinsed my face. I lay back down. I lay on the floor, just like I had done with my parents in the bush. I got up, and got into bed. When the first sun seeped into the room, I started to count all the pieces of dust floating above my head. At some point, I must have fallen asleep.

By morning, I was a wreck. I vomited up bits of mushroom and steak from dinner the night before and then I retched and retched but nothing came up. I cleaned the toilet, then went to the dining hall.

At breakfast, all I wanted was coffee. I looked around the hall, and Maurice waved. I slid in next to him. Steve, who was sitting next to him, reached over and put out his hand. I shook it. He told me that his drug dealer was an Indian.

"Not to be racist or anything," he said.

"Didn't take it like that."

"Good. You ever smoked?" he asked.

"Once or twice," I said. "Not really my thing."

"You're a good man," he said. "Best not to start. Started on the weed, went to coke, went to crack, lost my house and wife and came here. You?"

"I had a drinking problem. Have," I corrected myself.

He nodded and waited for me to go on.

"I thought I was doing well. But everyone wanted too much. I couldn't deliver. I kept fucking up." I stared into the distance. In my mind's eye I saw Joan. She was sitting on Albalina's bed, reading to her. "I let everyone down," I muttered. "Cheated on my wife."

"She stick around?"

"No," I said, in a voice near a whisper. "She's smarter than that."

In the afternoon we had a presentation. A counsellor named Bill stood at the front of the lounge. He looked like he was in his late thirties. He said we were lucky because this was one of the best drug and alcohol programs in the country. It emphasized a healthy body and mind so there were daily aerobics classes before breakfast. It offered behaviour therapy, group work, and Alcoholics Anonymous. For the natives, there would be some traditional healers delivering presentations in a few days.

Then Bill held up a book called *Alcoholics Anonymous: The Story of How Many Thousands of Men and Women Have Recovered from Alcoholism*. He called it the Big Book. He had several copies and he passed them around the class.

It was about the same size as the Bible. Inside were a lot of stories about finding God. One chapter was called "Crossing the River of Denial." Another was "The Keys of the Kingdom," another about some doctor who had lost his way until he realized that God, not he, was the Great Healer.

I remembered Father Gagnon's prayer. "Oh merciful God: have mercy on all Jews, Turks, infidels and heretics and also upon all those heathen nations, on whom the light of Thy glorious Gospel hath not yet shone: especially the Indians of this continent."

I shut the Big Book and took a deep breath.

A few days later, after the aerobics class, there was a morning lecture by a guest speaker named Julian. A medium-sized man, he was a counsellor and an expert in alcohol and psychic trauma.

"How does alcohol work?" He turned around and pointed to the blackboard on which he'd taped a poster of a brain. "It's a sedative. It affects the brain's neurotransmitters, which are the chemical messengers that transmit signals that control thought processes, behaviour and emotion. It causes us to lose inhibitions, and increases our levels of dopamine, causing us to feel good. So why is this a problem? Why should a chemically induced high become an issue?"

"'Cause you start to need it," Maurice said. "Every moment is spent craving the next drink."

"Excellent," Julian said. "Alcohol numbs psychic pain. In small doses, it can make you feel good. When it is used as a crutch, it causes serious problems. It affects our decision-making and our ability to assess risk."

I thought back to when I had started drinking socially. Nicholas, Erick and I had gone out and bought some cheap wine when we were sixteen. They had been grounded, so we didn't try again that year. The following year, I had come home from Montreal, and I knew that there was something wrong with me. I was marked. Damaged goods. Who was going to go for that? No girl. Drinking made things a bit easier. Gave me some confidence. Not much. But enough to take a few girls to the movies. I figured out how to kiss, but even with alcohol, it was hard for me to go further. Too much shame.

When I got back to Fort Albany after high school, I wondered if it would ever happen to me. The years had ticked by, eighteen, nineteen, twenty—they were supposed to be the time of your life. I saw my life accelerate, and me turning old before I had become a man. Then Joan had arrived in Fort Albany from down south. I was twenty. Alcohol made everything easy. I flirted with Joan. Opened up. She liked me.

I'd been without it now for a total of seven days, and every day stretched out like a treacherous icy river. I was deep in it, and I felt unable to swim or walk, weighed down—by my past, by my mistakes and by those I had hurt. Every day there were more questions, from the counsellors, psychologists, addicts and experts. Why *why* WHY? I started to explain, and then I tumbled into memory, images spinning ever faster until the words didn't matter, there was only thirst. I would say anything for a moment's relief. Give everything for a drink.

Things got better midway through when a Cree healer named Terry came in for the presentations that were aimed at natives. We sat in a circle—Terry, Maurice, me and Geraldine, a Stoney woman from Nakoda Nation, who was just here for a couple of days.

"You know, I used to be in your shoes," Terry said. "Managing my mood swings with alcohol. Always running from my past. Then I came here for some healing a few years ago, and never looked back. I started asking some hard questions about my life here. Had someone come in and give a presentation, just like I'm giving to you. That's when I realized I had to start figuring out my culture. That I was a little lost.

"Anyway. Enough of me. Let's talk about you. You've come here because you're probably drinkers. The other people at the addiction centre might have other substance abuse problems, but for us, it's probably booze. When the white man first brought alcohol, they knew what they were giving us. The beginnings of broken families.

"To start, let's go around the room. Loosen things up a bit. Natives have a lot of names for booze. Anyone know a few?"

I put up my hand. "Firewater," I said.

"Yes," Terry said. "The old people called it firewater because they used to make homebrew out of anything they could find. Real booze was banned for Indians. When you make booze in your backyard, it usually burns. Water that sets your throat on fire. Anything else?"

"We call it crazy water," Geraldine said. "*Gahtonejabee meenee*. Because it makes you crazy."

"You already were," Maurice said. She smiled at him. He had the hots for Geraldine. We weren't supposed to get together romantically at the centre, although I didn't think Maurice cared much for the rules.

"What else?" Terry said.

"In Mohawk we say *deganigohadaynyohs*," Maurice said. "The mind changer. Because whatever mood you're in before, it makes you happy."

"Yeah, I've heard of that. Of all the names, I think that's the worst of all. Because people do use it to change their minds. They try to change their minds instead of changing their circumstances."

I wondered whether I'd used alcohol to change my mind instead of my circumstances. I was sure I had. But what had been that wrong with my circumstances? Hadn't I already got all I wanted? After high school, I'd wanted to become a teacher, and I'd managed, and I'd loved my job. I'd wanted to marry Joan, and she took me even though I wasn't much to look at and she could have chosen anyone. I'd wanted to go to university, get my degree, and it had been hard, but I'd succeeded. Hell, I even had three amazing kids. Why had I screwed everything up?

It was evening, near the end of the program, when a middle-aged counsellor with red hair named Barb gave us Self-Monitoring Logs. She asked us to write down when we felt the urge to use drugs or drink. Everyone had to fill out that part except for the newbies because Barb said every newbie had urges so bad they might as well be teenage boys. She kept laughing long after the rest of the room had fallen silent.

The next part of the form dealt with the causes of our addiction. *What were the triggers for you wanting to drink alcohol/use drugs?*

I thought about all the things that made me want to drink. Why did they give us such a tiny box? I needed a filing cabinet. I felt embarrassed about my brown body. It felt small and weak. Unlovable. Every failure compounded my growing shame. I felt lost and out of control when I let my students down. My overwhelming remorse when I came home drunk and saw Joan looking tired and broken. The better question was when I didn't want to drink—that would be easier to answer.

When had I first tried alcohol? I thought back. I remembered finding Pa's bucket of homebrew when I was about five. I stuck my finger in and tried it. It set my mouth on fire, burning through my cheeks and throat. Ma got mad when Pa drank too much, and I didn't want her finding out.

After that, the memories took hold in Technicolor. I was seven, walking to the school with my dad, having my hair cut, playing soccer in the rain and seeing Mike fiddling with his umbrella. The memories sped up and I could smell the old meat and cologne and I just needed it to stop and for there to be space.

I looked down at my hands. They were shaking. So were my legs. I left that part of the form blank and excused myself.

When I came out of the bathroom, everyone had been paired off. We would be doing breathing exercises that were supposed to help take our mind off our cravings. A plump woman with messy, curly brown hair named Trish didn't have a partner so I became hers.

"Can you believe this shit?" she said, and pointed around the room.

"What shit?" I said.

She started to laugh. "You got the shits too?"

"No," I whispered.

"Come on, every addict gets them. Either it's stuck all the way up or it's flowing like the River Ganges."

"River what?"

"Brown river in India," she said. "Flowing like the floods of the monsoons."

"Can you keep it down?" said the woman who was sitting in a chair in front of us. "I'm trying to breathe properly."

"The problem is you are uptight," Trish said to her.

The women in front turned around again. "Be quiet," she said.

"Breathe on my shit, baby," Trish said. "'Cause it's coming at ya like roses about to burst."

"Hey, Trish," I whispered. "Let's not start."

"I ain't starting, I'm finishing!" She got up and began singing. It sounded a little like the Rolling Stones' "Brown Sugar," but with poop lyrics. As soon as Trish belted her first note, Barb got up and left the room. Once she left, more people began laughing. A few moments later Bill came in and led Trish away.

The next day Bill left a note on my door that he wanted to meet me one-on-one. I was already late for the AA meeting, but I stopped by his office on the way there.

"Sorry about what happened with Trish yesterday," he said. "There's a lot going on. Sometimes things get out of hand."

"It's fine."

"You didn't fill in all of your form," he said.

"Which part?"

"Question thirteen. 'What were the triggers for you wanting to drink alcohol/use drugs?'"

"It's difficult to say," I said.

"Difficult how?"

"I'm not sure which one to write down."

"Why don't you write down all of them?"

"All?" I asked hesitantly. There were some things in my past that I didn't think I could talk about.

He looked at me dubiously. "You know, Ed, we stress total honesty here."

"Yeah. I know." I looked at him. He had the same tone as Brother Goulet when he was lecturing boys about why they deserved the electric chair, and it was making it hard to concentrate.

"It helps with the healing process," Bill said.

"Healing process . . ." I repeated faintly.

His eyes narrowed. "I want you to go to AA now. When you've finished we can talk over question thirteen."

I left his office and went to AA, dazed. It felt like someone else had stepped into my body and taken over. I was so confused that I got lost on the way and arrived a few minutes late. I stuck my head in the room where I thought the meeting was supposed to be, but it didn't look right and made me feel dizzy.

"Why did you move the chairs?" I asked. They weren't in a circle anymore, but in rows so we were all facing the blackboard like at St. Anne's.

"It's easier for the exercise," Barb said, one hand on her hip. "Come in, you're late."

The AA 12 Steps were written on the board. Barb read number three aloud: "Made a decision to surrender our will and our lives over to the care of God *as we understood Him*." She asked if we were ready for the Lord to take us. If we were ready to surrender to a Superior Being.

I looked at the board, specifically the word "surrender." Pa had talked about that word. He said the Indians had surrendered their land to the white man who had moved us to the reserves. We had surrendered our culture and our way of being so that we wouldn't be killed and didn't starve. And then Ma had surrendered me to Father Lavois so that I became a ward of the church-state partnership that ran the residential schools. Then I had surrendered to Mike.

I looked back at Barb. She was dressed all in black, just like a nun's habit. Her face shifted and I saw Sister Wesley's face on top of her body. She was looking at me. There was vomit on the floor. She was going to make me lick it up.

"Where are you going?" Sister Wesley asked.

"Please!" I begged.

"Please what?"

"Please don't make me, Sister!"

"Sister?" she said.

"Please, Sister Wesley!"

"It's Barb."

"Who?"

"Barb." In front of me was a forty-something woman with red hair.

"Where am I?"

"At the addiction centre." I looked at her again. She was wearing the nun's habit. Was it her or Sister Wesley? Maybe they were lying. They did that. Wanted to catch you out.

"Please. Miss. Please. Please can I leave?"

"What for?"

"Please. Please . . . I'm . . . I'm going to be sick."

She looked at me dubiously. "Fine. Go and see Dr. Wozechowski."

I hurried out the door and went to the toilets. I tried to vomit for a while. Nothing came up. I washed my mouth and face, and went outside to search for the Standing Ones. Beside the centre there was a picnic table and some grass. A man was having a smoke.

"You look like you've seen a ghost," he said, offering me a cigarette. I looked at him. He looked too old to be at St. Anne's.

"Who are you?"

"Maurice. Remember?"

"Maurice?"

"Yeah buddy. Maurice from Wahta Mohawk First Nation. We met a few days ago."

"We did?"

He put his arm on my shoulder. "Hey brother. Come on. Calm down. Just breathe." We stayed like that for a few minutes.

"I know you," I said at last.

"You sure do."

"It's Maurice, right?"

"Yep."

"Sorry 'bout that."

"It's fine. What happened? Barb not floating your boat?"

"Not too keen on these classroom exercises," I replied. "They remind me of residential school."

"Flashbacks. We all get 'em. That's why we're here, isn't it?"

"I guess," I said.

"Mine are mainly at night."

"What happens?"

"Oh you know," he said. "All the people I've let down come back to tell me that I fucked up. How disappointed they are."

"How do you deal with them?"

"I just try to let them pass. Go through me."

"How do you do that?"

"I dunno. Sometimes I count."

"Count?"

"Yeah. You know. One Mississippi. Two Mississippi. Then I imagine a big stop sign."

"And that works?"

"It does for me."

—

On the day before I was scheduled to leave the centre, Bill came up to me.

"Ed," he said. "Can I speak to you in private?"

We walked to an empty therapy room and he shut the door.

"Did I do something wrong?" I asked.

"No. You were great."

"So why are we in here?"

"I'm worried about you. I think you should consider staying longer."

"What for?"

"Well, last week you got confused in Barb's class and we still haven't talked about question thirteen."

"I made it through," I said.

"Making it through isn't the point. It's about giving you the coping skills to manage outside."

"One Mississippi. Two Mississippi."

"Huh?"

"Just something I learned while I was here."

"Look, we can't force you to stay against your will. But the other counsellors and I have some serious concerns."

"About me?"

"Yes."

"Why?"

"We're just not sure you're ready."

"I'm good. I really need to get back. My wife is alone with our three kids. I need to try to get my job back. Or get a new one." I realized that Don probably didn't want me back.

"But if you don't deal with things thoroughly you'll be right back where you started. Trust me. I've seen this before."

"I know you are trying to help but I've learned a lot while I'm here. Coping skills. Boundaries. And I did some hard thinking about my triggers. And about being more honest. I've got it covered."

He raised his eyebrows. "Okay, Ed."

EIGHTEEN

Steve and I flew back to Toronto together, and he gave me a lift to Peterborough. He'd been sober for more than a month, but he said that he still got the cravings. I asked him what he was going back to.

"Well, not much."

I nodded. He'd told me in rehab that he'd lost his job in sales before he'd checked himself into the clinic. Said that he wanted to get his job back and then his wife. He thought it was possible. He just had to stay clean.

"You going to the daily meetings?" I asked.

"Yeah, I'm gonna try. You?"

"Yeah. Ninety in ninety, right?"

That was the magic number. Ninety meetings in ninety days. It was the mantra chanted by all our AA counsellors, the one that ex-addicts came and spoke to us about. It felt like a distant star, impossible to reach.

"You gonna be okay for money?" he asked.

"Sure," I said. Then I remembered the "absolute honesty" piece of AA and I said, "Actually, I have no idea. I'm trying not to worry about it. I just want to go to as many meetings as possible. I'm hoping to get my job back. And . . . if that doesn't work, then . . . I don't know. Go back home to Fort Albany, I guess."

"I guess."

He dropped me off at my house and told me to get in touch with Brian. I'd never met this guy, but apparently, he'd been through the same program, and was supposed to be my sponsor. I promised I would.

I unlocked the door. I could see that Joan hadn't been here much, because it was dusty. I walked down the hall to our bedroom. She still hadn't taken all her clothes, and I went through her tops, inhaling them. The scent of laundry soap, but her smell lingering, which made me feel less alone. I walked to the kitchen table and wrote her a letter.

"Thanks for agreeing to see me," I said. I had rented a car and driven to Wilberforce to pick her up. It was too cold to do much of anything and besides, neither of us had any money, so we were sitting in front of Buckskin Lake looking at the snow-covered frozen water. It was the first time I had spoken to Joan since she left.

"It was a good letter."

"What did you like about it?"

"That you were honest. You did hurt me. A lot. I'm glad you owned up to it."

"I know it's been hard for you."

She laughed. "That would be an understatement."

"Very hard," I said.

"You took me for granted."

"Yes, I did."

"You embarrassed me in front of my parents."

"Yes I did."

"You fooled around with that girl."

"Yes I did."

"While I'm at home, taking care of our three kids."

"Yes," I said softly. "I'm sorry."

"Why did you do it?"

"I was drunk and messed up."

"That doesn't explain it."

"I know." I told her then about being called disgusting at school. A dirty savage. Feeling ashamed of my body. About drinking to gain confidence. "I tried to be open. I tried to do the right thing. But it just never worked out."

"Why not, Ed?"

"It was too hard. So I started to wear the mask."

"What mask?"

"The face that everyone else wanted to see."

"What face does everyone want to see?"

"Everyone wants to see something different. I felt like I had to go along with it."

"What do you mean?"

"Well, I didn't want to go to St. Anne's but I had to. It was what all the kids did. And then when I was there I felt that I had to hollow myself out. To be the face that watched but felt and said nothing."

"How so?" I told her then about watching Amocheesh being electrocuted.

"God, that's so awful."

"During the school holidays, when I returned home, I had to swallow my anger and pretend that nothing had happened. Pretend like I didn't care that they just sent me back there. I felt they had betrayed me. Then . . ." I paused.

"Then what, Ed?"

"Then I was in foster care and there was no one to turn to even when . . ." The words "Mike raped me" resounded in my head. I blushed and they caught in my throat. I would tell her at another time. ". . . when bad things happened." I paused to let the shame of the memory pass. "It made me feel alone. And I thought that feeling was going to stay with me forever. Then I met you. You made me feel that I was worth something."

"So why did you treat me like dirt?"

"Because if you were cruel to me that would prove I was right all along. I would get what I thought I deserved."

"I don't know what to say, Ed."

"You don't have to say anything. I just thought I'd tell you, that's all."

We said goodbye soon after that. She said she needed time to think.

NINETEEN

"How's the recovery going?" Don asked. We were sitting in his office.

"It's good. My sponsor Brian has been helping me stay focused. And I've done lots of thinking."

"You know I can't let you anywhere near the students if there's a danger of a relapse."

"I know. I'm totally sober."

He stared at me. "Getting sober is the easy bit. It's staying sober that's hard."

"One day at a time," I said, repeating one of the phrases they'd taught us at AA.

"And what are your alternative coping mechanisms? How are you going to manage under high stress without alcohol?"

"I'm trying to let those feelings pass through me." I told him about Maurice's coping technique.

"Is that working?"

"Yes. It's been great."

"Maybe this isn't the best job for you."

I stared at him, feeling crushed. "What do you mean?"

"Well . . . dealing with abuse. You know, that sort of stuff. It can be hard for people with . . . difficult pasts." I wondered how much of my story he'd guessed.

"It has been hard. But I think a lot of it was to do with not establishing boundaries. We learned a lot about them in AA."

"How so?"

"It was hard for me to set them before. I'm much better now."

"I see," he said. "How's Joan?"

"She's good." I told him about driving to Wilberforce to take care of the kids and give her a break. "I'm trying not to get my hopes up. She's still . . ." My soulmate, I thought. "I still love her. But I can't undo all I've done. I just have to live this day right. Be good to her today. And then we'll see."

So I continued driving to Wilberforce to help take care of the kids, and after a while Joan wanted to know what compromises I was prepared to make if she agreed to move back in. I didn't have much to offer other than my time and love: I was broke and out of work.

Then Ma called a few weeks later, and told me that after an eight-year wait, a new house had become available in Fort Albany. She knew that there had been some kind of problem with my job, and that we'd had a hard time, and said she'd keep an eye out. If we wanted it, it could be ours. I called Joan with the news.

"I know it's a long shot, and I don't deserve it, but I thought you should know."

"I know. Your ma called me too." Joan and Ma had gotten closer over the years.

"She did?"

"Yes. She said that she would look after the kids if I wanted to go back to work."

"Do you?"

"Yes. I've wanted to for some time."

"I didn't know."

"I know you didn't know."

"I made a lot of mistakes."

"Yes, you did."

Then we went hiking together, just the two of us. We drove up to Chemong Lake, north of Peterborough, and went bird watching. The burr oak and black ash were opening to spring, the first tender shoots of green. We saw some blue jays bouncing up on a cedar tree, singing *woo-oh, woo-uh*.

"That's funny," Joan said. "It sounds like they're courting, but it's pretty early, isn't it?" It was only April, and they didn't usually look for mates until May.

"Maybe they're following my lead."

"You're terrible," she said, and mock-punched me. I felt elated. She was laughing at my jokes again.

We were back at my parents' house in Fort Albany, sleeping on the fold-out bed in the living room until the new place was ready. It didn't make me or Joan happy, but to have her back in my arms, to have my family close by, well, sometimes you just have to let that other stuff go. Besides, it was only going to be temporary.

I'd mentioned to Ma and Pa that I'd had some problems with drinking but had left it at that. Pa nodded and didn't pry, and Ma just squeezed my shoulder and told me she was glad I was home. We Crees try to give people their space.

We felt summer approaching as our time on the fold-out couch got stickier. A few weeks later, Pa and I got up before everyone else was awake. It was bath night, and in the pickup we had every type of bottle, bucket, jug and bin that we could find in the house. We needed enough water to sponge down seventeen people. We could hardly see out of that cramped truck.

When we swung around the bend, I glimpsed my friend Kelvin standing on the riverbank, fishing. He waved. We parked in the grass and begun to unload it all. Kelvin came up to ask if we needed a hand. I nodded.

"Thought you was at Peterborough," he said.

"I was."

"What happened?"

"Not much. It was time to come home."

"Thought you wanted out of here."

"I did. People change," I said.

He nodded. "You hear about Erick?"

"What?" I hadn't heard anything about Erick since high school.

"He died in a fire. In Kashechewan."

"Oh no. I'm so sorry." I shook my head. He'd made it through all that at St. Anne's, and then he was still cut down in the prime of his life. I remembered the time when he'd approached me after accepting the bread from Brother Jutras, and seeing his embarrassment. The pin game that we'd played together in St. Anne's. Teasing me about Connie, the girl I liked in high school. He was pretty withdrawn at St. Anne's, but he'd started to come out of his shell in high school. We hadn't been best friends, but he'd come through for me when I needed it most. I'd hung about with him in our bedroom at the Tekaucs' after returning from that summer with Mike Pasko. He'd asked me if there was anything wrong. I hadn't been able to talk, so he had sat beside me, and we'd both stared at the floor. It was comforting. I knew he was trying to help in the only way he knew how. He was like that. Always saw more than he let on. And now, he was dead. It felt unfair. Like we'd been cursed. "What happened?"

"We don't know yet. Might be arson or an accident." Fires were pretty common in reserves around here—a combination of bored teenagers and faulty wiring in our government-issued houses. What made it worse was that there was no fire department.

"Some of the guys are raising money for the funeral," Kelvin said. "Help support his wife and the little ones. You gonna help?"

"Sure. Of course. What can I do?"

"Anything you like, as long as it makes money."

I stayed up that night. Couldn't sleep. Why was there arson in our community? Were Indians burning up inside? Or so mad about their lives, they had to destroy others'? I thought about the fire that raged inside of me. My mind felt hot with a fever, and it burned in my heart and chest. I had tried to put it out in rehab. I had worked on those breathing exercises that Maurice taught me. And honesty. I'd worked hard on that too. But when I thought about Erick the memories began to burn again, spreading like wildfire after a hot dry summer.

I used to joke with my friends about reserve life when I was at Trent University. Clayton, Simone and me hanging around at the Commoner bar, laughing about the crowded little houses and the lengthy welfare lines. We had ridiculed the Indian Agents and the Indian Act. We japed the so-called Treaty Days, a government-enforced celebration, where the RCMP officers came to town to remind us that they'd ripped us off—sorry, to remind us of a historic agreement that no sooner was signed than ignored, like the rest of the broken promises. Each year, my parents lined up with the others, along the hallways of St. Anne's, to get their Treaty Day money. Four dollars per person, as stipulated by the treaties. Same as it ever was. Given to us in the places where we were whipped.

We laughed about it, just like we mocked the other injustices of history. It was all so goddamned funny, especially the reserves. Tiny

plots of land that we desperately clung to. We called them prisons—
the places that we'd been moved to against our will. We had rebelled
and died not to go there. So they'd imprisoned us, locking away
leaders like Big Bear, Crazy Horse and Sitting Bull. Or executed us,
like Louis Riel, Wandering Spirit, Round the Sky, Bad Arrow,
Miserable Man, Iron Body, Little Bear, Crooked Leg and Man
Without Blood. And when there was no one left to fight, they had
moved us to the reserves anyway. Assigned housing with an assigned
religion and assigned laws under the Indian Act. Jails for Indian
inmates, with the Indian Agent as the warden.

Why had I come back to my reserve? Clayton had been desperate
to leave, too. Most people were. I'd come back because of Joan, that's
why. Back to this place of arson and unemployment. Indian Agents
and broken windows. Drinking and debt.

God, I needed a drink. There was nowhere around here to get
one. Pa rarely made homebrew anymore and there was no way he'd
give me any. There was the bootlegger's but Fort Albany was small
enough that someone would see me, and word would get around. It
would ruin me.

I got out of bed and went to the cots where Albalina, Shannin
and Jassen were sleeping. I sat down next to my seven-year old daughter. She was getting so big. Her skin was so smooth, like the gentle
waters of the Albany at first light. I stroked her hair. It was auburn,
a colour midway between Joan's and my own. They were part of me.
Ni chi shannock. All my relations. I had helped bring them into this
world. I couldn't let them down again. I wouldn't.

TWENTY

We all went to Erick's funeral: Joan, Albalina, Shannin, Jassen and I, speeding along in our motorboat. It was the quickest way to Kashechewan, but three kids in a motorboat, even with life jackets, is pretty terrifying. Kash used to be part of Fort Albany, but it split away when I was in Grade 3 and moved directly across the river. The Kash elders said they were Protestants and needed to split from our Catholic community. I wondered if the behaviour of the nuns and priests at St. Anne's had anything to do with it.

When we got there, we went directly to the church, where a group of people were standing around outside. I hadn't been in a church since my wedding, and here I was again. I felt nervous and remembered back to my time in AA. "Come on, brother. Calm down. Just breathe." Maurice was a good man. I would call him when we moved into our new house and got a phone.

I caught sight of a tall clean-shaven man in his late twenties. I looked closer: there was something I recognized about his high cheekbones, and the slightly crooked bridge of his nose. It was Tony. We hadn't seen each other since he left St. Anne's in Grade 7. He'd fallen out with Brandon by then, and for a few months we were friends again, although never as close as before.

I stopped to chat while Joan took the kids inside.

"Hey man!" Tony said, hugging me. "I heard you were back."

"Yeah. Down south is crazy. Busy, busy."

"Tell me about it! I'm in Timmins. Place is booming. So crazy."

"Mining?"

"No. Tried that. But I couldn't take the dark, you know?" I knew. I'd heard about grown men who'd found it hard to sleep in the dark even years after being locked in the St. Anne's basement. "No, I'm working as a logger," he said.

"Good for you," I said. "What's it like?"

"Oh, you know. It's no walk in the park. But the money's good."

I nodded. "You going in?" I said, gesturing to the church.

"Yeah, in a moment." He lowered his voice. "Heard it was an electrical fire."

"Oh," I said. We would never know for sure. Since there weren't any fire investigators or fire department, the uncertainty would hang around, like the dust after one of those bad autumn windstorms.

Then Nicholas approached us. He'd moved back home after high school, and started working in construction and for the band council. "Glad I found you, Ed. Can I have a word?" Nicholas glanced at Tony, who took the hint and went inside. We walked a few steps toward the side of the church, away from the people milling around. He lowered his voice. "There's a rumour going around. It's probably nothing, but I thought you should know."

"What?" I said, although I saw the whole thing play out in my mind, him telling me that he'd heard about the drinking, and about the problems with my students.

"It's hard to say, but you have to be careful . . ." he said. I stared at him as he talked, my mind spinning, and pretended to listen. It felt like his words were beating down on my head. There was only the noise, and shame. I wanted to hide.

"You okay?" he said.

"What? Yeah," I replied, coming back to the present. "Yeah, fine. Thanks for telling me."

"These things are always hard."

"Yeah, I know. Thanks."

I went inside in a daze. The funeral had just started. I looked at Joan. She was singing. Everyone was singing, but I could hear her voice sweetest of all. The shame came over me like a waterfall. My face became hot, and everything—our house and town and the ground—fell away. Inside my mind were only angry accusations. What could I say to her? I had let her down, again. I had embarrassed and shamed her and now everyone would know about it.

Once the service was over, I wanted to get away. I wanted to be by myself long enough to get my head straight.

"You okay?" Joan said. "You look like you've seen a ghost."

"Yeah well . . . you know, funerals."

"We should get you home." She drove the boat. When we got to land, I said there was something I needed to take care of and that she should take the kids home. "Where are you going?"

"I just need some fresh air."

"Are you okay?"

"Yeah. Fine. I just need a bit of space, that's all. I don't feel well."

"What's wrong?"

"Nothing. Just the funeral. Erick. We were close, you know." She squeezed my shoulder.

"I love you, Ed."

"Yeah. You too," I said, hurrying off.

I needed to talk to my sponsor, Brian. I needed to ask him what to do. I thought about going to Father Daneau's house and calling Brian on the radio phone. It would mean the priest finding out about everything. Maybe I could ask him to leave while I talked. Was that a good idea? I couldn't tell. Everything was spinning and I just needed some space.

I knocked on the priest's door and stood there for a while before calling out his name. Next door, a window opened.

"Are you looking for Father Daneau?" A middle-aged woman leaned out.

"Yes."

"He's gone to Denny's house for a haircut."

I thought about waiting for the priest. About him listening in on my conversation with Brian about why I was so angry. Having the priest hear about what had happened with my students. About being a drunk. The memory of seeing the black robes in a "medical exam" and looking up at a face that was smiling, even as I turned red and the brother fondled my penis until it was hard.

It was a short walk from the priest's house to the bootlegger's. I searched in my pockets as I walked. I had fifty dollars in cash. Enough for half a mickey of vodka. It would have to do.

"I'm surprised to see you here," said Luke, who ran booze in and out of Fort Albany.

"Yeah. Well. We're having a celebration," I said, handing him the fifty dollars. In return, he gave me the vodka, which I put into my inner coat pocket so it didn't show. "Look," I said, "I'd appreciate it if this didn't get around. You know, me coming here."

He raised an eyebrow. "I'm not telling anyone. But that works both ways, right?"

"Yeah. Yeah. Of course."

I walked along the main dirt road toward the trees. I pulled up the hood of my coat as I walked, hoping that I didn't run into anyone.

When I got to the edge of the spruce forest, I looked at the charcoal sky. There were a few faint stars. I looked away. The Great Creator had turned some animals into stars to keep an eye on us. I didn't want them staring at me. They could see me in my despair, and I hated it. I wanted to curl into a ball. I headed into the shadows of the forest, unscrewed the vodka cap and took my first drink.

I got home a few hours later. Joan greeted me at the door.

"Can I have a word?" she said.

"Now?" I said.

"I really want to have a word."

"Okay. Speak."

"In private."

"Nowhere is private."

"For God's sake, Ed! Outside." Joan took my hand and pulled me out of the front door. Then we were in my dad's truck. Joan drove. Neither of us said anything until we got to the cemetery. Then she turned off the ignition and shifted to face me.

"How could you!" she said. "After all we've been through."

"What?"

"Ed! You're drunk!"

"It was only a couple."

"Bullshit! You think I'm stupid?"

"No! Joan, I'm trying!"

"Everyone is trying but you!"

"That's not fair. I love you."

"Oh, don't give me that love bull now. 'Oh, the Cree eagle,' he says. 'Oh, the Seven Sacred Teachings.' And to think I believed it! After all your lies, to think that I believed it!"

"I believe it," I said softly.

"No you don't! No you don't! You believe in your Cree Fucking Helper. And you believe in fucking yourself up. That's what you believe in."

"Joan!"

"I want you out of the house," she said.

"Where should I go?"

"I don't care. Stay at John's. Stay with Nicholas."

"Joan, what about the kids?"

"That's just it. They need role models. Not drunks."

"Joan. Please. I'm sorry."

"You're always fucking sorry."

"I'll try harder. I love you."

"This isn't about fucking love!"

I got out of the truck and walked away.

TWENTY-ONE

I stayed on Nicholas's couch that night. The next day I went to the ATM and took out some cash and then I went to our wooden shack of an airport and bought a plane ticket to Timmins, and onwards by bus to Peterborough. I wanted to say goodbye to my family, but I knew it would be too hard, seeing all those faces I'd disappointed.

Clayton picked me up from the bus station in my car. He'd been storing it for me until he could sell it.

"No luggage," he said.

"Didn't need any."

He didn't reply.

We drove back to his apartment. My car was as shitty as a worn-out Predator ATV. The engine didn't feel like it could pull more than a couple of dead geese. No wonder I had bought it so cheap.

"So what are you going to do now?" Clayton said.

"I'll probably get in touch with my sponsor. Try and figure out how to start again."

"Who's your sponsor?"

"A former addict. Brian."

"He any good?"

"He was. Is," I corrected myself. "I couldn't get hold of him up north."

"That part of it?"

"I guess."

"I don't understand what happened," Clayton said. "I mean, you were doing so well."

"Yeah. I was. My past caught up with me, I guess. All those people I'd let down. They were all there, stuck in that tiny house." I shook my head.

"You wanna talk about it?" Clayton said.

"Not really."

"You're going to have to talk about it sometime, you know."

"I know."

"A lot of AA programs don't really work for our people, you know."

"What do you mean?"

"I dunno, just stuff I hear."

"What stuff?"

"Just that it's hard to relate. All that pop psychology stuff. Behaviour modification. That's not what this is about."

I glanced at him as he drove, and wondered whether he'd been through any of the same things as me. He'd been in a residential school too: he'd likely seen and experienced things that troubled him. He probably had his suspicions. You started opening up and the memories came back faster and faster, swirling over your pit of dread. You tried to do the right thing and put that stuff behind you, but then it was right there, screwing up the present, and you were left with a trail of people you'd loved that you'd then pulled into your own hurt and misery.

We didn't say anything for a while. I was thinking about Joan and our children, and my eyes were wet. I looked out the window so he wouldn't see. The grass and the signs by the highway whipped by.

"You know, there's some interesting things happening in Edmonton," he said eventually. "I heard about it from my uncle Travis. He lives out there."

"What sort of things?"

"Well a bunch of people have been working with kids in residential schools. Eddie Bellerose, George Callingbull, Wilton Littlechild, Madeline Stout, Allen Benson."

"Never heard of them."

"They don't think the old models are working."

"What old models?"

"The wemistikoshiw models of healing."

"Why not?"

"It doesn't jell with our way of thinking."

I thought about reading the religious doctrine in the Big Book in our AA sessions in rehab, and seeing Sister Wesley's face replace Barb's. He got that one right.

"So what's different?" I said.

"I'm not too sure. They have traditional healing groups. Something about rewiring your brain with culture."

"With culture? What, so they play you music or something?"

"Nah, man. This is different. It's about figuring out how you can follow the Red Road."

I remembered Pa telling me about the Red Road after I'd hit my brother Alex. What had he said again? He was always talking about that, but after I'd gone to St. Anne's, I'd started to tune him out. I thought back to that summer. He'd been mad, and said he wanted me to understand what I'd done wrong. How I wasn't treating anyone with respect. How I was forgetting that we are all related, and all need each other to survive. All my relations. *Ni chi shannock.* That stuff felt like it had happened to someone else.

"How do they do that?"

"I don't know too much about it. But there are a lot of people who swear by it. They say that the groups help you find your true path."

"My true path," I said, and laughed harshly.

"No point being bitter," he said.

"Whatever."

"No, I mean it."

"Oh, we all mean it."

"You've got to try."

"I did," I said.

"Well, try again."

"Edmonton is a long way away."

"You're already a long way from home, brother."

TWENTY-TWO

EDMONTON, ALBERTA, 1977

Edmonton is built on top of old Cree bones. We named it Wheeskwaciwaskahikan, or Beaver Hill, because the mound where they laid the first foundations of the city used to be shaped like three stacked dams. Standing tall, it looked out over where our people—the Woods, Plains and Swampy Crees—lived and roamed. From the Atlantic to the Rockies, Newfoundland to Alberta, this was our land. We watched and listened to the land and animals, and picked up and moved according to their rhythms. Navigating the rivers Albany, Churchill, Saskatchewan, Nelson, St. Lawrence and Athabasca, we followed the caribou, moose and deer. Animals offered themselves to the hunt: flesh to sharpened rock, skin under teeth, blood for our blood. We lived like this for thousands of years, until there were strangers in our midst, people who came on tall ships. They knew not the ways of the land and water, so we fed them and gave them furs. They thanked us with guns and horses, but also with smallpox, and then they slowly pushed us out. Make way for Her Majesty, the Great Queen Mother. Away to the edges, to the tiny plots of land called the reserves.

I drove from Timmins to Edmonton faster than I should have, sleeping in my car. On the way, I listened out for Buffy Sainte-Marie on the radio. She got me every time with her rough and ragged voice that cracked me right open. For three days, I ate in places where I could load up on bacon and eggs and didn't have to eat for the rest of the day. It was pretty hard to call anybody. Payphones were plentiful but you never knew how many coins you needed until the operator broke in and demanded "please deposit three more dollars in quarters, please," and when you didn't have quite twelve quarters in your pocket, well, the line went dead. My calls were very limited. On the way, I did get through to Brian, who said he thought it was a good idea to try to join a traditional healing group. And I left messages with the priest for Joan. I asked him if he'd seen her about town, and he said that she looked more tired than usual. I felt a rush of love and protectiveness, and waited for him to go on, but the line on the radio phone was bad so we hung up.

Clayton had a friend with an empty place, just outside of Edmonton. I pulled up there, and after finding the key under a flowerpot, I walked in and fell asleep on his couch.

The next day, I arrived at the Canadian Native Friendship Centre and waited while the receptionist took calls. Then I met the director, Clive, who said they had a healing circle specifically for residential school survivors that met every other day. The centre also recommended taking part in some traditional healing ceremonies, and said they could put me in touch with George Callingbull, one of the elders Clayton had mentioned. Clive recommended going intensely if I was doing this work for the first time. I didn't have to worry about cost—it was paid for by the federal government.

"The healing circle meets in the middle of the day around lunchtime. Do you work nearby?"

"I don't have a job, right now. But I'm looking."

"Good. Then make sure you get something flexible."

"I'll try."

The following Monday, I showed up at a church basement down-town. It was nothing like the addiction centre in southern Alberta. The room was dark, lit by candles. In the middle of the room was a blanket covered in stones, arranged in a half-moon. Around the blanket, eight people were sitting, their eyes closed.

I tiptoed to an empty chair, trying to remove my denim jacket quietly. I wondered if we were going to pray to the Holy Mother or the Holy Spirit, or Priest Boy, which is what we used to call anyone native who was now a big shot in the church.

A native man of about fifty wearing a fringed leather jacket came in. He removed his knapsack, sat down, and introduced himself as Dennis LeRoy. He asked us to go around the circle, saying our names.

"You are sitting in the Circle of Trust," he said. "The Circle of Trust is something that we create. It's a place where we decide to trust ourselves and others. To trust in the process. To do that, you have to make a promise. Is everyone ready to make a promise?"

I was not ready to make a promise to someone I had never met, but I found myself looking squarely at Dennis, whose gaze stilled my restlessness.

"You need to silently promise that whatever people say in this circle you will not share it with the outside. I want you to look inside of yourselves and promise this to us, your brothers and sisters."

What have I got to lose? I thought. *I've already lost everything that matters to me.*

I made a promise to everyone in the group, then to Joan, the kids, Ma and Pa. A promise that I would try my best. That I would listen and be honest even when it was painful and difficult.

Dennis held up an eagle feather. A symbol, he said. Only the people holding the feather could speak. He asked us to share our stories, which he called our Knowings. No one could interrupt. No one could discount or ridicule or criticize what anyone else was saying or had just said.

"What about joking? Can we do that?" a woman asked.

"It's easy to be cynical about all this. But healing starts with trusting. So if you have to joke, you better make sure that it doesn't mock anyone's experience. And make it funny."

He stood and pulled a tobacco pouch from his shirt pocket.

"This tobacco is an offering to the ancestors. We offer it to the people of the east, the people of the south, the people of the west and the people of the north."

Everyone around me shut their eyes, and I did the same. Dennis stayed silent and the room was quiet except for the sound of the overhead fan, slicing still air.

"We have come here to learn from the ancestors. To open our minds to their teachings once more. Each of these people has a heaviness in their hearts. They are wounded. They have made mistakes in their lives. They have strayed from the Red Road. They are lost."

He told us to open our eyes, and he sat down. Turning to the woman on his left, he gave her the eagle feather. He asked her to introduce herself.

She was in her fifties and her name was Jo-Anne. Dennis asked her to relate her happiest memory from childhood.

She told us that it happened when she was seven, the same age as when I started at St. Anne's. It was Christmas. Some kids at the residential school had gone to visit their parents, but she stayed behind with those whose parents were too far away. The nuns handed out gifts that had been sent in by parents and other relatives. Everyone got one except her.

After Christmas lunch, the nuns came back with a big silver box. It was for her. A doll. She was so happy she cried.

Then Jo-Anne handed the eagle feather back to Dennis, and he gave it to a man in his thirties, named Paul, who was sitting next to her.

While Paul was speaking, I thought back to one of my happiest memories. The first time I saw Mike at the school, fiddling with his umbrella at soccer. Then him calling me by my name. Ed. A real name, not a number. He had smiled at me, and it felt good. How I had wanted to please him. How I kept trying to please him. My face burned. I could never say that. I settled on a different memory to tell the group, the time that Tony and I stole the canned meat.

As I spoke, I wondered if Dennis could tell that I was keeping something from the group, but he simply nodded and looked into my eyes. Once we were finished the exercise, he told us he was very proud of us, and then we took a coffee break.

When we came back, Dennis asked us to talk about a time in our childhood when we had been hurt.

An older guy named Lenny talked first about how in the residential school a nun would touch him too much when she gave him a bath. I felt sweaty.

"Where are you going, Ed?" Dennis asked.

"This isn't for me," I replied.

"Why not?"

"That didn't happen to me," I said.

"Were you at a residential school?" he asked.

"Yes, but no *nun* ever touched me," I replied.

"Lenny has his Knowings," he said.

"Yes," I replied.

"And you have yours."

"I don't understand," I said.

"The wemistikoshiw listen so they can gain advantage. This is different. You come here to listen to other people's Knowings. When you truly listen, yours become more real."

"How does my story make his real?" Lenny asked.

"Because for Ed to truly hear your story, he has to listen with an open heart."

"Can you explain?" Bridget said.

"Let me start with the medicine wheel," Dennis said. He got up, went to his knapsack and started handing around a stack of paper. I'd seen these at Trent University, but it had been in class after I'd had a fight with Joan and had been too upset to pay much attention. On each page was a drawing of a circle, divided into four with each quarter differently coloured. "There are four directions, same as points on the compass. Many people start in the east with the rising sun, but I want to start somewhere else. A long time ago, when I was in your position, my healer taught me about grass."

"Your healer taught you about getting high?" Bridget asked.

"That wasn't funny," Dennis said.

"Yes it was," she replied. He ignored her.

"Grass is on the south of your medicine wheel. Whenever we do any sort of work we need to embody the spirit of grass."

"Can we embody it through smoking it?" Bridget asked.

"Okay already, Bridget. A joke doesn't get funnier the more times you tell it. And I'm holding the eagle feather, remember?"

She shrugged.

"Seriously, grass is the symbol of kindness on the medicine wheel. Because whenever it is cut, it always grows back. We have to embody that spirit of kindness toward ourselves as we heal and remember than whenever we feel unloved or trampled on, if we are kind to ourselves, we will spring back."

Dennis asked, "Now, what teaching does fire give us?"

"Heat?" someone ventured.

"And?" Dennis prodded.

"Pain," Lenny offered.

"Yes, it can do that but at a higher level, fire symbolizes love. To feel the heat is to receive the touch of creation and you feel pain, yes, but at least you feel.

"We use the natural things to remind ourselves of what is important in life, to understand what defines us as the indigenous people of Turtle Island. Who knows about the tree?"

"The tree grows straight and tall. It teaches us how to stand proud," Jo-Anne said.

"Yes, straight and tall," Dennis repeated. "The tree teaches us about honesty. We must be straight in all things we do. Now one more. What about mountains?"

"Our cultures are like the mountains," Jo-Anne said, "old and ancient."

"We are immovable," I said.

"You are on the right path. The mountains, the rock teaches us to be strong. The strength of the rock, that's what we want to have. Some of you may know this already, and some may not."

There was silence for a while. Dennis held up the eagle feather for someone else to speak. As he looked about, Lenny spoke up.

"Maybe I'm like the grass. Maybe I'm tired of being trampled on," Lenny said.

"What do you mean?" Dennis said.

"Maybe I don't want to be the grass beneath someone else's feet anymore. Maybe I'm sick of being told that as natives, we're always at the bottom. Maybe I want more than that," he said. Several people nodded and there were yeahs heard around the room.

"Everyone gets tired, Lenny," Dennis said. "But we come here because we are tired of being drunk, angry and hurt. Who has hurt those they love?"

I put up my hand. He gave me the eagle feather.

"Who did you hurt?"

"Everyone."

"Who specifically."

"My wife, my sons, my daughter. My family. Don. Everyone, really."

"Are you angry inside?"

"Yes," I said.

"Have you been hurt?"

"Yes."

"At the residential school?"

"It started there. And it continued after. When I went to Montreal when I was sixteen."

"Tell me your worst memory," he said. I looked down at the eagle feather. It was white and fluffy at the shaft, then split to black, as if burnt. I remembered Albalina being born and the image of the hovering eagle flashing before my eyes. A symbol of love and truth, Pa used to say, before I stopped listening to him after being in St. Anne's. Was it a sign? I didn't know, but I began to talk.

A few days later, Dennis met me one-on-one in the church basement. He knew I was still having trouble talking about my past in front of the others. He told me it was okay that I had enjoyed some of my time with Mike. Common, in fact. And that I shouldn't feel ashamed of what had happened because I wasn't responsible. Mike was the one who "warmed me up" with gifts and built my trust. He betrayed that trust, and it was okay to feel angry at him. Good, in fact.

"Why didn't I leave? I stayed there the whole summer."

"Were you scared?" he asked.

"Yes."

"Did any part of you want to leave?"

"Yes."

"What happened to that part?"

"He tried and then he gave up."

"Why did he give up?"

"He was embarrassed about not having any money. Embarrassed that he had let himself be tricked. Embarrassed about what he'd have to say when he got home. And embarrassed that he just lay there and didn't fight for his life."

"Predators work by exploiting your fear and embarrassment."

"I could have fought. I could have strangled him. I could have killed him."

"Ed, you were scared."

"Why didn't I do anything?"

"What do you think? There must have been a reason."

"I don't know. He had such a hold over me."

"Predators are natural manipulators. They use our weaknesses against us."

"Maybe I like being weak. Maybe that's why I gave up. Give up," I corrected myself.

"Everyone feels weak sometimes. That's why we are here."

"I don't want to be weak anymore. I want to be strong. Alcohol makes me feel strong."

"We are a people who have endured. We have strength in our ceremonies. We have strength in our memories."

"What do you mean?"

"You'll have to live it before you understand."

"I see." I looked down at the eagle feather. "I've carried the memories for a long time. See, thing is, I worry sometimes. A lot. I'm afraid I wasn't the only one. Amocheesh went to his house in Montreal, too."

"It sounds like he was close to several boys. Where is Amocheesh now?"

"I don't know."

"Have you thought about contacting him?"

"Sure. But I don't know where he is."

"But you know his family name. And you know where his family lives."

I didn't say anything for a while. "Maybe I don't want to know," I finally replied.

"Why not?"

"Because what if the same thing happened and he never got over it?"

"Predators rely on your silence. And the silence of the nuns, priests and everyone else who worked at the school, and those in the community who suspected something. As soon as that silence is broken, it becomes dangerous for them."

"I don't know if I'm ready," I said.

"That's good. Good that you are being honest with yourself. We have a long way to go, Ed."

Then he took out some sage, lit it, and we began to smudge. I wafted the smoke toward myself. The burnt smell reminded me of sitting around our Fort Albany woodstove, of being a boy back home.

TWENTY-THREE

That weekend, Lenny and I drove to Enoch Cree Nation, northwest of Edmonton. It was a small reserve, on flat grassland with a few scattered buildings. Dennis had given us directions and told us that we would be meeting Mr. Callingbull, who would be leading the sweat.

In the car, I thought of my great-granddad, John Metatawabin. He did sweat lodge ceremonies in the night in the woods before he was taken away. The police found out about it. Who told them? The town's priest? The Hudson's Bay manager? So many questions, but my family were afraid to even talk about it. Fearful of being targeted by the police or stigmatized by the rest of the town.

I imagined my great-grandfather looking down on me from the Spirit World. As I thought about it, I felt the back of my head burn, as if someone was really watching me. His manitou was outside of me, but also within. His spirit danced in me, and guided me in times of trouble. It drew its power from Gitchi Manitou, who lived in me, and breathed in us all. We were all upwellings of the same pool of Spirit-Matter, all different manifestations of Gitchi Manitou. The

Standing Ones, the Four-Leggeds, the Two-Leggeds, the Grandfather Rocks, the River of Life. All my relations. *Ni chi shannock*.

Mr. Callingbull came to the car to greet us. Then he led us toward a mound-shaped tent made of saplings and blankets.

"You must be Lenny and Ed," he said. "I'm George. Dennis told me about you." Then he told us to strip down to our boxers and come inside.

We crawled through the narrow entrance. Inside was dark and hot, like being inside a woodstove. George began speaking.

"We came in through a door of new beginnings. An opening that faces east, the direction the sun rises."

I'm too hot, I thought. Sweat dribbled down my face.

"We honour the Great Earth Mother, the skies, and the fire, the air and the forest."

I heard a *pfft*, and my legs became prickly with steam. When the air hit my neck, my throat became tight.

"We honour the Seven Sacred Teachings and the Red Road. We honour Gitchi Manitou and all his spirit helpers."

Another *pfft*, and the temperature increased. My throat screamed *water*. My mouth was on fire.

"We honour the Standing Ones, the Four-Leggeds, and the Two-Leggeds."

My skin was going to unpeel raw from my body. My hair felt like it had trapped a burning restlessness inside. I shut my eyes again and tried to get more air. I felt faint. Something warm and wet on my hand. I looked down and saw the shadow of a wolf licking it. I rubbed my eyes. It was dark, but I could make out a muzzle and a pair of yellow eyes. The eyes disappeared for a moment then drew a tight circle around the spot where George was sitting.

"Wolf spirit, is that you?" I asked, the words resounding inside my head.

"Yes," she said.

"What are you doing here?"

"I never left."

"You didn't?" The eyes disappeared. I rubbed my own, and saw a glimmer of yellow.

"Are you there?" I asked silently.

"I'm right here, Ed."

"What should I do?"

"You already know."

"Tell me. Please."

The yellow eyes faded again and I saw an image of Ma tending to a knife wound Pa had self-inflicted while skinning a marten. He was sitting on the tree stump outside our house and she leaned over him, washing the cut with a pot of boiled water. Once she had finished, she stroked his hair. The image faded and I saw Joan holding the hands of my children, in a line, from youngest to oldest, then this too disappeared into black.

"Wolf spirit. Why go home?"

"You need to take your Knowings back home."

"What are my Knowings?"

She disappeared.

The heat was so intense that I could not breathe. It pulled me into a sadness that had been there for as long as I could remember. Tears mixed with the steam that drenched my face. I cried until I was nothing but dry heat.

I lay down on the floor, where it was cooler, and my chest sank into the damp earth. George began to sing, and one by one, the others joined in. Their voices resonated deep inside my flesh. I listened as my skin danced with their melodies. Until their last notes had faded into the heat. Then I tried to get up, but I felt a heavy weight, like a dog, on my chest. The weight began to fill my chest, pulling me into a darkness deeper than night. I let go and began to fall. The thick black air pulled me downwards, into the ground. I felt the soil between my fingers. I was on the floor, weak and part of the dirt. I was the Great Mother Earth. I was Gitchi Manitou and his Creation.

George began saying another prayer, signifying the sweat was over. I was exhausted and unable to move. Lenny helped me outside into daylight. The cool air soothed my near-naked body.

TWENTY-FOUR

In the valley
The walking people are blank-eyed
Elders mouth vacant thought.
Youth grow spindly, wan
from sap too drugged to rise.

Dennis read this poem to us twice. Marilou Awiakta was a Cherokee poet from East Tennessee, but she could have been from anywhere. The policy was universal, or at least the same across North America. Kill the Indian to Save the Man. Turned out when you killed the Indian, you just killed the Indian.

Dennis asked us what we thought it meant.

"It means it's hard to follow the Red Road," I said.

"Explain."

"The Red Road is the way we're supposed to walk right in the world. It's called a road, but really it's bigger than that. It's all of it—the Seven Sacred Teachings, the vision quests, the shaking tent, the sweat lodges, the animal spirit guides. Each of them offers a teaching on how to live well in the world. The sweat lodge offers a lesson on enduring discomfort. On letting go into pain. On trusting your body even when everything else seems unbearable. It teaches you through experience on how to stare death in the face. Thing is, we were taught that this stuff was shameful. We were taught to be fearful of who we were, and to turn our backs on our traditions, on our ancient coping mechanisms. We were taught not to listen to the elders, the keepers of those traditions. So we became lost. We lost faith in the road. We became afraid to put one foot in front of the other. So we block everything out with booze and drugs."

"Is that your story?"

"Mostly," I said. "Some of it was my own doing."

"What was your own doing?"

"Well, I've hurt a lot of people over the years, especially my wife. I had chances and I blew them. Chances to do right and to come clean and each time I didn't go there."

"Part of this healing is learning how to own your own story," Dennis said. "To acknowledge what has happened and what you have done and to stop running from it. It's there. It's done. People were hurt. Stop reliving it."

"How do I do that?"

"You're human and you made mistakes. That's okay. We all do it. Especially when you've been in a residential school. Seen and been part of things that shouldn't have happened. Then you come out and you're expected to pretend like it never happened. Go on with your life. Chances are it doesn't work out that way. There's a lot of hurt inside of you that wants to get out and be in the world. So you start to destroy those who are close to you. It feels inevitable. But once you finally realize what you've done, you still have to own that hurt. You still have to repair those relations, as much as you can. Remember, you've already taken the first steps."

"I have?"

"Tell everyone about your new job, Ed." I took hold of the eagle feather and told the group that I'd been trying to find stable work when I went to the University of Alberta to ask about their master's programs. I had bumped into Marilyn Buffalo-McDonald, who was working as director of its Native Student Services. We had an intense discussion about politics and she told me she was looking for an assistant to help her boost native enrollment at the school. I returned home for my CV, and after a couple of interviews, I got the job.

Everyone clapped.

"Sounds big shot. What's it mean?" Bridget asked.

"Oh, I'm pretty far down the totem pole. It just means that I'm helping kids."

After I started my job at the university, I continued going to cultural training workshops. One took place at Goodstriker's Ranch, near the Rockies. Each day we had a good breakfast, exercise and heard talks from elders. Nights we slept in teepees. What we found most helpful was to meet for ten or fifteen minutes at dawn by a nearby creek. For me it was not rational and least of all not scientific. What could be accomplished by gazing in wonderment at the coming sunrise?

But we sat there and watched the creek flow, saw the minute details of the rivulet cascading over pebbles and sand, and we began to understand appreciation. We realized that this gratitude took the form of acceptance: of ourselves and our situation.

I had never been on a horse before. The owner of the ranch, Rufus Goodstriker, gave me a small gelding to ride. Half an hour later I was navigating a narrow ledge, looking at the deep canyon below, rock face to my right and nothing on my left. I focused on staying atop the horse. My name became the Sandal-Footed Cowboy because I had no cowboy boots, unlike everyone else.

—

As the months went by, I went to more sweats, and Dennis said that I was ready to start helping others. That I should use Pa's teachings and what I had learned in our sessions and in the sweat lodge to get involved.

"I am involved. We're trying to raise native involvement at the university."

"Some of these people could do with your help," he said, gesturing around the room. "Have someone else listen to them and guide them along the way."

"I don't know," I said. "There's still a lot I'm dealing with."

"Ed, what you went through has left some pretty serious scars."

"Yeah."

"Helping others will help heal them."

"You sure?"

"No. But I'd like you to try."

The following Saturday morning I replayed this conversation as I sat in my car outside Sue-May's house. I didn't know much about her: she was one of the quiet ones in the healing circle. When she spoke, which wasn't often, we all leaned in, until Bridget singed her hair on one of the candles, jumping up, as the sacred space exploded with four-letter curses. Sue-May hadn't said much after that. I think she was afraid of causing third-degree burns.

I glanced at my watch, and looked around. She lived on the top floor of a building on a street filled with massage parlours and pawnbrokers. There was no front yard, just a rough mound of snow filled with Coke cans and tufts of prickly grass.

A few minutes later, she got in my car and said she wanted to go to the Camsell Hospital. What's at the Camsell? I asked. It was known to be an Indian hospital where they'd fly all the natives from up north. Mostly for TB. The rates of infection had come down since I'd attended school but the disease still freaked people out. Coughing up blood. Quick, get the children to hospital down south. Then wait. And wait. Any news? Please. No. Usually, the kids didn't come home. Only arrived in hospital once there was a hole in the lungs full of disease. Not much the doctors could do. Maybe that's why there were rumours of the ghosts of coughing children wandering the Camsell's lobby.

"It was where I had my operation," she said.

"What operation?"

She looked out the window and said nothing.

At the Camsell I parked the car and she went inside. To keep warm, I turned the car on every few minutes. Outside the hospital entrance, a mother was helping a five-year-old into his coat. They reminded me of Joan and Jassen. Not the way they looked, just the way the boy put his arms around his mother's neck for support and how she used her coat to protect him from the wind as she got him into his own.

After an hour, Sue-May returned. I asked her how it went. She said they were too busy to see her.

"What do you mean?"

"They told me to come back tomorrow."

"Why?"

"The supervisor will be there then."

"Do you want me to talk to them?"

"No. They said to come back tomorrow."

At our healing session that evening, Dennis took me aside and asked how it had all gone.

"It's like she's still on the reserve," I said. "She treats everyone with authority like they're an Indian Agent or something."

"That's why I partnered her with you," he said.

"Why me?"

"Because you're ready. You're steady enough that you can give back. You've done the hard work, and found your voice."

I had long wanted to call Joan. I wanted her back in my life. Every time I asked Dennis about it, he told me to wait.

"Why? I need my family. They are everything to me."

"What do they need?" Dennis asked.

"I think my kids need a dad."

"And do you feel ready? Do you feel ready in here?" and he put his hand on my heart.

I did some smudging ceremonies over the next few days, and cleansed my mind, preparing myself for the talk. I needed to be in a mindset where I felt I knew how to listen to her needs and take them seriously. I had to remember how to follow the Red Road.

"Joan. Is that you?"

"Yes. Who's this?"

"It's Ed. Your husband. Ex-husband," I corrected myself. We were separated, but she hadn't yet brought up divorce. Thank Gitchi Manitou for these small favours.

"Oh. Right. It's been a while." I couldn't believe that eight months had passed.

"I know. My healer said I shouldn't call until I was ready."

"*You* were ready?" She sounded bemused.

"There's a lot going on."

"Here too. I'm taking care of your three children."

"I know. I want to be involved."

"Yeah. I've heard that before."

"Things are different now."

"That one too."

"You're a hard woman." It was supposed to be a joke.

"No. I'm not. I'm too easy actually."

"Is there anything I can say that would impress you?"

"Actions speak louder than words."

"I'm doing an apology dance as we speak." I could hear her smile on the phone.

"I gotta go," she said.

I called again a few days later.

"There's a woman I'm helping," I said.

"A woman?"

"It's not like that. She's older."

"Oh, I see."

"She had some sort of operation. In residential school. It reminded me of something that happened to me. Something that I should have told you about a long time ago."

"What, Ed?" she said, sighing.

"There was a man. His name was Mike Pasko." And then I told her about the time I had gone with him to the Albany, and then about our trip to Montreal.

"Jesus, Ed," she said, once I'd finished. We were silent for a while.

"Are you going to say anything else?" I asked.

"I'm in shock."

"I should have told you before."

"Yes. No. God, I don't know."

At our next healing session, Dennis asked Sue-May and me to stay behind after our group work, then he left the room. Sue-May asked me to light a candle and turn out the lights. She wouldn't say why. We sat in the near dark, face to face.

"I had an operation. They cut me."

"Who?"

"The doctors at the Camsell."

"Why?"

"I don't know."

"When did it happen?"

"When I was sixteen at residential school in Alberta. I was a ward of the state."

"What happened?"

"They gave me a test. In math. There were three men sitting up high. Behind a table. They said I needed my appendix out."

"You had appendicitis?"

"No."

"So what happened?"

"I went to have surgery. I came out. I thought I was fine. But last year, I needed to have an examination, you know, for here." She pointed at her stomach. "After, the doctor said my insides are all chewed up. Like they've been in a food processor. That I'd never be able to have a baby."

I reached for her hand in the darkness. Her palms were as dry as moose jerky, but the tops felt soft like a baby's skin. We were quiet for a while.

I didn't know what to say. Years later we found out that she wasn't alone, that there were thousands like her—Leilani Muir and others—aboriginals, alcoholics, mentally handicapped and juvenile delinquents deemed unsuitable for procreation, who were sterilized without their consent.[8] When I met Sue-May in the winter of 1977, the Sexual Sterilization Act had been revoked five years earlier, but not before 2,800 people had been sterilized in Alberta. The Act allowed a residential school superintendent or principal to permit the sterilization of any student under their charge.

"Tell me about your kids," she said.

"My kids?"

"They are eight, six and five, right?" she asked.

"Yeah."

So I told her about the time that Joan and I had gone hiking with Albalina when she was a baby. We'd stopped in a spruce grove next to a creek and listened to the Standing Ones. I cradled Albalina and held Joan's hand. Near us the branches curled around each other.

"I hear something," Joan said.

"What?"

"I love you," she whispered in my ear.

"The Standing Ones didn't tell you that," I replied, laughing.

"Does it matter?"

Afterwards we had gone home and made love. I hadn't meant to tell Sue-May all that, but she listened expectantly every time I stopped, as if wanting more.

The next day at the Camsell, I went in with her. We explained the situation at the information desk. The clerk, a tall man with delicate hands, raised an eyebrow and said he didn't think anything like that had happened here.

"Are you a musician?" Sue-May asked. "You have musician's hands." The tall man blushed.

"I play jazz guitar," he said. "But only on weekends."

Sue-May nodded and looked him in the eyes. "It did happen," she said. He looked at her, embarrassed, then looked back at me before going off to get his boss. A man in his forties returned. He had a thin mustache, which he played with as he spoke. He told us he'd look into it.

That evening it got to me. All of it. Sue-May, Lenny, Amocheesh, Bridget, myself: everyone who'd had their lives picked apart by the residential schools. I called Joan and told her about Sue-May.

"Everyone is so unhelpful," I said. "And she doesn't even know why they did it."

"Why did they do it?" Joan said.

"I don't know. I'm still finding it out."

"Is she okay?"

"I think so. There's a sadness about her."

"I can imagine."

"Sometimes it sits heavy on her. Like in her shoulders. I try to help, but . . . anyway, I told her about you. About us."

"What did you say?"

"I told her about the time that we went hiking with Albalina."

"We did that a bunch of times."

"Remember the time when we listened to the Standing Ones?"

"You were always trying to get me to do stuff like that."

"Still am."

"You're such a flirt."

"I can't help it."

"Listen, I should go."

"Can I have five more minutes? There's something I want to tell you."

"Another secret? Should I sit down?"

"No, nothing like that. I'm tired, Joan. And angry. I think I need to take those bastards to court."

"Who?"

"The staff at St. Anne's. Mike. Everyone who has trampled on us and thinks they can get away with it."

"Wow. That's a lot of people."

"Joan, come on. Seriously."

"Seriously. It's going to be hard work . . ."

"I know."

"But I think you need to do it. I mean the whippings. The standing naked bed-wetting punishments. An electric chair. Being made to eat your own vomit. Brother Jutras's 'medical exams.' The solitary confinement in the basement. There's just so much."

"Yes. It's taken me a long time to come to terms with it."

"How did you survive while you were there? How did you get through every day?"

"I had friends at first. They helped me. We helped each other. But after a while, it took a toll. Lots of us just shut down."

"God. That's so sad."

"We lost our voices. Lost our way. Didn't know what was right in our hearts."

"Do you think that's why so many people in Fort Albany drink?"

"Yeah. That's part of it. For sure."

"Well then I think a court case is a good idea. It will help people find peace."

"All the records are in Fort Albany. I'd need to come back. How do you feel about that?

"You mean to move in here?"

Joan was working as an ESL teacher, and had taken over my parent's old two-bedroom when they got their bigger band house.

"Well . . . I guess I could live with my parents."

"I'll have to think about it. I mean I can't just pick up . . ." She paused. "A lot has happened, Ed."

"I know. I just wish there were some way to make things right."

"So do I."

"Joan?"

"Yeah."

"That guy. Mark. Is he . . . still . . . in the picture?" I had heard through the grapevine that she was dating.

"Funny. I didn't know you knew. No."

"I love you, you know . . ."

"Yes, I know."

"What do you see right now?"

"What do you mean?"

"Outside the window."

She got up to check. "Trees."

"Today when I was driving home, I thought that the icicles hanging from the branches looked like phantom leaves. They're like all of us. Numb and just hanging there. Just a wind's breath away from falling off."

"I can't be there anymore to catch you, Ed."

"I know. You've already done so much. I just miss you, that's all. I miss your voice, your eyes, your skin. I miss everything about you."

"I miss you too," she said.

TWENTY-FIVE

FORT ALBANY, 1988

With these two hands, I build my home. I split the spruce wood, and plant my foundations in the earth. I hammer the roof, and ask for shelter from the wind and snow for my children . . . *what was it?* The prayer came to me.

> *And I saw that the sacred hoop of my people was one of many hoops*
> *that made one circle, wide as daylight and as starlight,*
> *and in the center grew one mighty flowering tree to shelter*
> *all the children of one mother and one father* [9]

"Hey man!" Nicholas interrupted my thoughts. I looked up at him from my pit. He was standing up on his idling quad. "What you doing down there?"

"Building a house. These are gonna be the foundations," I said, pointing to some spruce planks.

"Sure looks big."

"It will be. Five bedrooms."

"Does the chief know you're doing this?"

"Yeah. I've told him."

"You know it's illegal, right?"

Sections 18, 20, 35 and 53 of the Indian Act made it illegal for us to have our own land or houses on the reserves. We couldn't build or sell or buy on our reserve or treaty land without first getting permission from the minister—an empty clause, since he hadn't yet been known to give it.

"I know," I said.

"And he's okay with it?"

"Yep."

"What if everyone does it?" Nicholas said.

I looked around the spruce forest, imagining what it would look like if we took possession of the land we had once roamed. If we built our own houses, instead of the cheap, clapboard houses issued by the Department of Indian Affairs and Northern Development (DIAND). I saw a street of hand-built wooden houses, each with its own unique character, and kids laughing and playing out front.

"Maybe they should," I said.

I built my house after returning home for good. After Edmonton, Joan and I moved to Toronto where I did a master's in Environmental Studies at York University; a choice based on the healing sessions I had done with Dennis LeRoy and George Callingbull. I wanted to take my Knowings back home, but knew that if I was ever to make any wemistikoshiw understand the importance of nature, and how it defines us, I needed to speak their language. I loved the degree; it was easier to concentrate and study once I had stopped drinking.

During that time, Joan took some university courses in education, and then we moved back to Fort Albany in 1987. We decided to build a house one kilometre from Fort Albany. I wanted to be as far away from St. Anne's as possible, but there was more to it than that. Lots of my classmates had similar issues to me. I'd been through several cultural training workshops, healing circles and sweat lodges in Alberta, but you can never escape these things, not completely. They are always there, like the ghosts of the ancestors, whispering in your ears. The drinking in our community had worsened, as had the drugs—now the bootleggers were bringing in coke, speed, valium and painkillers. The effects were hardest on the kids, especially as the parents imitated people like Sister Wesley, Brother Jutras, Brother Goulet and the like who had raised them.

Youth grow spindly, wan
from sap too drugged to rise.

"What did he want?" Joan had come to chat. I looked at her. Man, I am *so* lucky. After all that, she'd taken me back. *One last chance*, she had said. *For the kids. I better not regret it.*

Did she? I looked at her as she handed a bottle of water to me. No. Maybe. Hard to say. I hoped not.

"Wanted to tell me I was breaking the law," I said.

"What did you say?"

"I said that I had permission."

"Do you?"

"Not really. From the band, but not the Ministry."

"Do you think that's right?" Joan said.

"Yes, I do." I paused. That we would need permission from the Ministry to build on the tiny parcel of land reserved for us by Treaty No. 9 symbolized what was wrong with the laws that govern my people. All the power rested with the Ministry. Every decision, whether it was chopping down a tree, or building your own home, had to be cleared with the higher-ups.

And we were Crees. We were used to giving everyone their freedom, letting them do as they would as long as they didn't harm others, not suffocated with oppressive rules. This was supposed to be our land. It was where we had lived and hunted and prayed for thousands of years. Sure, we had negotiated its use with the Crown in the early 1900s. Her Majesty's representatives had canoed here and asked our opinions on our land. We fed them and then we spoke together for several days via translators. They said they wanted to use our land in exchange for a few dollars. No one gets something for nothing, and so we asked what they wanted us to give up. They told us that the treaty would not interfere with our lifestyles, or our hunting and fishing. Things would continue as before. When we expressed concerns about these words, they assured us that we shouldn't worry because they were here to help us. We were nervous, especially because we could not read the words they had written on the paper and had to rely on translators, but they assured us that we were signing a treaty. Any treaty, by definition, meant that they acknowledged that we were a sovereign nation with land rights and attendant powers. For us, treaties meant more, being a totem of respect, honour and good will toward the other side.

"I'd never get permission if I wrote to the Ministry," I said. "Once I finish this place, Alex and Madeline can live in our old place." Alex and his wife Madeline had nine kids and had already been waiting seven years on the band's housing waitlist. They were currently living with my parents.

"What if one of the DIAND guys flies in and says it's illegal?" Like the Indian Agents, the Department of Indian Affairs and Northern Development sometimes flew in to check whether we had broken the Indian Act laws.

"Well that's a risk we have to take. Besides, *Amistagoshow ootu na shway we na*. It's only one of those white man's laws." It was a Cree phrase that poked fun at all the ridiculous laws imposed on us from above.

"Just don't teach that saying to our kids," she said. "I don't want them growing up on the wrong side of the law."

"I won't," I replied, and I blew her a kiss.

There are some people who can silence you with a glance. I don't know what it is about them, but you look into their eyes, and you see something that you can't put a finger on, something that lays you bare. Oliver was like that. He was an old hunting buddy of my pa's. I had started seeing him when I got back to Fort Albany, trying to record all those practices and rituals that help us follow the Red Road before elders like Oliver passed into the Spirit World.

I'd packed my recorder, microphone and notepad. The paper was because in the best moments, people asked me to turn the tape recorder off. *I have something special to tell you. Turn it off.* No please, I said. *This is important. Turn it off.* That's when you knew you were getting the best bits. The stuff that you were supposed to score onto your memory, the words to embed in your heart.

Outside it was brisk. The sun was just burning off the last of the Albany's morning mist.

"Ed. How's it going?" Oliver said coming to the door.

"Pretty good. Been building a house."

"I heard. Same as your pa. Built it from the ground up."

"Ours is going to be a bit bigger."

"That was some squeeze, eh?" he said.

"Made dinnertimes fun."

"And how's Mattawasini?" That was the name of the drumming group I had founded. I had been keen to introduce our traditions back to the community, and so had brought in several aboriginal drumming groups from Manitoulin Island and North Bay. The musicians had inspired some Fort Albany men, who had started their own drum group and called it Mattawasini, meaning "the singers of

the powerful rock," named after an ancient stone located 50 kilometres up river that was said to possess spiritual powers that had long
anchored our people. The drum is a powerful tradition, as it strikes
the heartbeat of Mother Earth. We drop into that rhythm to sym-
bolize the many coming together as one. My time with Dennis
LeRoy and George Callingbull had taught me that these teachings,
rituals and practices could help us heal as a people and find our place
in the world. We could use them to know who we were, build community, and find our voices again.

"It's good. I'm getting the kids involved."

"That's good. Lots of them don't listen to us anymore. Off partying or playing video games."

"Some do."

"Yeah. Jassen and Shannin are good," he said.

"And Albalina."

"Yeah. She's turning into quite the woman." Albalina was eighteen, and had those effortless good looks that strike fear into every
father's heart. I looked at Oliver to see what he was driving at, but he
was already preoccupied with the kettle, putting it on the stove for
bush tea. Once we were finished, I took out my microphone and
turned it on. Oliver put his hand over the mic.

"Just a minute, Ed. You once told me that you wanted to bring
the St. Anne's nuns and priests to justice."

"Still do. Eventually."

"So when is eventually?"

"I have to become chief first."

"So you're running?"

"Ahh . . . I dunno. All that work and answering to the Ministry.
It's a bit of a headache."

"You're starting to sound like a wemistikoshiw," Oliver said.

"I'm living in their system."

"The wemistikoshiw have built many prisons. Don't let them build one inside your mind."

"What's that supposed to mean?"

He pointed to his heart. "You already know, Ed."

A few months later, we were in the St. Anne's school hall. The government took over the building in 1969 and, in 1973, kicked out all the nuns and replaced them with lay people, but the place still freaked me out. I hated it when they had meetings in here, but there was no other space. A memory flashed before my eyes: the faces of 140 boys just before I was electrocuted, all transfixed, some scared, hardened or upset, and a few with the glint of sadistic curiosity. Those were the ones that terrified me, as they wore an expression that I saw in myself. I could feel myself being pulled back into anger, and I reached into my pocket. My fingers curled around a tight ball—a cloth bag filled with tobacco. Oliver had given it to me as a reminder not to get pulled into emotion, to let it pass through you so you can follow the Red Road. The herb that teaches us about giving thanks for our own existence. How to follow a spiritual path. I had forgotten to take it out of my pocket, and here it was in my time of need.

I was sitting on a row of chairs, facing an audience of one hundred and fifty adults and about fifty kids. Not everyone in the town—we couldn't squeeze everyone in here; besides, in a population of eight hundred, there were six hundred kids. Next to me were the two other candidates for chief, the incumbent Louis Nakogee, and Simeon Soloman. Louis spoke first. He said the usual stuff, the things that all chiefs tell their constituents. *I'll get the Ministry to make good on their treaty promises. There will be more services. There will be more fresh water. There will be houses for all.*

I looked about the room. We have these elections every two years. Almost without fail, the candidates make the same promises. And every time, my people buy it and vote for them. Or maybe they don't buy it but they still vote for them. The candidates do their best, I guess. They mean all their promises, even if they don't have the power to keep them.

You wanna build a fence? Talk to the Minister. Want to set up a business? Write him a letter. You wanna get a mortgage on your house? Ask his permission. Then learn the reserve's favourite activity: the gentle art of waiting.

The Indian Act is written like they are doing us a favour, but that's what it means. The Minister decides how we should keep our land, roads, fences and houses. We are not allowed to do anything on reserve land without getting his clearance. Then they wonder why Indians don't take more initiative. When it was my turn, I walked to the front of the stage and looked out across a packed hall.

"You know," I said, "when I was a kid my parents sent me away to the residential school just over the bridge. St. Anne's. Where we're sitting today. They told me that it was necessary to learn the way of the wemistikoshiw. They said that would be the only way we could get jobs and get out of debt. We had to give up our culture because it was holding us back.

"So we did. We learned that the vision quest and the shaking tent were wrong. We learned that Jesus Christ, not Gitchi Manitou, was our lord and saviour. We learned that we were backwards and needed to be civilized by people whose idea of civilization was to stick us in electric chairs. We were told we were dirty savages by people who would make us stand naked with feces-covered clothing on our heads. That we were dogs, by people who made us eat our own vomit." I paused, looking out at the audience. Some people looked shocked. Like this was not what they had expected from an election speech. It was getting too heavy, and I had to bring us all back to safer waters.

"We accepted all these ideas because we were used to being

silenced, because any resistance—whether it was against the terms of the treaties or the Indian Agents or the Potlatch laws—was put down.

"So this morning, I walked past the band office, and you know what I saw? I saw a big lineup for welfare. And I heard people complaining there were no jobs. Unemployment at 80 percent. And talking about their debt.

"Many of you gave away your children so that our community would no longer have these problems. So we would have more jobs. So that our kids could look forward to a better life. That's what my parents did. They put me in a place where kids were being abused. Whipped. Half starved. They told me the nuns would look after me.

"They did it because they wanted a different future for me. They were prepared to make great sacrifices. But it turns out that those promises couldn't be kept. St. Anne's has been in the community for almost a hundred years, and yet those issues—the joblessness and debt—have gotten worse.

"I think it's time that we stopped accepting the wemistikoshiw solutions to our problems. I think it's time that we return to the treaties and the traditions. The wemistikoshiw have taken our land and resources. They put Indian Agents, Hudson's Bay managers, priests and the RCMP in charge. They fly experts in here to fix things and take care of our problems, but they don't listen to what needs fixing. They ignore us when we say that we want to do these things for ourselves. We have long been a resilient people. Self-reliant. Resourceful. In my dad's day, nature had a quick way of punishing those who were lazy. They didn't survive the winter. They starved.

"A long time ago, before any of us were born, Chief Big Bear used to remind his people that the Crees were a proud, independent people. We took care of each other and of ourselves. He warned us not to get too dependent on the handouts of the white man. I am telling my people that we need to do the same. We have the intelligence and will to do everything that the wemistikoshiw does. We need to start believing in ourselves again. To know that however hard it is, we can do it. We are worthy. We need to take our power back.

"So if you elect me, I can't promise that I'll get the Ministry to build more houses. I can't promise that I'll get them to install a new sewage plant or running water. I will try to do all of these things. But what I will focus on is giving each of you more control over your own destiny. If you elect me, I will focus on taking our power back from the Ministry and giving it to our people, the Mushkegowuk. We are the Crees of Northern Ontario. We are a sovereign nation. A proud, independent people. We must remember what it is to follow the Red Road. What it is to stand tall and say, 'This is who I am. This is what is right. This is what I believe in.' We must be strong in our struggle and strong in ourselves."

I finished talking and looked at Oliver across the room. He nodded, then pointed to his heart, a sign that I had spoken from my soul and in the spirit of the eagle, with love and wisdom.

We voted by secret ballot. I won by a landslide—110 people voted for me. That evening we celebrated at my parents' house. Ma had cooked smoked pike, goose, mashed potatoes, cranberry jam, and mac and cheese. We were all there: Ma and Pa, Alex and his wife Madeline and their daughter Evelyn, Mary-Louise, Chris, Leo, Jane, Denise, Mike, Marcel, Danny, Albalina, Shannin, Jassen, Joan and myself squished around a long wooden table.

"When will we have this at your place?" Ma said.

"We're getting there. Right, Jassen?"

"Yep," he said, grabbing some homemade bread.

"You know your pa tried to take our power back," Ma said. "Tried to take control over policing on the reserve. The Indian Agent didn't think much of the idea," she said.

"Things are different now, Ma," I said. We'd gained a little more control over our own affairs when the Indian Act had changed three years ago in 1985. Now our band council could make their own hires for construction, reserve services and cultural programs. Of course, they still needed wemistikoshiw supervisors, but it was a start.

"I hope so," Pa said. "Remember when I tried to fight the Indian Agent on housing? No one was interested. They said why do the work when the government was giving everything for free." He helped himself to some more goose. "Then I tried to pass a Band Council Resolution on it. But the Indian Agent didn't think much of the idea. Said it wasn't my land to begin with." He laughed bitterly.

"Well, times have changed," I said.

"People say that but—"

Ma interrupted him. "We're proud of you, aren't we, Keshayno?" He and Ma exchanged glances.

"Yeah," he said gruffly.

There's a story about Chief Big Bear at the end of his life. It was the 1880s, and the buffalo were already dead and his people were starving. He decided to ride from the Cypress Hills in Saskatchewan to Ottawa to meet the head of Indian Affairs. Chief Big Bear was said to be tired of explaining his issues to various officers only to be told that it was out of their hands and he would have to ask someone higher up. But as he rode east, he began talking to various wemistikoshiw officials, Indian Agents, police officers, newspapermen. Each told him that it would be near impossible. Eventually, he gave up.

The first year I was chief I didn't ride or fly to Ottawa. I wrote to the politicians, explaining my grand plans and taking control of our destiny. Sometimes I got a polite reply.

Dear Mr. Metatawabin,

Thank you for your suggestions. We have taken them on board and are investigating accordant to Sections 53–60 of the Indian Act. We will be in touch following due processing with the correct jurisdiction.

Usually I got nothing.

So after a year, I had made good on a few of my election promises. I had given a couple of speeches to our local school, now called St. Anne's Catholic School, about how the Red Road could be adapted to provide important life lessons that apply today. I had organized a youth muskeg run, where we ran 10 kilometres through the muskeg, to champion youth fitness, as more kids were turning away from the traditions, to spend their days watching TV and eating junk food. I had done some youth training sessions, teaching them how to write cover letters, and how to prepare for a job interview.

I was reintroducing ancient and sacred aspects of our culture, but I had nothing to show for my ideas on native empowerment. I realized I was about to be shifted around in the revolving door of elected chiefs who are ejected faster than puking kids on a merry-go-round. I decided to take my band councillors to Sudbury.

Compared to other great native resistances, whether led by Sitting Bull, Crazy Horse or Louis Riel, ours might seem tame. The band council and I set up a meeting with the Department of Indian Affairs in the morning and told them what we wanted: to become manager of our own affairs, that is, prime contractor on all development work undertaken in our community. Normally, the bulk of taxpayers' money spent on our community went to hiring wemistikoshiw consultants who had to be flown in and put up in Fort Albany's grotty hotel and fed overpriced food. Or on renting machines—all construction machinery had to be brought in on the winter road, which meant that we usually had to rent it for a year and return it when the winter road next opened, regardless of how long it was needed. Construction equipment usually couldn't be rented without hiring the company's people to operate it, so we lost valuable jobs too. We wanted to take control of DIAND grants so that we could buy our own secondhand equipment, rent it out to other communities and use the savings to train our people.

The Indian Affairs representatives—two middle-aged men and a woman, all of them in suits—met with us on the morning of February 15, 1989. They took notes and coughed a lot. They thanked us for our idea and said they'd give it the appropriate thought and consideration. They got up to leave, and we stayed sitting. The representatives cleared their throats. They shuffled from side to side. Finally, the man in the middle spoke up.

"Can you wait outside?"

"No thanks," I replied.

That was it. Very Canadian. We sat there until four p.m., and then they gave us our paperwork. We'd made history by becoming the first native community in Ontario to gain control over its own affairs, a small victory in the fight for First Nations sovereignty. It wasn't as drawn out as other occupations, such as the Blue Quills school sit-in in 1970, or as high profile as the Occupation of Alcatraz. But for my people whose family members had been taken away under the Potlatch laws, and who had tried and failed to resist the Indian Agents on many issues of personal autonomy, such as the size and area of their trapline, or whether they could expand their businesses, or whether they could practise their religion or culture, or if their kids were allowed to grow up with their parents or had to go to St. Anne's, it felt like more than the outcome of a day's peaceful resistance—it felt like a long, hard-won victory.

We returned to our Sudbury hotel and I called Joan.

TWENTY-SIX

You might think that with everything going so well, I would have already started proceedings against Mike Pasko and the nuns and priests, but it would take me another three years. At the time, I told myself that I was too busy. I wanted to help my community snap out of its stupor—the daze left behind from the residential schools, the Indian Act, cultural loss and welfare dependency—and there was always so much to do.

As prime contractors, we'd started a construction company, Neegan-o'chee. We were building a stone dike, using the abundant aggregate on the dry riverbed, to stop Fort Albany from flooding, a sewage treatment plant (previously people dumped their sewage in the woods, buried it in their backyards, or threw it into the river), and a filtration plant to supply houses with running water. We had halved unemployment to 40 percent, and were making profits on our DIAND grants: we had bought some used construction equipment to build our dike and houses, and were renting it out to other First Nations communities, rather than renting machines on a daily rate from the wemistikoshiw, and paying exorbitant shipping costs. We reinvested the profits into cultural projects for the community. I was re-elected in 1990 on the basis of these successes, and still I dragged my heels for another two years on the court case. Partly it was the power of the church in town: they ran everything from the yearly Christmas concert and Thanksgiving feasts, to the hockey fundraisers to buy equipment for the kids.

But if I'm honest, there was much more to it. I had dinner with Tony in the fall after I was first elected, and our conversation stayed with me. He had left mining and started his own consulting business, helping First Nations communities get grants from DIAND. He had dinner with the family, and afterwards I said I had something to talk to him about and we went for a drive.

"So," he said. "What's on your mind? I don't see you for five years and then suddenly a call out of the blue."

"Yeah man. I've been busy. It ain't easy being chief."

"Easier than not being chief," he said.

"Probably," I laughed. "Listen. Remember when Sister Wesley used to beat us up and all?"

"Yep. Eat like a dog!" He shook his head. She had made Tony eat vomit from the floor, too.

"I've been thinking of taking her to court."

"You should."

"Her and the others."

"Which others? The staff or students?"

"What do you mean, the students?"

"It was a pretty rough place, Ed."

"I know. I was there."

"Right. So you remember how the boys used to copy the staff. Beat each other up. Hit them with sticks. Force themselves on each other."

"What?"

"Yeah. I told my parents about it and said I wasn't going back. That's why they pulled me from the school."

"I don't remember that . . . I mean, I remember the kids beating each other up, but not them forcing themselves on each other." God, did kids rape others like Mike had done to me? I couldn't even imagine it.

"Well, I do remember it," Tony said. "It shouldn't stop you though. I mean, everything is always passed from one generation to the next, right? That's why we have to stop it here. Punish those responsible . . ." He continued talking, but I couldn't hear. My mind was spinning. I couldn't focus.

A few weeks later, after I had gone out on the Albany to canoe and fish, I felt calm enough to discuss Tony's conversation with Joan.

"After all that has happened," I said, "we can't let the students take the blame. It will mean Mike and Sister Wesley and the others won."

"Ed," Joan said. "I don't think that's going to happen. I mean, you said it yourself. There have been other court cases and the only ones prosecuted were the staff and the government."

"Maybe they didn't have any student abusers at those schools."

"That seems hard to believe. Kids learn through imitation."

"All kids?"

"Well, not all. But enough to generate some hardcore bullies and maybe a few abusers, especially if everyone is turning a blind eye."

"So what do you suggest?"

"I think you should do what you feel is right."

"What if we go through with this and it's just the natives who are punished? I mean, if there's a native guy and a white guy charged with the same thing, then the native guy will be convicted."

"Ed, I just don't think that's true. You can say what you like about the wemistikoshiw, but our courts are fair."

"Joan, I think you're being naive. Remember my great-granddad, John Metatawabin?"

"Well, that was eighty years ago."

"Yeah, but it's not so different today."

"Ed, you're exaggerating.

"No, I'm not. A native guy shows up in court, and he looks down to avoid confrontation, and then he's called shifty. Or he doesn't speak English well enough to paint a compelling picture, and people assume he is lying. Or he damns himself by assuming that he must have done something wrong, because why else would they have arrested him, and he admits his guilt. Or he assumes that he's broken an Indian Act law that he didn't even realize existed, since the Indian Act bans most things considered essential to a good Cree life. There's a reason why the jails down south are full of Indians."

"So what are you going to do?"

"I'm still figuring that out."

After that conversation with my wife, I watched anxiously as other people came forward. In 1990, eight Secwepemc men, former students of St. Joseph's Mission in Williams Lake, B.C., launched a case alleging sexual abuse against the Catholic Church. As the case unfolded, I waited to see if there was any mention of student-on-student abuse or if any charges were laid. None were—just a settlement against the Catholic Church and the federal government. Asking around when I was next in Sudbury, I found the same was true of the first residential school case two years earlier, *Mowatt v. Clarke*, where eight Nlakapamuk boys from out in Lytton, B.C., came forward and said they'd been abused at St. George's Residential School. No charges were laid against the boys, and the federal government and the Anglican Church admitted fault before the case went to trial.

Did that mean that these schools weren't as bad as St. Anne's? That the boys there did not repeat the behaviour of their abusers? Or were the lawyers just focusing on prosecuting those in charge?

Then Phil Fontaine, leader of the Assembly of Manitoba Chiefs, spoke out against his own sexual abuse and called for an inquiry. I decided to act.

To expose the abuse at St. Anne's, I started small. Working with my band council, I arranged for everyone who had ever been at the school to come together in the summertime. We called it the St. Anne's Reunion and Keykaywin Conference—part school reunion, part safe space to talk about some of the issues that had affected us, as *keykaywin* is Cree for "healing."

Despite the innocuous title, many people tried to stop it from happening over the next few weeks. They likely figured there would be serious consequences from discussing what had really happened at the school. They came to my door to talk about how their relatives had gotten jobs at the school, and would now be punished for all their hard work. They gossiped about me and stared at Joan at the Hudson's Bay store. I ignored them all. It's hard to embarrass an alcoholic. To heal, they've already buried all their shame.

"Thanks for coming, man," I greeted Tony at the airport, one of three hundred students coming to the St. Anne's Reunion and Keykaywin Conference. They came from all over—Peawanuck, Attawapiskat, Moosonee, Kashechewan, Timmins, Toronto, Ottawa, Sudbury, Cochrane, North Bay, Thunder Bay—and we put them up in people's houses and at the nurse's station, which was the only place in town with any spare beds.

"Good to see you," he said, hugging me. "Sorry I didn't get back to you about Amocheesh. I was asking around." I had been trying to learn Amocheesh's whereabouts. I needed to know whether he had been abused, too, when he had gone to stay with Mike in Montreal.

"That's okay," I said. "I actually wanted to ask you about something else. Do you know anything about Mike Pasko?"

"The Hudson's Bay manager?"

"Yeah, that's him."

"He was a good man. Real nice."

I blushed. "You never heard . . ."

"What?"

"You never heard that he took boys to his place in Montreal."

"Yeah, I heard that."

"Who?"

"Amocheesh. And some others, I think."

"He took me," I said quietly. I looked down, and my shoulders tensed.

Tony stared at me. I could feel his eyes on the top of my head. I met his gaze, and a flash of understanding passed through his eyes. "Are you getting at what I think you're getting at?" he asked.

"Yeah, I am."

"Did he, you know, touch you?"

"Yeah."

"When?"

"When I was sixteen. I went with him to Montreal."

"Have you told the police?"

"No."

"Are you going to tell the conference?"

"I haven't decided."

"You should."

"Yeah, I know."

"Sorry man. Wow. Fuck. I don't know what to say."

"It's okay."

"Are you okay?"

"I am now."

He put his arm around my shoulder and squeezed me, and looked at me with sad eyes. I met his gaze at first, then I could tell that we both wanted to be alone with our thoughts so I drove him to Nicholas's, where he was staying.

At the St. Anne's Reunion and Keykaywin Conference, we had worked hard to create a safe space for people to open up about abuse, inviting social workers, mental health workers, a justice of the peace, elders, First Nation chiefs, and a professor of native history to speak about the effects of residential schools and child abuse. In the mornings, there were presentations by experts about how residential schools can affect someone's life, and then we asked anyone to open up about their experiences. We knew they'd be in a raw and vulnerable state after talking, so we searched for a Cree healer who could come to Fort Albany to help out. No one whom I'd worked with in Edmonton was available, so my colleague, Mary Anne Nakogee-Davis, arranged for a Navajo healer whom she had met and said was renowned among his people, Albert Damon from Window Rock, Arizona.

Where to put all these people? That was a constant challenge. We rented an outdoor tent for some of the presentations, but we also had to hold some of the sessions inside St. Anne's school for lack of any extra space. The only place we could find with any privacy was an old classroom where a committee involving myself and two others—Andrew Wesley, director of aboriginal child family services in Timmins, a distant relative of Sister Wesley, and Alex Spence, director of the Timmins Ojibway and Cree Cultural Centre—would listen to the testimonies in private. Many came to us to begin to tell stories. It was difficult for them. You could tell by the way they spoke with their eyes lowered. Soft voices. Weight shifting between dusty running shoes. Most people didn't mention names. They said, "a man came upstairs, and he made me kneel down"; "they came into the bedroom, and I couldn't see their faces."

Over the next seven days, we heard accounts of homosexual and heterosexual rapes, forced masturbation, fondling, and the cover-up of a murder.

A boy several years younger than me, Simon John Thomas, took me aside and told me three support staff at St. Anne's took him and his friend down to the basement. They raped them among the sacks of potatoes, then took them back upstairs to the dorm.

Joel Wesley, who was a few years below me, and Andrew Wesley's brother, said he and his friend, Abraham Nakogee, both sixteen, were running around the school's track. Nakogee complained of chest pains to Brother Lauzon. He was told to stop whining and to keep going because he was fat. He had a heart attack and died. Joel was told that if he ever talked about it, he would be punished.

A woman in her forties, Lucy, stood up in an open session and told the crowd of about two hundred people that when she was fourteen, a nun came into her bedroom and led her to one of the storage rooms. Two brothers were waiting and they raped her. After it was over, they told her that she would be whipped forty times if she said anything. A few months later, she was taken to the infirmary and made to have an abortion.

"I miss him. I miss my baby," she said. She stared off into space, like she was lost in another world, the world where her baby still lived.

She sat back down and her story seemed to hang there, silencing the room.

Later Andrew Wesley, Alex Spence and I escorted Lucy outside. She said she wanted to go to the place where she was made to have the abortion. We walked across the school grounds, over the bridge to the site of the old infirmary, which had since closed down. Andrew said a prayer for the baby. Then we all took it in turns to hug Lucy. Afterwards, she said she wanted to be alone.

We left her and I walked across the grass to the Albany. The sun had started to set, and the spruces across the river had sunk into shadow, the rocks' reflections rimmed by darkness. I started to cry.

After the healing conference, I gave the Ontario Provincial Police a booklet of testimonies from the conference and they flew in from South Porcupine, near Timmins, 500 kilometres away, to lay charges. Four investigators and one detective sergeant took statements from approximately 750 people. Eighty of them alleged sexual abuse. Almost all of them alleged physical abuse, but most of it was not severe enough to be considered a crime. The 1950s Criminal Code allowed corporal punishment for parents on their children, and as the school was our official legal guardian, the kicks, punches and whippings were acceptable. So too were some of the punishments that terrified us: standing with our soiled underpants on our head and being locked in a dark basement without food and water. These punishments were not considered serious enough for criminal charges since the harm done was mainly psychological.

I was sitting in the Crown lawyer's office in Sudbury. Diana Fuller was prosecuting all the St. Anne's cases. She had a nice space—there were papers everywhere, but the window looked out onto some flowerbeds and a park.

"So, no students?" she asked. I had told her about the conversation with Tony. I had asked her to limit the court case to only the staff, and not to prosecute any of the allegations of physical and sexual abuse committed by St. Anne's students.

"No," I said. "It's not fair to them. Lots of them were just repeating the behaviour that they learned from the staff."

"God. Poor things," she said.

"And I don't think they want to testify anyway. St. Anne's was a lawless place. There was a lot going on. It was difficult to survive."

"And did anything like this happen to you?"

"No student touched me, no."

"What about the staff?"

I told her about being sexually assaulted by Brother Jutras.

"And this happened when you were seven," she said.

"Yes. Seven or eight."

"Which is it? Seven or eight?"

"I'm not sure."

Diana sighed. "This is hard, isn't it?"

"Yes," I said.

"That's the hard thing about memory. It changes. Especially when there's alcohol involved."

"Yes," I said.

"I'm not here to judge. But before we put you on the stand, we need to iron this stuff out."

"Good idea."

"And we have to be a bit careful here."

"What do you mean?"

"If I put bad cases on the stand, it weakens the good cases."

"Bad cases?"

"That's not the right word. Sorry. Cases where we don't have much hope of a conviction."

"We don't have much hope of a conviction?"

"Let me tell you about sexual abuse cases. First, all of them come down to indecent assault. We won't even try for male rape because it's so hard to prove whether penetration occurred. In your case, you were fondled. So that's indecent assault."

"Oh," I replied.

"And there's the timing. I mean it happened during a medical exam, right? So maybe he was actually examining your penis. I mean, who knows?"

"But he wasn't a doctor."

"I thought there weren't any doctors up there?"

"There weren't."

"Exactly. Which is how the defence will argue it. Then there's also the case of the testimony. In sexual abuse cases, it's always your word against theirs. Rarely are there witnesses. So then it comes down to believability and alibi. You have to describe what happened in a way that makes the jury see and feel the event. That convinces everyone beyond a reasonable doubt."

"Oh," I said again.

"I'm just your lawyer. But given what's at stake, I urge you to be very careful before proceeding further."

I never told the police what happened with Mike. Technically, it wasn't part of our case against St. Anne's, as he wasn't employed by the school and it happened after I had graduated.

Because of my memory lapses due to repeated trauma and alcoholism, they did not use me as a witness against Sister Wesley or Brother Jutras. Still, I went down to Cochrane for some of the court cases so I could support others.

There were seven people charged. Only the staff, thank Gitchi Manitou. Sister Anna Wesley was charged with five counts of assault, three counts of assault causing bodily harm and five counts of administering a noxious substance with intent to aggrieve or annoy, which is how the prosecution charged her with her favourite punishment—forcing the kids to eat their own vomit. Initially, we didn't think the charge would stick—the defence argued the punishment was legal since the substance was a natural bodily secretion. But Diana brought in an expert witness who argued that vomit, while natural inside the stomach, was unnatural as a food. The judge agreed and Sister Wesley was convicted of five counts of assault and three counts of administering a noxious substance with intent to aggrieve or annoy, and sentenced to eleven and a half months' house arrest.

The supervisor of the girls' part of the school, Jane Kakeychewan, was convicted of three counts of assault causing bodily harm, and also sentenced to house arrest.

The only men who were convicted of sexual abuse came to the school after I had graduated. Claude Lambert, fifty at the time, of Saint-André-Avellin, Quebec, who took over once Sister Wesley left, helping the boys with showering, bathing and getting changed, and Marcel Blais, forty-nine at the time, of Ottawa, a kitchen aid—were charged with indecent assault on a male and convicted.

David Murray Stein, forty-nine, of Timmins, who was a few years younger than me, went back and worked at the school as a cafeteria helper in the late 1960s, and was accused of molesting four boys. He was charged with indecent assault and gross indecency. He pleaded guilty and was sentenced to one year in prison. Afterwards, four more boys came forward, and he was sentenced to another year.

Brother Goulet, who built the electric chair, was never charged for his role in electrocuting the boys, as he had already died. The lawyer decided not to pursue charges against anyone else who electrocuted us because it was too hard to prove that the shocks were an excessive use of force.

Brother Lauzon was never charged for his part in Abraham Nakogee's death because he'd died several years earlier of cancer.

Brother Jutras was never charged either. Joe decided not to testify that he'd allowed himself to be masturbated in exchange for a slice of bread, as he was too embarrassed. Others came forward, but then we discovered that it didn't matter as he was already dead. On

November 21, 1979, Brother Jutras passed away due to complications relating to gangrene and a broken leg.

A few months after the reunion, Fred called me. He was still living in Timmins, but had come to Fort Albany for the Keykaywin conference where I'd put out the word that I was looking for Amocheesh.

"So about Amocheesh," Fred said. "I asked around."

"And?"

"You know he had that drinking problem?"

"Yeah."

"It's not good. He died. Drank himself to death."

"Oh my God. What?"

"Sorry, man."

"How?"

"I dunno. I just heard it. I thought you should know."

"Was it an accident or a suicide?"

"An accident, I think. Although he was drinking so much that maybe that was a suicide."

"So what did he actually die of?"

"I don't know. His family are being a bit vague. Just told me that he passed and that I should pray for him."

"Is there going to be a funeral?"

"It happened a few weeks ago."

"Oh," I said.

"Sorry, man."

"Yeah, me too."

"I know you used to be close."

"Yeah, we were," I said. Now I will never know, I thought. I will never know what happened when Mike Pasko took him to his house in Montreal, and whether he raped him, too.

TWENTY-SEVEN

There is no concept of justice in Cree culture. The nearest word is *kintohpatatin*, which loosely translates to "you've been listened to." But kintohpatatin is richer than justice—really it means you've been listened to by someone compassionate and fair, and your needs will be taken seriously. We had peacemakers before we had judges, whose responsibility was to listen to all those affected by the crime: the victim, the offender and their relatives. Justice was a matter of coming together to talk about what had happened, how it had affected all those involved and to find a form of payment that would smooth the ill feelings and repair the harm.

I believe that today's version of kintohpatatin would start with us being heard when we tell our stories. In the residential schools, they forcibly took us from our parents, banned our language, dehumanized us by replacing our names with numbers, and turned us into the subjects of medical experiments on the effects of prolonged malnutrition by starving us, a fact that only came out in 2013 when food historian Ian Mosby went to the national media with his research. At St. Anne's, we were usually hungry, a deprivation that allowed Brother Jutras to bribe the boys with food for sexual favours, although whether this was because of the poverty of the school or by the design of the nuns or government is one of the issues we may never know. We were used to being silenced—whether through the Potlatch laws, which banned our culture and religion, the Indian Act, which gave the Indian Agent total power over the reserves, or the Canada Elections Act, which forbade us from voting.

Many chiefs and parents spoke out about the abuses in the residential schools, including in St. Anne's. These statements were usually met with disbelief or indifference, or they were ignored. What gave many of us the courage to step forward was an unrelated case. In 1989, the wards of Mount Cashel Orphanage took the Catholic Church to court in what became Canada's—and one of the world's—largest sexual abuse scandals. Hearing those testimonies day in, day out gave us the confidence and the voice to start to say that this had happened to us, too.

In the mid-1990s, having been ignored for years, we were able to raise public awareness of what had happened at St. Anne's Residential School with articles in the *Globe and Mail* and the *Toronto Star*. After the healing conference, we went to court, as did others: we were part of a wave of cases against the authorities—the churches and the federal government—that ran the schools. Once word was out, the numbers of cases and victims escalated. In 1995, Mi'kmaq activist Nora Bernard filed what would become the largest lawsuit in Canadian history, representing 79,000 survivors. The Canadian government settled the lawsuit, the Indian Residential Schools Settlement Agreement (IRSSA), for $5 billion, which included payment for our experiences—$10,000 for being sent to the school and $3,000 for every year attended. The settlement detailed an additional payment, if the abuse was severe, calculated by the length of time it was experienced. This was called Independent Assessment Process (IAP) compensation.

While the IRSSA was a step in the right direction, it did not go far enough. In 1998, we began raising our concerns with the federal and provincial governments, and representatives from the church that ran the school, the Oblates of Mary Immaculate and the Grey Nuns. I went down to Toronto for the Alternative Dispute Resolution meetings as representative for the St. Anne's Residential School Survivors (Peetabeck Keway Keykaywin) Association. After a few meetings, it soon became apparent that the government did not take seriously the cultural genocide that had happened at the school. When they offered us $30,000 per student, we declined, as we did not want our concerns to be reduced to a dollar figure.

The issue lay dormant for a few years as the Indian Residential Schools Settlement Agreement moved through the cogs of bureaucracy. In 2006, it came time for us to file our IAP compensation. To qualify, the student would have to give testimony and provide supporting documents to secure an IAP hearing. In turn, the government, as part of the IRSSA, was obligated to release any records relevant to the case, and issue evidence "narratives."

The problem first surfaced when my friends and others from St. Anne's Residential School tried to access their records. Many of us were told that our attendance records were missing, so we had problems proving basic facts, like the years we attended St. Anne's. Others could not access their medical records. When students tried to prove that they had gone to the infirmary for infractions such as being beaten so hard they bled, they were told that those records had gone missing.

It did not stop there. When we tried to prove the issue of widespread abuse, the Department of Justice said they did not have any of the official documents, such as the OPP investigation and court records. And in the official evidence narrative, they denied that the abuse against us had ever taken place. "No known documents of sexual abuse at Fort Albany IRS," it said. "No known incident documents of sexual abuse at Fort Albany IRS."

It was hard to understand how such a flagrant misrepresentation of the truth could come from Department of Justice lawyers. For this reason, many residential school survivors lost faith in the IAP process, and no longer wanted these government lawyers at their hearings. In a letter that was covered by the national press, I wrote to Justice Minister Peter MacKay to remove them.

As we still needed to prove that the abuse had happened, sixty students began to work with lawyer Fay Brunning, tracking down the official records of abuse, with me working as a translator starting in early 2012. Two years later, in January 2014, in a landmark ruling covered by most major national media, we won. Justice Paul Perell of the Ontario Superior Court ruled that the federal government had to hand over all the OPP and court documents to support students' claims for compensation.

With the media attention, a larger pattern of obstruction and secrecy surfaced. It wasn't the first time that Ottawa had dragged its heels on releasing records; the federal government is now under criticism for failing to release millions of residential school documents currently held at Library and Archives Canada. Nor, I'm sure, will it be the last.

In the residential schools, the secrecy began at dawn: we were beaten from the time we first awoke. Speaking out against the injustice in letters home was also cause for punishment. We coped in whatever way we could, often by imitating our oppressors. At St. Anne's, the stronger boys beat the weaker boys either with their fists or with tamarack branches. Sexual abuse was rampant too, with the staff forcing themselves on the girls and boys, and the students forcing themselves on each other. As parents, we continued to imitate the cruelty of the school, ignoring our children or worse, abusing them emotionally, physically or sexually. Joan suffered my emotional abuse and indiscretions, and my kids endured a drunk and absentee dad. Others, such as Lucy, Amocheesh and Abraham Nakogee, fared far worse.

Children often survived these things by shutting down. There are blanks in my memories, and those of my classmates'; the horrific trauma of fifty years ago becomes today's disjointed, tragic fragments. This, combined with the resultant alcoholism, meant that many of us were considered unreliable witnesses in the subsequent court cases, and so the number initially accused diverged greatly from the number found guilty. Many in the community were angry that I had gone to the police, and then at the final outcome, where the number found guilty did not accurately represent the scale of the horrors we had experienced. That anger turned to a burning hot rage. In 2002, St. Anne's Residential School burned down. Many suspected it was arson, as the building had become symbolic of the abuse, sexual and physical, and the psychic scars that continue to the next generation.

Still, I have to believe it was worth it: the court cases have become part of a growing awareness that has shifted the public's understanding of native history. Residential school syndrome is now a recognized phenomenon, with a body of historical and psychological literature behind it. Each person who comes forward adds to this deepening awareness. If trauma is the wounds of the mind, then the court cases, the media interest, the Truth and Reconciliation Commission and the prime minister's 2008 Statement of Apology have given us valuable ways to talk about those wounds. These successes have helped us externalize the shame, slowly shifting our anger from the self to the wider system, easing the burden of rage and memory.

How to repair the harm of St. Anne's? That's a journey that I shall spend the rest of my life navigating. I've been on it for a while. My counsellor in Edmonton, Dennis LeRoy, and George Callingbull helped me along the way, as did Joan, Albalina, Shannin and Jassen.

Now we are helping others along their way, too. In 1988, we started looking after Terry, the son of my middle sister, Jane. She was unemployed, and it was hard for her to find her feet, moving between Toronto and Manitoulin Island. He stayed with us, from age ten until he moved to North Bay for high school. In the summer of 1992, before the healing conference, we adopted another daughter, Cedar, eighteen months, whose grandmother had gone to St. Anne's. I don't know if she suffered as I had, but I know that her daughter, Angela, ended up on the streets, pregnant at fourteen. Cedar became our fifth child.

After I stopped being chief in 1996, I started doing whatever I could to preserve our ancient traditions and knowledge and bring them to the youth. I built a sweat lodge in my backyard, and began bringing the youth and elders together, to close the generational divide left by the residential schools. I brought writers such as Joseph Boyden to our community to promote youth literacy and Cree culture. I became a member of the Ontario Chiefs Traditional Knowledge Keepers group, to discuss how to preserve and pass on our traditions in a respectful manner. I introduced Indian Days, an annual event where we would celebrate the sweat lodge, the shaking tent and other spiritual traditions. I started a sawmill that employs four people in the summer months and two during the winter. I would like to expand to offer more employment, although it is hard for any business to grow on reserves because the Indian Act means that we do not own our land, so cutting down trees on reserve land is illegal. There are other provisions in the Indian Act that hold us back: without any assets, we cannot use our businesses as collateral to get mortgages or insurance. The inability to buy insurance discourages budding entrepreneurs, especially because of the high rates of vandalism. Any business investment becomes a personal risk. Without a trained and energetic fire department, and with arson a strong risk, there's always the danger that we will wake up one morning and have lost everything.

For this work, I have won a couple of awards, including the western elders honorary headdress, "for leadership shown in the fight for the rights of First Nations," and a community leader award by Nishnawbe Aski Nation, a political union of forty-nine First Nations communities across northern Ontario in honour of "raising the profile of the residential school issue."

After I heard about my friend Amocheesh's death, I carried the burden with me for a few months, wondering why I hadn't done more to reach out to him. Finally Joan told me to stop bottling it all up. I called Tony. We had gotten closer ever since the conference; he was one of the few people who knew about Mike.

I picked him up at the airport, and with fishing rods in the back of my pickup truck we drove down to my beauty, the Albany. It was a gentle fall day, the sky dotted with a few clouds that moved slowly, despite the occasional burst of wind. In the early morning, trout and walleye like to rest in the back-eddies swirling by the rocky outcrops mid-river, but by late afternoon, they'd moved to the warmer shallows where we cast our lines. I had some mayfly worms, but Tony, he could make anything dance, and the metallic light from his lure flitted along the gently lapping lake.

We laughed about the time in Grade 5 when Amocheesh had broken character in a school play and had danced across the stage dressed up as a witch. Tony remembered a few more anecdotes, and I laughed along, but to be honest, I couldn't remember them. I've blocked out the good as well as the bad.

"How's the kid?" he asked. I had already told Tony that I was worried about Cedar having fetal alcohol syndrome because of Angela's history.

"I think she's fine."

"You're lucky," he said. I nodded. I hadn't been a great dad when my own children were young. I'd almost drowned under the weight of memory and dragged everyone around me into my whirlpool of rage and hurt. And yet, here I was, with all the trappings of success: a chief, married and raising five kids. Cedar had given me a second chance. How had I gotten here? Did I get what I deserved? What about Amocheesh? Did he deserve the life he got? What did anyone deserve?

"Ed?" Tony said, snapping his fingers in front of my eyes.

"Sorry, man." Easy to get lost in those thoughts.

"Remember that time when you told me not to break the rules?"

"Which time? I was always saying things like that."

"Damn right . . . goody two-shoes."

"Meant I got whipped less."

"Meant you sucked up more. Geesh. I was talking about the time when we tried to run away."

"What about it?"

"I tell it to my kids," he said. "Then I tell them all those Cree stories you told me."

"Which ones?"

"Rita dying . . . that kind of stuff."

"That was a long time ago."

"Yeah, but when our *gookum* died, we did the same."

"You carried the body and buried her upstream?"

"Nah. We buried her with pemmican. Pemmican and cigarettes. We put it right in the coffin."

"Good for you. Now that's something."

EPILOGUE

For thousands of years, we have crossed the waters of sufferings to seek the path of healing. We take a trip along the landscape of our forefathers to honour the memory and the harms done to the ancestors. We respect their lives so that we can stand proud. We walk and paddle in their shadows to remind ourselves they are still here, all around us, guiding those who listen.

Those traditions continue today. Each year the Dakota Nation revisit their tragic history by marching along the route of their forced dislocation from Fort Snelling, Minnesota, to Lower Sioux Reservation, Minnesota, to honour the harms done to the ancestors. Each year, I dip my paddle into the river of healing, by taking ten youth 480 kilometres along the Albany so they can learn their culture and history, and start to reclaim what was lost in the residential schools. I teach them ancient traditions that have been passed down for millennia, spiritual teachings that helped me heal from my alcoholism and the abuse I endured at St. Anne's. Fundraising for the trip takes place all year round. Some filmmakers even made a documentary about it called *Paquataskamik Is Home.*

In late 2012, such journeys became threatened by a series of laws that were considered a direct attack on the environment and native sovereignty. Bill C-45 and other similar legislation by the Harper government made it easier for development to occur on our land and waterways without our approval. Targeting the health of our land, they jeopardized our ability to fish, hunt and trap, and the deep healing and peace that comes from settling the mind into nature, and connecting to the beyond. And they silenced one of the few remaining rights accorded to First Nations people: consultation over our traditional land. In response, Idle No More was born.

In my household, the political movement became a family affair. Joan, who has for the past twenty years worked toward improving kids' nutrition, received the Queen's Diamond Jubilee Medal for her volunteerism. Charlie Angus, the Member of Parliament for Timmins–James Bay, and Gilles Bisson, the Member of Provincial Parliament for Timmins–James Bay, travelled to Fort Albany for the ceremony, just as Idle No More ramped up. Joan went to the ceremony but refused the award, as she didn't want to accept a medal from the Crown given the current political situation. I signed petitions, and talked about Idle No More with the Fort Albany youth.

The Harper government's bills set fire to years of frustration pent up from the residential schools, racism, broken treaty promises, the Indian Act, and everything else that has kept us down. The movement began as rallies in a few Canadian cities, but then exploded across Canada and beyond, spreading ideas and native engagement around the world. There were protests in more than fifty countries, with international indigenous groups offering letters of support.

"I invite all who support my activities to also support Idle No More and I invite all those who support Idle No More to also support the struggle of my people, the Kayapo, for the protection of the indigenous territories and the opposition to the Belo Monte dam," wrote Chief Raoni Metuktire, who has been fighting to stop the flooding of 400 square kilometres of Amazon rainforest, predicted to displace twenty thousand people, a fight that film director James Cameron has compared to a real-life version of *Avatar*.

The movement's outreach and peacefulness led many to describe it in prophetic terms. "The news about what's happening in the North, in these cold lands that we call Canada, came like hot hurricane winds," Oscar Olivera, one of the leading indigenous organizers in Bolivia's battle against water privatization wrote on the Idle No More website. "It is our struggle like all of the battles that our brothers of the South are fighting: brothers and sisters in Argentinean Patagonia, Mapuches in Chile, Quechuas of the Cajamarca in Peru, Quichuas from CONAIE, peasants in Paraguay, indigenous people from the lower lands of TIPNIS in Bolivia . . ." Many saw it as a movement of hope, as predicted by an ancient indigenous teaching, the Seven Fires prophecy. The Anishinaabe prophecy was woven onto a wampum belt around the year 1400 CE, but has become pan-indigenous, with Crees, Ojibways, Stoneys, Iroquois, Denes, Haida and many others talking about it from coast to coast. Each Fire describes a period of native history, with the Sixth Fire usually interpreted as the creation of residential schools and the rise of Christianity.

Grandsons and granddaughters will turn against the Elders. In this way the Elders will lose their reason for living. They will lose their purpose in life. At this time a new sickness will come among the people. The balance of many people will be disturbed. The cup of life will almost become the cup of grief.[10]

The Seventh Fire explains what we must do now to move forward:

In the time of the Seventh Fire New People will emerge. They will retrace their steps to find what was left by the trail. Their steps will take them to the Elders who they will ask to guide them on their journey . . . If the New People will remain strong in their quest the Water Drum of the Midewiwin Lodge[11] will again sound its voice . . . The Sacred Fire will again be lit.

The series of marches to protest Idle No More was symbolic of young people finding their voices by retracing "their steps to find what was left by the trail." As part of Idle No More, the Youth for the Lakes, many from Jackhead First Nation in Manitoba, marched to Ottawa to seek protection for Lake Winnipeg, which has become severely polluted. The Crees of northern Quebec walked 1,600 kilometres from Whapmagoostui to Ottawa. They named it the Journey of Nishiyuu, a word that means how humans are interconnected with nature and all living beings. Hundreds of aboriginals and others joined them along the way.

What was accomplished by Idle No More? With Stephen Harper's parliamentary majority, it was hard for us to stop the Acts from becoming law. And yet, it soon became apparent that the movement was bigger than the original legislation that sparked it. We organized and demonstrated politically and spiritually, championing those aspects of our culture that the residential schools had tried to destroy. At the protests worldwide, we raised our voices and sang to the four directions to show that we are still here. We banged the moosehide drum because it symbolizes the union between the heartbeat of Mother Earth and our people, still beating strong after centuries of oppression. We rose up, strong and united, to return to the Red Road. We took to the streets and retraced the ancient trails. We found our spirits and our voices, and told our stories of renewed pride and strength in powerful traditions. We took a healing journey, as I have been doing ever since I left St. Anne's. We honoured the memories of our living ghosts.

GETTING INVOLVED

How do we heal? I'll begin with the words of Viktor Frankl, a psychiatrist and Holocaust survivor:

> Regarding our "provisional existence" as unreal was in itself an important factor in causing the prisoners to lose their hold on life; everything in a way became pointless. Such people forgot that often it is just such an exceptionally difficult external situation which gives man the opportunity to grow spiritually beyond himself.[12]

For Frankl, the external situation was the hard fight for survival in the camps, an existence that pitted man against man, guard against prisoner, father against son. In the camps, people died for hunger, thirst, by bullets and gas, but perhaps most tragically, for lack of hope. The pointlessness of the suffering itself became the trial to endure, and extinguished the qualities of humanity that we hold most dear: pleasure, generosity, kindness, and even the ability to experience real love. And yet, out of this emptiness, from this spiritual wasteland, Frankl found value. We suffered greatly in the residential schools, but finding a worthwhile response to my past has become my life's mission, and led to my own search for meaning. As First Nations people, we have long endured oppressive laws and policy that tested our own will to live, and as yet, as the rise of the Idle No More movement demonstrates, the spark of the soul is not easy to eliminate.

It seems that for any First Nation, community or individual to be reminded of their own inner strengths, uniqueness and power, they must periodically undergo a trial. This trial will test their resolve to exist, and can be so severe it will threaten them with extinction. We Mushkegowuk Cree have been blessed to have undergone our trial. To say we have passed it successfully is premature because we are still being tested. Recognizing it as a challenge and giving ourselves the authority to find a solution will assist our youth in aspiring to bigger goals. Claiming authority is important for us because we, as the targets of institutionalization, can too easily identify with the position given to us by our victimizers.

Where do we go from here? How long do we yell and scream that the promises of the treaties have not been fulfilled? How long can we complain to the Canadian public that our houses are dilapidated, our roads bad, and our education system broken before we take the reins ourselves? Somehow the mental effort to step outside, grab a hammer (if you have one) and climb onto the roof to fix it is missing. Frankl calls living under this spell of inaction and blames a "provisional existence," as the person suspends forward motion while waiting for this uncomfortable period to be over. But Frankl reminds us that we are the ones who can affect change. It is by our shining through that we can help others overcome injustice. Acknowledge first what your life looks like now; and secondly, consider what about your life needs to change to benefit yourself and your community.

When I ask myself what needs to be done, I recall a dream:

We are on Parliament Hill in a procession that stretches as far as the eye can see. Drums guide us past the Centennial Flame toward Peace Tower and we walk toward the open doors. Waiting outside are Mounties in official uniforms, and political dignitaries.

"Welcoming Committee," I say to myself. "They will walk us inside."

It is a very important moment, unexpected and long fought for.

As we reach the entrance, we pause and move to either side. Across the walkway I see an elder, tears in his eyes, holding an eagle staff in one hand, and the hand of his friend in the other.

People shake bells, and with the noise, young men wearing

traditional clothing sway, twirl and jump to the beat. My body moves to their rhythm, and the fringe of my beaded vest flies as I dance.

And now the moment has come. I see our National Chief, walking down the pathway toward the open doors. Some chiefs said she should be carried, but she wanted her feet on the ground with her people. Just days before, the Government of Canada had issued an official statement. To recognize the treaties, and align all policy and laws according to the spirit of their promises. And to give the Office of the National Chief some political power, with her own seat to represent us in the House of Commons . . .

That is my dream, and you can help make it a reality by getting involved.

"Reconciliation with Native People is still the most pressing social justice issue Canada faces." If you agree with that quote from Ojibway journalist Wab Kinew, or think he has half a point, I hope you might consider getting involved. There is still much work to be done before First Nations get a fair and just deal in Canada. Here are a few ways to help:

Abolish the Indian Act: The Indian Act is a piece of legislation that profoundly affects every aspect of life on reserves. It makes it impossible for us to own our land or build wealth, and highly limits the creation of jobs and economic investment. Rob Clarke, MP for Desnethé–Missinippi–Churchill River, has actively campaigned to abolish this discriminatory piece of legislation. You can support his campaign by writing to rob.clarke@parl.gc.ca.

Support native sovereignty: The current top-down approach, where indigenous people are treated like children to be managed rather than a sovereign people, disempowers and frustrates my people. Idle No More campaigns to restore a just relationship between the Crown and indigenous people. You can support their campaign at www.idlenomore.ca.

Advocate for political change: The widespread movement of First Nations people away from towns and cities into isolated, marginal land that was government policy from the 1700s onwards dispersed and scattered our populations. As a result we are underrepresented in Parliament. Other countries, such as New Zealand, have successfully moved to change this situation, to give fair representation to their aboriginal population. This could be Canada's destiny too, with your help. Please consider supporting political reform by writing to your local MP.

Help youth in education: One of the legacies of the residential schools is elevated high school dropout rates among First Nations students. DreamCatcher Mentoring is an e-support program that encourages native kids to stay in school by partnering professionals with northern students. Get involved—become a mentor at www.dreamcatchermentoring.ca.

The Martin Aboriginal Education Initiative also supports education for aboriginal students across Canada. Visit the website at www.maei-ieam.ca.

Target youth suicide: The North-South partnership for children or Mamow Sha-way-gi-kay-win is a charity that supports First Nations culture, education, mental health and skills training. It organizes counselling and mentorship to aboriginal youth, suicide support, native art and music exhibitions, and education exchanges between northern and southern high schools, publishes First Nations youth magazines, and provides machines that create safe drinking water on reserves. For more information, see www.northsouthpartnership.com.

Support native artists: There are many talented First Nations writers, visual artists, musicians, filmmakers, dancers, drummers and historians that rely on your interest and support. Our stories are vital to understanding the ongoing narrative of the country, yet we are often told, "your work doesn't sell." And if you enjoyed this book, please consider spreading the word. My income as a writer and teacher supports my volunteer work, including taking the youth along the Albany River, preserving Cree culture through the Ontario Chiefs Traditional Knowledge Keepers group, and advocating for the survivors of St. Anne's Residential School.

SUGGESTED READING

If you want to learn more about the issues described in *Up Ghost River*, the following books on native history and rights make for some interesting bedtime reading.

Adams, Howard. *Prison of Grass: Canada from a Native Point of View.* Saskatoon: Fifth House, 1989.

Assembly of First Nations. *Breaking the Silence: An Interpretive Study of Residential School Impact and Healing as Illustrated by the Stories of First Nations Individuals.* Ottawa: Assembly of First Nations, 1994.

Backhouse, Constance. *Colour-Coded: A Legal History of Racism in Canada, 1900–1950.* Toronto: University of Toronto Press, 1999.

Brown, Dee Alexander. *Bury My Heart at Wounded Knee: An Indian History of the American West.* New York: H. Holt, 2007.

Cardinal, Harold. *The Unjust Society.* Vancouver: Douglas & McIntyre, 1999.

Carlson, Hans. *Home Is the Hunter: The James Bay Cree and Their Land.* Vancouver: UBC Press, 2008.

Dei, George Jerry Sefa, Budd Hall and Dorothy Rosenberg. *Indigenous Knowledges in Global Contexts: Multiple Readings of Our World.* Toronto: OISE/UT book published in association with University of Toronto Press, 2000.

Department of Indian and Northern Affairs. *The Historical Development of the Indian Act.* Treaties and Historical Research Centre, P.R.E. Group, 1978.

Diamond, Jared. *Guns, Germs and Steel: The Fates of Human Societies.* New York: W. W. Norton & Co., 1997.

Dyck, Erika. *Eugenic Frontiers: A Social History of Sexual Sterilization in Alberta.* Toronto: University of Toronto Press, 2014.

Fiddler, Thomas and James R. Stevens. *Killing the Shamen.* Newcastle, ON: Penumbra Press, 1985.

Frazier, Ian. *On the Rez.* New York: Farrar, Straus and Giroux, 2000.

Iannone, Catherine. *Sitting Bull: Lakota Leader.* New York: Johnlin Watts, 1998.

King, Thomas. *The Inconvenient Indian: A Curious Account of Native People in North America.* Toronto: Doubleday Canada, 2012.

LaPointe, Ernie. *Sitting Bull: His Life and Legacy.* Layton, UT: Gibbs Smith, 2009.

Mann, Charles C. *1491: New Revelations of the Americas Before Columbus.* New York: Knopf, 2005.

McCaslin, Wanda D. *Justice as Healing: Indigenous Ways.* St. Paul, MN: Living Justice Press, 2008.

McDonnell, Roger. *Justice for the Cree: Customary Beliefs and Practices.* Ottawa: Grand Council of the Crees (Quebec), Cree Regional Authority, 1992.

Miller, J. R. *Lethal Legacy: Current Native Controversies in Canada.* Toronto: McClelland & Stewart, 2004.

———. *Shingwauk's Vision: History of Native Residential Schools.* Toronto: University of Toronto Press, 1996.

Milloy, John Sheridan. *A National Crime: The Canadian Government and the Residential School System.* Winnipeg: University of Manitoba Press, 1999.

Niezen, Ronald. *Defending the Land: Sovereignty and Forest Life in James Bay Cree Society.* Boston: Allyn and Bacon, 1998.

Robertson, Heather. *Reservations Are for Indians.* Toronto: J. Lorimer, 1991.

Sellars, Bev. *They Called Me Number One: Secrets and Survival at an Indian Residential School.* Vancouver: Talonbooks, 2013.

Wiebe, Rudy. *The Temptations of Big Bear.* Toronto: McClelland & Stewart, 1973.

———. *Big Bear.* Toronto: Penguin, 2008.

York, Geoffrey. *The Dispossessed: Life and Death in Native Canada.* Toronto: Lester & Orpen Dennys, 1989.

The following books are helpful guides for learning about traditional knowledge and native spirituality.

Abram, David. *The Spell of the Sensuous: Perception and Language in a More-Than-Human World*. New York: Pantheon Books, 1996.

Ahenakew, Edward. *Voices of the Plains Cree*. Regina: Canadian Plains Research Centre, University of Regina, 1995.

Benton-Banai, Edward. *The Mishomis Book: The Voice of the Ojibway*. Minneapolis, University of Minnesota Press.

Black Elk. *Black Elk Speaks: Being the Life Story of a Holy Man of the Oglala Sioux* as told through John Neihardt. Lincoln: University of Nebraska Press, 1972.

Bouchard, David and Joseph Martin. *Seven Sacred Teachings / Niizhwaaswi Gagiikwewin*. More than Words Publishers, Canada.

Buhner, Stephen Harrod. *Sacred Plant Medicine: The Wisdom in Native American Herbalism*. Rochester, Vermont: Bear & Co., 2006.

Castaneda, Carlos. *The Teachings of Don Juan: A Yaqui Way of Knowledge*. Berkeley, CA: University of California Press, 2008.

Couture, Ruth and Virginia McGowan, eds. *A Metaphoric Mind: Selected Writings of Joseph Couture*. Edmonton: Athabasca University Press, 2013.

Ehman, Dan. *Cree Stories from Moose Lake*. Winnipeg: Native Education Branch, Manitoba Department of Education, 1980.

Hogan, Linda, ed. *The Inner Journey: Views from Native Traditions*. Sandpoint, ID: Morning Light Press, 2009.

Young, Shinzen. *The Red Road*. Audiobook. Dundas, ON: Vipassana Support International.

ACKNOWLEDGEMENTS

So many people generously gave their time and help to make this book possible. We would like to thank the following:

Allen Benson, Chief Executive Officer of Native Counselling Services of Alberta, for his knowledge of treating substance abuse and historic trauma.

Tali Boritz, psychologist, for sharing her knowledge of addiction, memory and mental health issues.

Marilyn Buffalo-McDonald, President of the Indian Association of Alberta, for her time, knowledge and expertise.

Wil Campbell, aboriginal activist and film director, for his time and expertise on Alberta's First Nations history.

Lewis Cardinal, aboriginal activist and educator, for his invaluable insight on Alberta native rights.

Hans Carlson, author of *Home Is the Hunter*, for his invaluable knowledge of the history of the James Bay Cree.

Gordon Christie, Director of the Indigenous Legal Studies Program, University of British Columbia, for guiding us through the thorny complexities of Canadian and First Nations law.

Anne Collins, publisher of the Knopf Random Canada Publishing Group, for her insight, vision and guidance.

Travis Enright, Canon Missioner for Indigenous Ministry in the Chair of St. John de Brebeuf at All Saints' Anglican Cathedral, Edmonton, whose guidance on all things Cree was hugely helpful.

Diana Fuller, lawyer for St. Anne's Residential School students, for sharing her impressive understanding of the law.

Isaac Glick, managing director of Team Products, a non-profit selling First Nations crafts, for his understanding of native issues in Alberta.

Angelika Glover, copy editor, for her careful eye and attention to detail, which saved this book from grammatical embarrassment.

Moyra Lang, Project Coordinator, Living Archives on Eugenics in Western Canada, for her knowledge of Alberta's sterilization laws.

Amanda Lewis, Associate Editor at the Knopf Random Canada Publishing Group, for her intelligence and patience, and for helping us to go ever deeper.

Leo Loone, former student, for his knowledge of St. Anne's Residential School.

Mike Lusty, writer and historian, for his encyclopedic knowledge of First Nations and Métis history.

Jennifer Mair, National Film Board of Canada Ontario Centre publicist, for helping us access a wealth of First Nations programming.

Diane Martin, acquiring editor, for her tireless support and for believing in this book.

Paul Martin, former prime minister and founder of Martin Aboriginal Education Initiative (MAEI) and the Capital for Aboriginal Prosperity and Entrepreneurship (CAPE) fund, for his insight on First Nations politics.

Don McCaskill, Professor in Indigenous Studies at Trent University, for his insight into the department and the program.

Jesse McCormick, law clerk at the Federal Court of Canada, for his supreme knowledge of the law and Aboriginal Affairs and Northern Development Canada bureaucracy.

Sheelah McLean, co-founder of Idle No More, for her insight on the world-wide political movement.

John Milloy, author of *A National Crime: The Canadian Government and the Residential School System*, for guiding us around the available residential school resources.

Gerald Morin, judge and creator of Canada's first Cree court, for his inestimable understanding of Cree justice.

Bridget Perrier, for her time, humour and knowledge of the law and First Nations women.

Roy Piepenburg, First Nations civil rights activist, for guiding us around Alberta's native history.

Andrew Reuben, Cree elder and former Chief of Kashechewan, for his knowledge of aboriginal history and traditions.

Alex Spence, former project manager for Fort Albany's water and sewers, for his boundless knowledge of all things Fort Albany.

Greg Spence, former student at St. Anne's, for his vast knowledge of the residential school.

Andrew Wesley, Elder-in-Residence at First Nations House, University of Toronto, whose generosity of time and knowledge of Cree spirituality were crucial.

Dr. Cynthia Wesley-Esquimaux, Vice Provost (Aboriginal Initiatives) Lakehead University, Thunder Bay, for her expertise on residential school resources.

Sandra Willock, consultant and operational manager Neegan-o'chee, for her insight on Fort Albany politics and the Department of Indian Affairs and Northern Development.

Nina Wilson, co-founder of Idle No More, for explaining the political movement's expansion and growth.

Shinzen Young, vipassana teacher and creator of the CD *The Red Road*, for his wisdom and understanding of First Nations spirituality and deep equanimity.

On a personal note, I would like to thank:

Albalina Metatawabin, Shannin Metatawabin, Jassen Metatawabin, Alex Metatawabin, Mary-Theresa Metatawabin (my mother) and Joan Metatawabin for her endless patience and love.

I would also like to thank the Canada Council for the Arts and the Ontario Arts Council for their generous granting support.

Alexandra Shimo would like to thank:

Ailsa Barry and Jonathan Sakula; Steven and Eva Shimotakahara; my brothers and sisters Augusta, Sidonie, Tim and Danielle; Mary Albino, whose ideas and guidance were a blessing; Patricia Pearson; Lucille and Milton Maskalyk; James Maskalyk; Jeff Warren; Sudha Krishna; Elaine Wong; Alexandra Grimanis, for her translation help; my agents Chris Casuccio and John Pearce; and my partner Lia Grimanis, for her guidance, love and wisdom.

ENDNOTES

1. From the Historical Development of the Indian Act, Treaties and Historical Research Centre, P.R.E. Group, Indian and Northern Affairs, August 1978.

2. The Seven Sacred Teachings are a way of being in the world that respects Mother Earth and all of Creation. To live with honour, the Sacred Teachings say that we should observe the animal kingdom, and understand how each species interacts, eats, hunts, plays and lives in harmony with the rest of the environment. Each animal has a teaching for us, a way of doing things that we can bring into our own lives. The wolf, for example, walks with its head down, and lives for the pack, showing us how to be humble. The wolf's virtue is humility. The other animals that embody the sacred lessons are bear (courage), eagle (love), beaver (wisdom), raven (honesty), deer (respect) and turtle (truth). The Seven Sacred Teachings are common to many First Nations peoples, although the animals differ depending on the geographic region.

3. Many years later, I began looking into what had happened to him. Under the Indian Act, what was illegal was "Indian participation" in any "show, exhibition, performance, stampede or pageant" in "aboriginal costume," and encouraging any form of participation. However, it was up to the Indian Agent to decide whether or not a person had encouraged what were called "savage rites," what encouragement entailed, and to decide on our punishment. Since Indian Agents were liberal with their interpretation of the law, it was hard to know what was legal: we assumed that being aboriginal, e.g., having long hair, was not legal. Arrests, imprisonment, threats, refusal to issue "off-reserve" travel passes, or stopping of food rations were all common punishments. The Fort Albany Indian Agent decided that my great-grandfather's activities were worthy of arrest but he left no records as to why, or at least none that I have been able to access. This is not uncommon: the Indian Agents were not obliged to keep documents, and other information was destroyed because it was considered "culturally insignificant." No one knows the true number of arrests; however, scholars estimate that hundreds went to jail between 1884 and 1951, when the Potlatch laws

were finally repealed. For more information, see Constance Backhouse's *Colour-Coded: A Legal History of Racism in Canada, 1900–1950* (Toronto: University of Toronto Press, 1999).

4. Racist insults heard growing up included "savage," "wild," "beast." More than a reprimand by our teachers, "half-breed" institutionalized the racism: it was the official category for Métis children until the government changed it with the 1982 Constitution Act.

5. Years later I found out that it wasn't just school policy, it was the mandate for all residential schools across North America. "Kill the Indian, Save the Man," were the words of Richard Henry Pratt, a U.S. Army officer who developed the Carlisle Indian School in Pennsylvania, the first (off-reservation) Indian boarding school, whose principles and practices came to guide Canadian and American policy. The dictum "Kill the Indian, Save the Man" has come to represent the cultural genocide that took place for more than a century in the continent's residential schools.

6. The Trent-Severn Waterway was built to connect two of the Great Lakes, Huron and Ontario, to streamline and improve water trade and transportation. To make room, the government flooded First Nations land, beginning in 1837. Three aboriginal communities were affected: Curve Lake (Anishinaabe), Hiawatha and Mississaugas of Scugog Island. The First Nations were not consulted before it happened. In October 2012, 175 years after the first of the government-controlled floods, the federal government settled with these communities for $71 million.

7. In 1969, Prime Minister Pierre Trudeau, and his then-Minister of Indian Affairs Jean Chrétien, introduced the White Paper, which would abolish the Indian Act and dismantle the legal relationship between Canada and First Nations in favour of equality, and by implication, assimilation. Cardinal's book *The Unjust Society: The Tragedy of Canada's Indians* argued that the White Paper imposed legal equality on an unequal situation, ignoring First Nations' history of oppression and colonialism, and the desire of aboriginals to be a "red tile in the Canadian mosaic." It was, he said, equivalent to "cultural genocide." In his book, Cardinal argued that any solution should restore a respectful relationship between the Crown and First

Nations, with Ottawa recognizing us as a sovereign people with resource rights over our traditional lands.

8. Several forces gave rise to the eugenics movement: the rise of social Darwinism, scientific racism and increasing interest in genetics. Many countries, including Canada, convinced by the theories of prominent biologists such as Francis Galton and Charles Davenport, became interested in improving the intelligence and productivity of their citizenry by removing unwanted persons and persons deemed "racially inferior" from their gene pools. From 1928 to 1972, under the Sexual Sterilization Act of Alberta, the province sterilized approximately 2,800 people considered unfit for procreation, including mentally and physically challenged ("mental defectives"), persons "incapable of intelligent parenthood," juvenile delinquents, Indians, Inuit and Métis. Aboriginals and residential school students were disproportionately targeted because these groups were more likely to be seen as mentally defective due to language and cultural differences. If a student was misbehaving, the principal, acting as the student's official guardian, could recommend the student went before the Eugenics Board, which did an interview, often lasting five to ten minutes, to decide whether or not the child should be sterilized. Often, children were not told what was happening; instead they were told they were having their appendix out, or another operation—and would not realize they were infertile until adulthood. British Columbia passed a similar law in 1933 that was repealed in 1979. The number of people sterilized in B.C. remains uncertain since the records have been destroyed. The scope and details of Alberta's law gained national exposure with the 1995 court case of Leilani Muir, who was sterilized without her consent or knowledge at Alberta's Provincial Training School for Mental Defectives in 1959. She sued the provincial government and won. Since then 850 Albertans who were sterilized have been awarded $142 million in damages.

9. "Then I was standing on the highest mountain of them all, and round about beneath me was the whole hoop of the world. And while I stood there I saw more than I can tell and I understood more than I saw; for I was seeing in a sacred manner the shapes of all things in the spirit, and the shape of all shapes as they must live together like one being.

And I saw that the sacred hoop of my people was one of the many hoops that made one circle, wide as daylight and as starlight, and in the center grew one mighty flowering tree to shelter all the children of one mother and one father. And I saw that it was holy . . ."

(From *Black Elk Speaks: Being the Life Story of a Holy Man of the Ogalala Sioux* as told through John Neihardt, University of Nebraska Press, 1972.)

10. *The Mishomis Book: The Voice of the Ojibway,* Edward Benton-Banai, University of Minnesota Press, 2010.

11. A religious practice involving fasting and smoking a sacred pipe that helps people drop into higher place of consciousness so that they can communicate with the Spirit World.

12. Viktor Frankl, *Man's Search for Meaning,* Beacon Press, 1959.

Edmund Metatawabin, former Chief of Fort Albany First Nation, is a Cree writer, educator and activist. A residential school survivor, he has devoted himself to righting the wrongs of the past, and educating native youth in traditional knowledge. Metatawabin now lives in his self-made log house in Fort Albany, Ontario, off the reserve boundary, on land he refers to as "My Grandfathers' Land." He owns a local sawmill and also works as a consultant, speaker and researcher. www.edmundmetatawabin.com

Alexandra Shimo is a former radio producer for the CBC and former editor at *Maclean's*. An award-winning journalist, she is the author of *The Environment Equation*, which was published in twelve countries. She volunteers as a communications consultant for the non-profit Up With Women, which works with at-risk women, and with DreamCatcher Mentoring, which helps native youth. She lives in Toronto. www.alexandrashimo.com

A NOTE ABOUT THE TYPE

The body of *Up Ghost River* has been set in Adobe Garamond. Designed for the Adobe Corporation by Robert Slimbach, the fonts are based on types first cut by Claude Garamond (c.1480–1561). Garamond was a pupil of Geoffrey Tory and is believed to have followed classic Venetian type models, although he did introduce a number of important differences, and it is to him that we owe the letterforms we now know as "old style." Garamond gave his characters a sense of movement and elegance that ultimately won him an international reputation and the patronage of Frances I of France.